VOICES OF REASON IN CHRISTIAN HISTORY

VOICES
OF REASON

IN
CHRISTIAN HISTORY

THE GREAT APOLOGISTS:
Their Lives and Legacies

By Gannon Murphy

Published by
✠ CHRISTIAN PUBLICATIONS, INC.
CAMP HILL, PENNSYLVANIA

and

Christian History Institute
WORCESTER, PENNSYLVANIA

CHRISTIAN PUBLICATIONS, INC.
3825 Hartzdale Drive, Camp Hill, PA 17011
www.christianpublications.com

Faithful, biblical publishing since 1883

Voices of Reason in Christian History
ISBN: 0-88965-233-3
LOC Control Number: 2005926704
© 2005 by Gannon Murphy
All rights reserved
Printed in the United States of America

05   06   07   08   09   5   4   3   2   1

Note: Italicized words in Scripture
quotations are the emphasis of the author.

Contents

To Dad

Introduction

This book was born from my work with the Minnesota Apologetics Project fielding questions from skeptics, seekers and those interested in learning about key players in the apologetical legacy. Over the years, inquiries have come through our Web site, http://mn-apologetics.org, asking, "What can you tell me about the apologetics of so and so?" While many excellent works deal with apologetics in general, no work—that I am aware of—has put together a brief, substantive compendium of the great Christian apologists offering snapshots of their lives and ministries. I must admit, however, in the words of John McKenzie, that "my professional colleagues will read this book, as they read all such popular presentations; but will not be surprised if they find nothing here they could not have done themselves . . . and better. My excuse for doing it is that no one else has done it."[1]

L. Russ Bush's *Classical Readings in Christian Apologetics* is a highly recommended compendium of apologetical readings, but it is not a biographical and intellectual chronicle of the great apologists themselves. Norman Geisler's *Baker Encyclopedia of Christian Apologetics* is an excellent resource on the great apologists, but it lacks detailed biographical data and primary readings. Robert Grant's *Greek Apologists of the Second Century* is restricted to a specific historical epoch as opposed to surveying the gamut of the great defenders of Christendom for the past two millennia.

A few words are in order about the criteria involved in putting this project together. First, this book is not about apologetical methods (e.g., classicalism, evidentialism, presuppositionalism, integrativism, etc.). For this I recommend Robert Bowman and Kenneth Boa's *Faith Has Its Reasons*. Rather, this book traces the use of apologetics over two millennia of Christendom as represented in the lives of some able defenders. Readers will become familiar with key names in apologetics over the history of the Church from its beginning to the present day. The most difficult task was choosing such representatives, for every age has had its great apologists. Christians will recognize that God has raised up the right persons to make a sturdy *apologia* against those attacking the truth of Christ's Church. The Lord has used such persons to defend the Church against the intellectual scrutiny that has plagued it since its birth. A stringent methodology was necessary to choose representatives of the apologetical legacy forged within each epoch of redemptive history.

I had originally decided to pick ten persons who 1) penned apologetical works; 2) had lasting impacts in the history of apologetics; 3) lived sound and Christian lives; and, 4) remained orthodox Christians from the point of their conversion onward.

I began with a list of about forty apologists. The remaining task consisted of a process of elimination. Tertullian (c. 160–220), for example, was omitted, not because of his lack of effect on apologetic history, but because he later immersed himself in the apocalyptic sect and aberrant teachings of Montanism. Yet he not only coined the word *Trinity* but also bequeathed to the Church notable phrases such as "The blood of the martyrs is the seed of the church" and "What hath Athens to do with Jerusalem?" He also defended the faith in his *Apologeticum,* which appealed to the fulfillment of Old Testament prophecy and various historical evidences to establish Christianity's truthfulness. Thus, Tertullian easily passed the first and second criteria, showed signs of meeting the third, but—for the criteria of this book—fell short of the fourth. Though Montanism eventually died out, it helped spawn later heretical movements such as Catharism, pneumato-Marionism, Swedenborgianism and other cults that focused on the Holy Spirit rather than the Father and Son.

Of course, other cases weren't so dramatic. Quadratus (c. 124), for example, was possibly the first bona fide apologist following the Apostle Paul, giving him a unique historical standing. Unfortunately, however, none of his works are extant (with the exception of a short passage quoted by Eusebius), and his historical effect is small in comparison to the others. G.K. Chesterton was an able defender but lacked many characteristics of a true Christian apologist. Francis Schaeffer defended Christianity against liberalism, relativism and existentialism but had a lesser historical impact than his contemporary, C.S. Lewis. Edward Carnell, a major twentieth-century apologist, was omitted for similar reasons. Any student of apologetics should read Carnell, but from a historical standpoint he helped develop a sound apologetical methodology rather than actively practicing apologetics.

I also omitted accounts of the lives and ministries of the Reformers Martin Luther and John Calvin. The reason for their omission is twofold: 1) Neither of them penned apologetical works defending the basic tenets of Christendom. Rather, their polemical writings primarily targeted the Roman Catholic Church; 2) Their lives and ministries cannot be adequately covered in this compendium. Fuller tomes are available when studying them, such as *Here I*

Stand by Roland Bainton on Martin Luther and *The Life of John Calvin* by Alister McGrath. The Men of Faith Series offers a short book on Luther by Mike Fearon and one on Calvin by William Linder.

Cornelius Van Til was omitted because he was more an apologetical theorist than an active apologist. In fact, he conceded as much in a letter he wrote to Francis Schaeffer saying, "You have the advantage over me. You converse constantly with modern artists, modern existentialists, etc., as they eat at your table, study their literature. Whereas I am only a book-worm."[2]

Ultimately, I reduced the list of great apologists to Justin Martyr, Irenaeus, Origen, Athanasius, Anselm, Augustine, Aquinas, Pascal and C.S. Lewis, while becoming inextricably stuck between retaining or dropping either Joseph Butler or William Paley. Instead I included Joseph Butler and William Paley in a joint chapter. Together they offered a powerful apologetical combination against the deistic/naturalistic philosophical climate of the day.

The appendix at the rear of this work offers a survey of major apologists over the centuries. This provides a context of the age in which the apologists practiced their ministry and will alert the reader to their major apologetical works. Internet resources are now available to the student of apologetics. Web sites, such as the *Christian Classics Ethereal Library* (http:// www.ccel.org/) and *New Advent* (http://www.newadvent.org), offer opportunities to read the original writings of many apologists. Other Web links are listed in the endnotes to offer more information on each apologist. Many Web sites are devoted to apologists' lives and ministries and sometimes provide information for an in-depth study.

Soli Deo Gloria!

Gannon Murphy
Minnesota Apologetics Project
http://mn-apologetics.org

Justin Martyr
The Lover of Wisdom

Our doctrines are not shameful, according to sober judgment, but are indeed more lofty than all human philosophy.
—Second Apology, *Chapter 15*

Events in the Life of **Justin Martyr**

c. 100	Born in Flavia Neapolis in Palestine.
c. 115–130	Studied and taught philosophy.
130	Converted to Christianity in Ephesus.
138	Wrote the *First Apology* to Antoninus Pius.
161	Wrote the *Second Apology* to Marcus Aurelius and the Roman Senate.
157–161	Wrote the *Dialogue with Trypho.*
167	Executed in Rome under orders of the court.

*L*uke tells us in Acts that, after appearing before the Sanhedrin and being flogged, the apostles began "rejoicing that they had been considered worthy to suffer shame for [Christ's] name" (5:41, NASB). According to the Church historian Eusebius, Peter was crucified in Rome upside down. "He had requested that he might suffer in this way"[1] since he didn't consider himself worthy of suffering and dying in the same manner as his Lord. Other such accounts abound in Christian history, including that of the life and ministry of Justin the Martyr.

The second century was the toughest of times and the best of times for Christians. It was the toughest because persecution ran rampant, and distortions about Christians were widely circulated and believed by many. One rumor claimed that followers of Jesus practiced cannibalism since they ceremonially ate Christ's body and blood (see Mark 14:22-24). Things got worse when they heard of Christian love feasts (see Jude 1:12), which many Romans construed to be quasi-orgiastic banquets where Christians engorged themselves with erotic and culinary pleasures. To trap initiates, one rumor said, Christians hid babies in huge loaves of bread during their love feasts and invited newcomers to slice into them. The initiates killed the newborns in preparation for the feast, thus fastening their silence forever.[2] Christians also were accused of atheism because they denied the divinity of Rome's pagan gods. Someone even started the ridiculous rumor that Christians worshiped an ass.[3]

The emperor at the time, Antoninus Pius (138–161), followed the principles of Trajan when dealing with those who did not follow the popular emperor cult. The Roman guard did not actively seek out Christians, but should they receive any "evidence" about believers, they took them to court. Unfortunately, such indictments were most often synonymous with convictions.

The persecution of Christians during this period often resulted in public beheadings. Numerous artifacts bear mute testimony to their suffering; one example is an ancient mosaic depicting forty martyrs left to die outside by freezing in the dead of winter. A letter from churches in Gaul speaks of so many Christians held in a small Roman jail that several died of suffocation. Much of the persecution was due to gross misconceptions and distortions of Christian beliefs and practices.

On this tumultuous backdrop, Justin emerged. God used him not only to dispel the falsities circulating about Christianity but also to explain its veracity as the true and "divine philosophy."[4] The apologetics of Justin Martyr were the most important and influential of the second century. He was the first to show the fulfillment of predictive prophecy. He demonstrated Platonism's inadequacy and then used it to guide people to Christ Jesus. He tore down the Roman rumor-mongers' myths about Christians and showed the folly of pagan worship. Finally, he described the superiority of Christianity over all other religions and philosophies. Justin was the first postapostolic pioneer to explain Christianity logically, in terms that his contemporaries could understand.

From Pagan Philosopher to Great Apologist

Justin was born around the year 100 in Flavia Neapolis in Palestine to pagan parents. Schooled in Greek philosophy, he wore the *pallium,* a cloak that Eusebius referred to as "the philosopher's garment."[5] Apparently, this illustrious garment identified its wearer as a philosopher and scholar.

Justin tried various philosophies to satisfy his hunger for truth. At the philosophical epicenters of Alexandria and Ephesus, he studied Stoicism, Pythagoreanism and Platonism. The latter of these placated him for a time, but it lacked any connection with the real world. Platonism taught that the physical world is filled with the imperfect manifestations of the transcendent, metaphysical world of forms and ideas. Because this world of perfection, the *Logos,* is unreachable and unknowable, human beings are locked on this side of the ontological boundary between perfection and imperfection. Justin's agony due to this existential disconnect was a chasm waiting to be bridged by the joyous news of the incarnation of Jesus, the Word made flesh. In his despondency, Justin was ripe for the good news of Christ Jesus, who bridges the gap between God and humankind. All that was needed was the bearer of this good news. God provided such a bearer in the form of a mysterious man whom Justin met on a walk by the sea. Justin said,

> While I was thus disposed, when I wished at one time to be filled with great quietness, and to shun the path of men, I used to go into a certain field not far from the sea. And when I was near that spot one day, which having reached I purposed to be by myself, a certain old man, by no means contemptible in appearance, exhibiting meek and venerable manners, followed me at a little distance. And when I turned around to him, having halted, I fixed my eyes rather keenly on him.
>
> And he said, "Do you know me?"

I replied in the negative.

"Why, then," said he to me, "do you so look at me?"

"I am astonished," I said, "because you have chanced to be in my company in the same place; for I had not expected to see any man here."

And he says to me, "I am concerned about some of my household. These are gone away from me; and therefore have I come to make personal search for them, if, perhaps, they shall make their appearance somewhere. But why are you here?" said he to me.

"I delight," said I, "in such walks, where my attention is not distracted, for converse with myself is uninterrupted; and such places are most fit for philology."

"Are you, then, a philologian," said he, "but no lover of deeds or of truth? and do you not aim at being a practical man so much as being a sophist?"

"What greater work," said I, "could one accomplish than this, to show the reason which governs all, and having laid hold of it, and being mounted upon it, to look down on the errors of others, and their pursuits? But without philosophy and right reason, prudence would not be present to any man. Wherefore it is necessary for every man to philosophize, and to esteem this the greatest and most honourable work; but other things only of second-rate or third-rate importance, though, indeed, if they be made to depend on philosophy, they are of moderate value, and worthy of acceptance; but deprived of it, and not accompanying it, they are vulgar and coarse to those who pursue them."

"Does philosophy, then, make happiness?" said he, interrupting.

"Assuredly," I said, "and it alone."[6]

A lengthy philosophical discussion ensued, wherein Justin's mysterious counterpart demonstrated the limitations in the system of his beloved Plato. The man showed that the only way Platonists could hold their opinions would be to posit a Creator in which all things have their source. Justin soon found himself at a lack for an adequate response. Platonism tried to say much about what is fundamentally unknowable. Justin saw that for all his wisdom, he had no grounds for what he believed. His frustrations and despondency—

perhaps even fear—about the inadequacies of his own philosophy became apparent. He lamented,

> "Did such notions, then, escape the observation of Plato and Pythagoras, those wise men," I said, "who have been as a wall and fortress of philosophy to us all?"
>
> He replied, "To me, it makes no difference whether Plato or Pythagoras, or any other man held such opinions. For the truth is so . . . and the soul [from whence man even contemplates all these things] assuredly has life . . . that the soul lives, no one would deny. But if it lives, it lives not as being in itself, but as the partaker of life. But that which partakes is different from that which it partakes in. . . . Thus, its Source wills it to live."
>
> "I wonder, then, should *anyone* employ a teacher?" I said. "How can anyone be helped, if not even in *them* there is truth?"

The man had a bold reply:

> "There existed, long before this time, certain men more ancient than all those who are esteemed philosophers, both righteous and beloved by God, who spoke by the Spirit, and foretold events which would take place, and which indeed are now taking place. They are called prophets. These alone both saw and announced the truth to men, neither reverencing nor fearing any man, neither being influenced by a vain desire for their own glory, but speaking those things alone which they saw and heard, being filled with the Holy Spirit. Their writings are still with us, and he who reads them is *very* much helped in his knowledge of the beginning and end of things, and of those matters which the philosophers ought to know, provided he only believes them. For they did not use a lofty demonstration in their treatises, seeing that they were witnesses to the truth above all demonstration, and worthy of belief; and those events which have happened, and those which are happening. And they compel you to assent to the utterances made by them, although, indeed, they were entitled to credit on account of the miracles they performed, since they both glorified the Creator, the God and Father of all things, and proclaimed His Son, the Christ, sent by Him to

earth, which, indeed, the false prophets, who are filled with lying spirits, have neither done nor do, but venture to work certain wonderful deeds for the purpose of astonishing men, and glorify the spirits and demons of error. But pray that, above all things, the gates of light may be opened to you; for these things cannot be perceived or understood by all, but only by the man to whom God and His Christ have imparted wisdom."[7]

Justin was cut to the core. . . .

When he had spoken these and many other things, which there is no time for mentioning at present, he went away, bidding me to attend to them; and I have not seen him since. But straightway a flame was kindled in my soul; and a love of the prophets of whom he spoke, and of those men who are friends of Christ, possessed me; and while revolving his words around in my mind, I found *this* philosophy alone to be safe and profitable. Thus, and for this reason, I am a philosopher. Moreover, I would wish that all, making a resolution similar to my own, do not keep themselves away from the words of the Savior. For they possess a terrible power in themselves, and are sufficient to inspire those who turn aside from the path of rectitude with awe; while the sweetest rest is afforded those who make a diligent practice of them. If, then, you have any concern for yourself, and if you are eagerly looking for salvation, and if you believe in God, you may—since you are not indifferent to the matter. Become acquainted with the Christ of God, and, after being initiated, live a happy life.[8]

The *Apologies* also shed light on another phase of Justin's conversion: "When I was a disciple of Plato, hearing the accusations made against the Christians and seeing them intrepid in the face of death and of all that men fear, I said to myself that it was impossible that they should be living in evil and in the love of pleasure."[9] Church historian Justo Gonzalez recounts from the Gaulian letter alluded to earlier that such accusations against Christians appeared suddenly "like a bolt of lightning," they reported. Paralyzed by fear, some weakened and fled, leaving "the womb of the church like abortive ones."[10] But others stood their ground, which provoked even further wrath from their persecutors, as Gonzalez explains:

Torture was ordered. A certain Sanctus, when tortured, simply answered, "I am a Christian." The more he was tortured, the more he persisted in saying nothing but these words. Moved by this and many other signs of courage, some who had earlier denied the faith returned to confess it and die as martyrs.[11]

Justin was speechless over this commitment. Nothing in Stoicism, Platonism or Pythagoreanism provoked this kind of devotion. As Irenaeus later put it, "No one trusted in Socrates so as to *die* for [his] doctrine."[12] Thus, finding none of his former philosophies satisfying, Justin finally arrived at the truth of Christianity and discovered "this philosophy alone to be safe and profitable."

The cavernous void in Justin's soul was filled at last, and he spent the rest of his life defending the truth of Christian theism. As he traveled he wore the *pallium* to demonstrate that he was now a philosopher with real answers instead of new ideas and nebulous riddles. The truth, he believed, would set people free (see John 8:32), not the endless speculation of the Greeks who spent their time "doing nothing but talking about and listening to the latest ideas" (Acts 17:21). Mere ideas do not set people free; truth does.

Defending the True Philosophy

At considerable risk, Justin founded a school in Rome. He taught that pagan philosophy, especially Platonism, was not altogether wrong, but as he had discovered in his conversation journey with the man on the beach (who some suppose was an angel), it can help gain a partial grasp of the truth. Just as the Old Testament Law is fulfilled in Christ but still convicts of sin, so too philosophy can often point us to Christ.[13]

Justin also debated and disputed with pagans, Jews and heretics. One heretic named Crescens later caused Justin's arrest and martyrdom by decapitation. During this time Justin wrote his most important works defending the Christian faith, three of which are extant: the *First* and *Second Apology*, and the *Dialogue with Trypho*. Some additional fragments of Justin's work have also been preserved, covering such topics as the resurrection and the Marcionite controversy.

Unlike later theological systematicians, such as Anselm and Augustine, Justin's apologetic approach was free and loose, even digressive. He apparently addressed various topics as they entered his mind. They were not haphazard topics, however, for they had calculated and decisive aims. In fact, his emphasis on the importance of careful reason has led some to conclude, wrongly, that he was a rationalist who concentrated more heavily on reason than on revelation. However, Justin believed firmly in the trustworthiness of revelation and the inspiration and authority of Scripture. He also believed that clear thinking was godly and would lead to God's truth. As Augustine would later affirm, all truth meets at the top in God, "who art truth itself."[14]

Thus, Justin affirmed that Greek philosophy contained some truth but not enough of it. It was like making observations about a vast stage but knowing nothing of the architecture undergirding it. At its best, philosophy possessed only dim shades of truth, whereas Christianity possessed it in full.[15] Interestingly, Justin even went so far as to say, "Whatever things were *rightly* said among [the philosophers], are the property of us Christians."[16] This only makes sense if God, as Justin held, is the Father of all truth and the wellspring from which all good and profitable things find their source. Justin said more on this:

> Our doctrines, then, appear to be greater than all human teaching; because Christ, who appeared for our sakes, became the whole rational being, both body, and reason, and soul. For whatever either lawgivers or philosophers uttered well, they elaborated by finding and contemplating some part of the Word. But since they did not know the whole of the Word, which is Christ, they often contradicted themselves. And those who by human birth were more ancient than Christ, when they attempted to consider and prove things by reason, were brought before the tribunals as impious persons and busybodies. And Socrates, who was more zealous in this direction than all of them, was accused of the very same crimes as ourselves. For they said that he was introducing new divinities, and did not consider those to be gods whom the state recognized. But he cast out from the state troth Homer and the rest of the poets, and taught men to reject the wicked demons and those who did the things which the poets related; and he exhorted them to become acquainted with the God who was to them unknown, by means of the investigation of reason, saying, "That it is neither easy to find the Father and Maker of all, nor, having found Him, is it safe to declare Him to all." But these things our Christ did through His own power. For no one trusted in Socrates so as to die for

this doctrine, but in Christ, who was partially known even by Socrates (for He was and is the Word who is in every man, and who foretold the things that were to come to pass both through the prophets and in His own person when He was made of like passions, and taught these things), not only philosophers and scholars believed, but also artisans and people entirely uneducated, despising both glory, and fear, and death; since He is a power of the ineffable Father, not the mere instrument of human reason.[17]

Founder of Classical Apologetics

In terms of apologetical method, Justin is the father of classicalism, that is, using reason and argument to defend both the truth of God's existence and the Christian faith as a whole.

The biblical invitation to "Come now, let us reason together" (Isaiah 1:18) is a fitting verse to assign to Justin's manner. To meet Hellenism on its own terms and turn its philosophical blade around on itself would prove a powerful approach. An excellent example of this is the manner in which Justin used the biblical language of the *Logos* and showed his audience its true meaning as revealed in Christ. Justin dialogued with his contemporaries after studying the *Logos* passage in the first chapter of John's Gospel: "In the beginning was the Word, and the Word was with God, and the Word was God. . . . And the Word became flesh, and dwelt among us, and we saw His glory, glory as of the only begotten from the Father, full of grace and truth" (John 1:1, 14, NASB). The word translated here as "Word" is the Greek *Logos,* the center point of Platonism. Thus, in order to support his claim that Christianity is the true philosophy where the transcendent meets the temporal, Justin was the first apologist in history to correlate John's doctrine of the *Logos* with Greek philosophy. He argued that whatever truth is found in philosophy is lifted from the teachings of Moses in the earlier Hebrew Scriptures.[18] The cross of Christ brings the unreachable musings of the Greeks to palpable reach in Christian praxis. Christ is the nexus through which God, the true *Logos,* touches humanity.

First Apology

Justin's *First Apology,* addressed to Antoninus Pius, urged the emperor to listen to the case of Christians by virtue of his own reason without the venom of the Roman mob. Justin challenged Rome's official attitude toward Christians. Since the Romans prided themselves in their advanced justice system, Justin used this as the fulcrum on which to pivot his defense.

> Reason directs those who are truly pious and philosophical to honour and love only what is true, declining to follow traditional opinions. . . . For not only does sound reason direct us to refuse the guidance of those who did or taught anything wrong, but it is incumbent on the lover of truth, by all means, and if death be threatened, even before his own life, to choose to do and say what is right. Do you, then . . . guardians of justice and lovers of learning, give good heed, and hearken to my address? . . . For we have come, not to flatter you by this writing, nor please you by our address, but to beg that you pass judgment, after an accurate and searching investigation, not flattered by prejudice or by a desire of pleasing superstitious men, nor induced by irrational impulse or evil rumours which have long been prevalent, to give a decision which will prove to be against yourselves.[19]

Justin objected against the senseless manner in which the Roman justice system prosecuted Christians. Punishment, he contended, should only be imposed on those who have been convicted of wrongdoing. The charge that Christians were atheists, for example, was utter nonsense.

> For not only among the Greeks did reason (*Logos*) prevail to condemn [the pagan gods] through Socrates, but also among the Barbarians were they condemned by Reason (or the Word, the *Logos*) Himself, who took shape, and became man, and was called Jesus Christ; and in obedience to Him, we not only deny that they who did such things as these are gods, but assert that they are wicked and impious demons, whose actions will not bear comparison with those even of men desirous of virtue. Hence are we called atheists. And we confess that we are atheists, so far as [pagan] gods are concerned, but not with respect to the most true God, the Father of righteousness and temperance and the other virtues, who is free from all impurity. But both Him, and the Son (who came forth from Him and taught us these things, and the host of the other good angels who follow and are made like to Him), and the prophetic Spirit, we worship and adore, knowing them in reason and truth, and de-

claring without grudging to every one who wishes to learn, as
we have been taught.[20]

Justin contended that worshiping statues is patently absurd and the teachings of their own philosophers demonstrated the fact. Christians fear the
judgment of God and thus will never bow before idols. In fact, this fear of God
impelled Christians to be model citizens despite their refusal to acquiesce to
pagan rituals or the emperor cult. They shunned crime and licentious behavior and supported justice, civil virtue, honesty and paying taxes on time.

Justin then appealed to the manifold Old Testament prophecies fulfilled in
Christ. Jesus, for example, was predicted by Moses:

> A star shall rise out of Jacob, and a flower shall spring from
> the root of Jesse; and His arm shall the nations trust. And a
> star of light has arisen, and a flower has sprung from the root
> of Jesse—this Christ. For by the power of God He was con-
> ceived by a virgin of the seed of Jacob, who was the father of
> Judah, who, as we have shown, was the father of the Jews;
> and Jesse was His forefather according to the oracle, and He
> was the son of Jacob and Judah according to lineal descent.[21]

Justin also quoted from Scripture various passages foretelling the manner
and place of Christ's birth (see Isaiah 7:14; Micah 5:2); His advent and crucifixion (see Psalm 22; Isaiah 53); His ascension to heaven (see Psalm 110:1;
Daniel 7:13); the desolation of Judea (see Isaiah 1:7; 64:10-12; Leviticus
26:33; Jeremiah 44:6); Christ's work (see Isaiah 35:6; 57:1); His rejection by
His people, the Jews (see Isaiah 65:1-3; 5:20); His humiliation (see Isaiah
53:1-8); His majesty (see Psalm 24:7; Daniel 7:13); and numerous other fulfilled prophecies. The composite sketch that Justin gave of the fulfillment of
the promised Messiah showed Christ at the center of history. Justin brought
harmony to this evidence and summarized it:

> Though we could bring forward many other prophecies, we for-
> bear, judging these sufficient for the persuasion of those who
> have ears to hear and understand; and considering also that
> those persons are able to see that we do not make mere asser-
> tions without being able to produce proof, like those fables that
> are told of the so-called sons of Jupiter. For with what reason
> should we believe of a crucified man that He is the first-born of
> the unbegotten God, and Himself will pass judgment on the

whole human race, unless we had found testimonies concerning Him published before He came and was born as man, and unless we saw that things had happened accordingly—the devastation of the land of the Jews, and men of every race persuaded by His teaching through the apostles, and rejecting their old habits, in which, being deceived, they had their conversation; yea, seeing ourselves too, and knowing that the Christians from among the Gentiles are both more numerous and more true than those from among the Jews and Samaritans? For all the other human races are called Gentiles by the Spirit of prophecy; but the Jewish and Samaritan races are called the tribe of Israel, and the house of Jacob. And the prophecy in which it was predicted that there should be more believers from the Gentiles than from the Jews and Samaritans, we will produce: it ran thus: "Rejoice, O barren, thou that dost not bear; break forth and shout, thou that dost not travail, because many more are the children of the desolate than of her that hath an husband." For all the Gentiles were "desolate" of the true God, serving the works of their hands; but the Jews and Samaritans, having the word of God delivered to them by the prophets, and always expecting the Christ, did not recognise Him when He came, except some few, of whom the Spirit of prophecy by Isaiah had predicted that they should be saved. . . . So many things therefore, as these, when they are seen with the eye, are enough to produce conviction and belief in those who embrace the truth, and are not bigoted in their opinions, nor are governed by their passions.[22]

After dispelling false rumors about Christian practices such as baptism and communion, the *First Apology* ended with a final appeal to the emperor to treat Christians with greater jurisprudence and evenhandedness.

Second Apology

Justin addressed his *Second Apology* to the entire Roman senate. It invited the noblemen to hear his case and then recounted the beheading of three Christians who had committed no crimes but were killed because they affirmed their faith in Christ. The circumstances lying behind these events were equally dismal and wretched. Apparently, a certain woman—whose name is not mentioned—had led a debauched life before converting to Christianity,

one full of drinking and illicit sex "and every vice."[23] Shunning the path of his
wife, her husband continued in these things. The woman procured a bill of divorce against him despite the counsel of her new Christian friends. He did not
take it lightly. He brought an accusation against her, knowing it could cost
her her life. By God's grace, however, the woman submitted a paper to the
emperor, requesting that she be permitted to make a defense. This the emperor granted.

Unfortunately, however, this only further incensed the woman's husband.
This time he went after the woman's Christian mentor, Ptolemaeus, a catechetical teacher. Justin describes how the jilted husband set him up.

> He persuaded a centurion who had [already] cast Ptolemaeus
> into prison, and who was friendly to himself, to take
> Ptolemaeus and interrogate him on this sole point: Whether
> he were a Christian? And Ptolemaeus, being a lover of truth,
> and not of a deceitful or false disposition, when he confessed
> himself to be a Christian, was bound by the centurion, and for
> a long time punished in the prison.[24]

After suffering in miserable conditions, Ptolemaeus was brought before
Urbicus, the prefect of Rome at the time (144–160). Urbicus asked him point-
blank, "Are you a Christian?"[25] Ptolemaeus replied in the affirmative. Urbicus
immediately ordered him to be led away to punishment.

Having witnessed this grave injustice, a Christian man named Lucius came
to his defense, asking Urbicus for the grounds on which he cast such a stern
judgment. Urbicus replied, "You also seem to me to be one of them." Lucius
also stood his ground and answered, "Most certainly I am."[26] And thus Lucius
was also led away to his death. Justin recounted that still a third came forward and was condemned as the others with no court or case, just straight to
the executioner. Justin followed this narrative with these interesting and
prophetic words:

> I too, therefore, expect to be plotted against and fixed to the
> stake, by some of those I have named, or perhaps by Crescens
> [Justin's frequent opponent], that lover of bravado and
> boasting; for the man is not worthy of the name of philoso-
> pher who publicly bears witness against us in matters which
> he does not understand, saying that the Christians are athe-
> ists and impious, and doing so to win favour with the deluded

mob, and to please them. For if he assails us without having read the teachings of Christ, he is thoroughly depraved, and far worse than the illiterate, who often refrain from discussing or bearing false witness about matters they do not understand. Or, if he has read them and does not understand the majesty that is in them, or, understanding it, acts thus that he may not be suspected of being such [a Christian], he is far more base and thoroughly depraved, being conquered by illiberal and unreasonable opinion and fear. For I would have you to know that I proposed to him certain questions on this subject, and interrogated him, and found most convincingly that he, in truth, knows nothing. And to prove that I speak the truth, I am ready, if these disputations have not been reported to you, to conduct them again in your presence. And this would be an act worthy of a prince. But if my questions and his answers have been made known to you, you are already aware that he is acquainted with none of our matters; or, if he is acquainted with them, but, through fear of those who might hear him, does not dare to speak out, like Socrates, he proves himself, as I said before, no philosopher, but an opinionative man; at least he does not regard that Socratic and most admirable saying: "But a man must in no wise be honoured before the truth." But it is impossible for a Cynic, who makes indifference his end, to know any good but indifference.[27]

Justin spent the remainder of the *Second Apology* defending the virtue and purity of Christian teachings and further dispelling the rumors and misapprehensions disseminated by the vicious critics. He further contended that demons caused them to be so persecuted. Justin also discussed why Christians did not commit suicide even when confronted with execution, as well as some other christological items, the persistent hatred of Christians, the doctrine of hell, an interesting comparison of Jesus versus Socrates and finally the Christian view of death. Particularly striking is Justin's boldness. He apparently saw his own martyrdom looming on the horizon, but this only galvanized him in his apologetical work. No matter what awaited him, he did not stop proclaiming the truth of the risen Christ. Justin concluded with these words:

Our doctrines are not shameful, according to a sober judgment, but are indeed more lofty than all human philosophy:

and if not so, they are at least unlike the doctrines of the [philosophers and artisans], and such other teachings of the poets, which all are allowed to acquaint themselves with both as acted and as written. And henceforth we shall be silent, having done as much as we could, and having added the prayer that all men everywhere may be counted worthy of the truth. And would that you also, in a manner becoming piety and philosophy, would for your own sakes judge justly.[28]

Dialogue with Trypho

Justin's third work, *Dialogue with Trypho,* is unique because his focus is taken off his usual defense of Christians against their Roman persecutors, angry mobs and spiteful philosophers. Instead, he tried to convince his readers, especially Jews, that Jesus Christ was the Messiah promised in the Hebrew Scriptures. Justin made a lengthy appeal to predictive prophecy and its meticulous fulfillment in Christ alone. Modern mathematician Peter Stoner, for example, calculated the odds of forty-eight of the major messianic prophecies being fulfilled in any one person (there are approximately sixty altogether). Stoner found the odds to be something on the order of 1 in 10^{157}.[29] That's a "1" with 157 zeros after it. This number is so remote as to not even be within the realm of intelligibility, and its value is greater than the number of atoms in the universe.

Justin's interlocutor, Trypho, was a learned Jewish rabbi with whom Justin had a lengthy conversation in Ephesus sometime in the 130s. Trypho possibly was the "Rabbi Tarphon" mentioned in the Mishna, the Talmudic section that summarizes much of Jewish oral law with legal interpretations of the Pentateuch.[30] Though this is the longest of Justin's extant works (142 chapters), we do not possess the entire text.

In the first section of the *Dialogue,* Justin described both his intellectual development and his conversion experience. After this, the first part of the main section (chapters 9-47) explained the Christian understanding of Old Testament revelation: "The Mosaic law had only temporary jurisdiction. Christianity is the new and eternal law for all mankind."[31] The second part (chapters 48-108) justifies the exaltation of Jesus Christ as God.

The third part (chapters 109-142) demonstrates that the kings and nations who believe in Christ and follow His teachings represent the new spiritual Israel, the true chosen people of God.[32] In these main sections, Justin marshaled the detailed fulfillment of Old Testament prophecy as proof of these claims. He gave particular attention to Psalm 22, a veritable Polaroid snapshot of Christ's crucifixion written nearly five hundred years before.

> My God, My God, why have You forsaken Me?
> Why are You so far from helping Me? . . .
> All those who see Me ridicule Me;
> They shoot out the lip, they shake the head, saying,
> "He trusted in the LORD, let Him rescue Him;
> Let Him deliver Him, since He delights in Him!" . . .
> Many bulls have surrounded Me;
> Strong bulls of Bashan have encircled Me.
> They gape at Me with their mouths,
> Like a raging and roaring lion.
> I am poured out like water,
> And all My bones are out of joint;
> My heart is like wax;
> It has melted within Me.
> My strength is dried up like a potsherd,
> And My tongue clings to My jaws;
> You have brought Me to the dust of death.
> For dogs have surrounded Me;
> The congregation of the wicked has enclosed Me.
> They pierced My hands and My feet;
> I can count all My bones.
> They look and stare at Me.
> They divide My garments among them,
> And for My clothing they cast lots.
> (Psalm 22:1, 7-8, 12-18, NKJV)

Justin argued that "the whole Psalm refers thus to Christ."[33] He then catalogued many other messianic prophecies from the Psalms, the Mosaic writings and Isaiah, which were all fulfilled in Christ.

At the end of the proofs, Justin stressed that to reject Christ as the fulfillment of these prophecies is tantamount to rejecting God Himself:

> For he who knows not Him, knows not the will of God; and he
> who insults and hates Him, insults and hates Him that sent Him.
> And whoever believes not in Him, believes not the declarations of
> the prophets, who preached and proclaimed Him to all.[34]

The *Dialogue* is an invaluable resource for all admirers of the great apologists. It affords us an insight into the development of early Christian thought concerning Judaism and the relationship between God's law and Christ's grace. It also allows us to sit in on a remarkable apologetical conversation as Justin modeled for us the proper manner in which to share our faith with wisdom, gentleness and respect (see 1 Peter 3:15).

At the end of the *Dialogue,* we are left with the parting words among Justin, Trypho and several of Trypho's associates. Trypho said,

> "You see that it was not intentional that we came to discuss these matters. I confess that I have been particularly pleased with the interchange and I think that my friends are of quite the same opinion. For, indeed, we have found more than we expected, and more than we could have. If we could do this more frequently, we might be greatly helped in our search of the Scriptures themselves. But since," he said, "you are preparing to depart, and expect daily to set sail, please do not hesitate to remember us as friends when you are gone."

Justin replied,

> "For my part, if I remained, I would wish to do the same thing daily. But now, since I expect, with God's will and aid, to set sail, I exhort you to give all diligence in the great struggle for your own salvation, and to be earnest in setting a higher value on the Christ of the Almighty God than on your own teachers."[35]

After this, Trypho and his associates left Justin, wishing him well on his voyage. Justin then prayed for their salvation, saying, "I can wish no better thing for you all than this, that recognizing in this way that intelligence is given to every man, that you may be of the same opinion as ourselves, and believe that Jesus is the Christ of God."

Justin Becomes Justin Martyr

We conclude our look at the life of this great apologist with the occasion that gave him his last name—the day on which he sealed his apologetical testimony in his own blood. His last words before being scourged and then laying his head under the executioner's blade are recorded in *The Martyrdom of the*

Holy Martyrs, a document based on an official court report. In 167, having charged his critic Crescens with being a fool for distorting Christian beliefs and practices, Justin stood before an audience of the Roman court presided over by the prefect, Rusticus, who began his interrogation by demanding:

> "Obey the gods at once, and submit to the kings." Justin said, "To obey the commandments of our Savior Jesus Christ is worthy neither of blame nor of condemnation." To which Rusticus replied, "What kind of doctrines do you profess?" Justin said, "I have endeavored to learn all doctrines; but I have acquiesced at last to the *true* doctrines, those of the Christians, even though they displease those who hold false opinions." Rusticus, "Are those the doctrines that please you, then, you wretched man?" "They are," Justin said, "since I adhere to them as correct dogma." Rusticus said, "And what dogma is that?" Justin said, "It is that we worship the God of the Christians, whom we reckon to be one from the beginning, the maker and fashioner of the whole creation, visible and invisible; and the Lord Jesus Christ, the Son of God, who had also been preached beforehand by the prophets as about to be present with ordinary men, the herald of salvation and teacher of good disciples. And I, being a man, think that what I can say is insignificant in comparison with His boundless divinity, acknowledging a prophetic power, since it was prophesied concerning Him of whom now I say that He is the Son of God. For I know that the prophets of old foretold of His appearance among men."
>
> Rusticus said, "Where do you assemble?" "Wherever each one chooses and can," Justin answered, "for do you wish that we all met in the same place? Well it is not so, since God is not confined by place but being invisible, fills all heaven and earth, and everywhere is worshipped and glorified by the faithful." Rusticus said, "Tell me where you assemble." Justin replied, "I live above one Martinus, at the Timiotinian Bath and during the whole time I am unaware of any other meeting than this. And if anyone wished to come to me, I would communicate to him the doctrines of truth." Rusticus said, "Are you not, then, a Christian?" Justin said, "Yes, I am a Christian."[36]

Conclusion

Justin Martyr stands as the greatest intellectual defender of Christianity against the paganism and statism of the second century. In his *Apologies,* he showed that Christ was the fuller revelation of what reason demanded in the positive aspects of Greek philosophy. Traces of the truth about God were contained within the philosophical reasoning of such figures as Socrates and Plato, who were even persecuted for their insights. These philosophies spoke some truth, but they fell short of grasping the true nature of the *Logos,* which was manifested only in Jesus Christ.

The need for this kind of apologetic is far from over in our day. Justin provided us with a model for defending Christianity by appealing to those aspects of our cultural environment that may also bring people to Jesus. It is a model derived from Paul's Mars Hill discourse in which he too appealed to pagan poets and philosophers to direct attention to the true living God.

We should never be afraid to study philosophy and modern cultural movements. Rather, we should attempt to identify ways that current modes of thought may be used for the advancement of the gospel. This is, no doubt, a difficult process. The possibility of absorbing more of these philosophies into our thinking than we should is an ever-present danger. The task, then, calls for prayer and discernment. But Justin's approach should encourage us to dialogue with unbelievers using concepts to which they can relate and that we can use as a fulcrum for propping up the true philosophy of the gospel.

Irenaeus
2 Champion of Orthodoxy

We must avoid the heretic's doctrines and take careful heed lest we suffer injury from them; but to flee to the Church, and be brought up in her bosom, and be nourished with the Lord's Scriptures.
—Against Heresies, 5.20.2

Events in the Life of Irenaeus

c. 140	Born to Greek parents in Asia (modern Turkey).
c. 1551–60	Left Smyrna for Lyons in Southern Gaul (modern France) as a teenage missionary.
177	Clergy of Lyons sent Irenaeus to Rome with a letter concerning Montanism.
178	Irenaeus became bishop of Lyons after his predecessor, Pothinus, was martyred.
180	Wrote *Against Heresies*.
190–191	Interceded with Victor, the Roman bishop, and mediated the Easter controversy.
202	Irenaeus died in Lyons (as a martyr, according to tradition).

*P*opular actress Shirley MacLaine contends that "we are at any given moment living the totality of everything. . . . The vibrational oscillation of nature is quickening. . . . Just remember that you are God, and act accordingly."[1] MacLaine may suppose that she is being novel with her New Age views. But as theologian R.C. Sproul has observed, "There's really nothing new about the New Age."[2] Sproul is right. Many so-called New Age practices are repackaged Gnostic doctrines that flourished chiefly in the second and third centuries (though they existed well into the fifth) and are built on shirleymaclainian pantheism. Gnosticism could always attract disciples despite its absurd doctrines. As two well-known scholars put it,

> That the intolerable absurdities of Gnosticism should have gained so many disciples, and proved itself an adversary to be grappled with and not despised, throws light on the condition of the human mind under heathenism, even when it professed "knowledge" and "philosophy."[3]

They add that, "Nothing more absurd than these has probably ever been imagined by rational beings."[4] Yet the rapidly spreading tentacles of Gnosticism's poisonous and nonsensical teachings provide Church father and our second great apologist, Irenaeus, with a lifelong apologetics ministry.

Beginnings

Irenaeus was born around the year 140 to Greek parents in the proconsular territory of Asia (possibly Smyrna), roughly corresponding to modern-day Turkey. The manner of his conversion is not known. Irenaeus developed spiritually and intellectually under the guidance of Polycarp, the great Smyrnian bishop and student of the Apostle John. As a bold defender of the faith, Polycarp provided the pedagogical and practical training for Irenaeus to develop the skills for his later ministry. Irenaeus mentions his formative years with Polycarp in his *Letter to Florinus*.

> Polycarp having thus received [information] from the eye-witnesses of the Word of life, would recount them all in harmony with the Scriptures. These things, through God's mercy which was upon me, I then listened to attentively, and treasured them up not on paper, but in my heart; and I am continually, by God's grace, revolving these things accurately in my mind.[5]

After the reign of Antoninus Pius, his successor, Marcus Aurelius, came to power. Sometime between 155 and 160, Irenaeus left Smyrna for Lyons in southern Gaul (modern France) as a teenage missionary. Lyons was the perfect place for his introduction to missiology. It was an epicenter for the European trade market with Asia Minor and the largest city in Roman Gaul. Irenaeus' gifts as an adept communicator of the faith were soon evident, and he was ordained to the priesthood. The clergy of Lyons, many of whom were suffering persecution under Aurelius, later commissioned him in about 177 to go to Rome with a letter to the bishop there concerning Montanism. That journey provided further occasion for him to use his skills as a defender and moderator of the Church. Shortly after his return from Rome around 178, he was made bishop of Lyons, following his predecessor, the martyred Pothinus.

Under previous emperors, the Roman policy toward Christians was one of loose tolerance, but things changed dramatically under Aurelius. Eusebius tells us that in southern Gaul an imperial order inaugurated a new and brutal era of persecution.[6] In Asia Minor and Syria, historical records indicate that believers suffered severe persecution. One historian refers to "the blood of Christians flowing in torrents."[7] Irenaeus' chief task during this time was to shepherd his flock, instruct them and help them weather the storm of aggression that engulfed them.

Irenaeus' ministry took a radical shift, however, around the year 180 when Commodus succeeded his father, Aurelius, as Roman emperor, and his rule was marked by greed, suspicion, cruelty and scandal. Yet a paradoxical consequence of this fact was that his personal interests diverted his attention away from Christian persecution, resulting in a veritable cessation of it. Christians, then, enjoyed a measure of respite with opportunities to grow and continue in their learning.

As a result, Irenaeus complemented his bishopric with missions and developed his apologetic skills. During the next two decades, Irenaeus gained a place in Church history as a pastor, litterateur, apologist *par excellence* and "the most important theologian of the 2nd century."[8]

Specific information concerning the circumstances of Irenaeus' death around 202 are not known. Jerome (342–420) and Gregory the Great (c. 540–604) apparently believed he was martyred with a multitude of other Christians under the persecution of Septimius Severus.[9] However, Eusebius, who detailed the events of Irenaeus' life, made no mention of this.

Irenaeus is chiefly known for four main items:

1. His development and defense of essential Christian doctrine
2. His polemical apologetics against the growing tide of Gnosticism
3. His attempts to broker peace between the opposing parties of the so-called "Easter controversy"
4. His evangelistic zeal, especially in and around Lyons

We will deal primarily with the first three items.

Against Heresies

Only two of Irenaeus' great works are extant, though there are many fragments and quotations from his other writings, especially in Eusebius and Hippolytus. The most notable works are *Against Heresies* and the *Demonstration of the Apostolic Preaching* (a.k.a., the *Demonstration*).

We begin with *Against Heresies: The Detection and Overthrow of the Gnosis Falsely So-Called*. *Gnosis* in Greek means "knowledge," and obviously refers to the Gnostic sects of which the treatise is primarily concerned.

Against Heresies consists of five books:

- Book 1 identifies Gnostic errors and various Gnostic sects.
- Book 2 systematically tears down these errors, especially the Gnostic systems of Marcion and Valentinus.
- Book 3 outlines and explains sound Christian doctrine over Gnostic blunders. Special attention is given to the doctrine of God and Christology.
- Book 4 lists the Old Testament promises of Christ and His glorious fulfillment of them. It also refutes the Marcionite error of divorcing the passage of the old covenant into the new covenant.
- Book 5 continues repudiating Gnosticism point by point, with an emphasis on the literal bodily resurrection of Christ. Since Gnostics denied the physicality of the resurrection, this was a crucial discussion. Irenaeus argues that the resurrection of Christ was literal. To deny this is to deny the capstone in the arch of Christianity, for as the Apostle Paul said, "If Christ has not been raised, your faith is futile; you are still in your sins" (1 Corinthians 15:17).

The voluminous *Against Heresies* took immediate aim at Gnostics in hope of dispatching their erroneous teachings once and for all. Because of its thorough treatment, it continues to be used as source material against the New

Age movement today. So exhaustive is it, that its English translators lament that in reading it "the patience of the reader is sorely tried in following [Irenaeus] through those mazes of absurdity which he treads, in explaining and refuting these Gnostic speculations."[10] Johannes Quasten concurs: "Prolixity and frequent repetition make its perusal wearisome."[11] Nevertheless, for the diligent student of apologetics and historical theology, its perusal is well worth the effort for its apologetical sharpness, its insight into the development of doctrine and its reminder that much of Christian theology has been cultivated in times of controversy.

One English translator of *Against Heresies* said concerning Irenaeus' possible motivation in composing this great work that:

> He had the mortification of finding the Montanist heresy patronized by Eleutherus the Bishop of Rome; and there he [also] met an old friend from the school of Polycarp, who had embraced the Valentinian heresy. We cannot doubt that to this visit we owe the lifelong struggle of Irenaeus against the heresies that now came in, like locusts, to devour the harvests of the Gospel.[12]

In terms of the historical influence of Gnosticism, *Against Heresies* was for many years the only good source of material on the sect prior to the discovery of the Nag Hammadi documents in 1945 in Upper Egypt. Gnosticism as a whole is difficult to pinpoint. One prime hallmark, however, was its syncretism, the melding of various religious beliefs, including those of Christianity, into a conglomeration of philosophies, dogmas and rituals to acquire the divine knowledge, or *gnosis*.

Most Gnostics considered this world to be the ill-conceived project of evil archons or undergods who kept human souls entrapped in physical bodies. Therefore, people needed secret knowledge to release them from bondage and provide an escape from this evil world. Gnostics considered physical or material objects as bad things right from the start instead of God's good creation. This was the inevitable mystical connection with the rational Platonism with which the Gnostics flirted. Platonism espoused the imperfection of all material things, since they were only dim reflections of the otherwise perfect forms and ideas in the unattainable metaphysical realm of the *Logos*. The rub, though, was that this cryptic knowledge could not be attained rationally. Rather, it was procured through subjective, esoteric, mystical rituals, practices and incantations. The intellect or mind was the enemy of the spiritually attuned person, quite unlike the Christian axiom given by the Lord Himself that one must bring all human faculties into worshipful submission to God, specifically, heart, soul, strength and mind. This is, in fact, the greatest Christian command of all (see Luke 10:27). This is another major carryover into modern New Age and Eastern mysticism, which is built on the art of meditation to separate the distractions of the mind from the mystical wanderings of the soul. It is indeed a practice akin to the "kingdom of the cults," as the late Walter Martin called it, and is very dangerous.

Irenaeus made no bones about the true reality that people toy with when they do these things: "[When] they practice [their] magical arts and incantations, philters, and love-potions and have recourse to their familiar spirits," they are but "dream-sending demons."[13] Irenaeus saw Gnosticism and Christianity as nothing less than the powers of darkness feebly contending against the glorious forces of Light. This struggle between good and evil has eternal consequences, he argued. For those who flirt with the fleeting doctrines of the latter, they are foolishly inviting doom on themselves. The Christian Church alone is the keeper of truth and life.

> The Church, though dispersed throughout the whole world, even to the ends of the earth, has received from the apostles and their disciples this faith: [She believes] in one God, the Father Almighty, Maker of heaven, and earth, and the sea, and all things that are in them; and in one Christ Jesus, the Son of God, who became incarnate for our salvation; and in the Holy Spirit, who proclaimed through the prophets the dispensations of God, and the advents, and the birth from a virgin, and the passion, and the resurrection from the dead, and the ascension into heaven in the flesh of the beloved Christ Jesus, our Lord, and His [future] manifestation from heaven in the glory of the Father "to gather all things in one," and to raise up anew all flesh of the whole human race, in order that to Christ Jesus, our Lord, and God, and Saviour, and King, according to the will of the invisible Father, "every knee should bow, of things in heaven, and things in earth, and things under the earth, and that every tongue should confess" to Him, and that He should execute just judgment towards all; that He may send "spiritual wickednesses," and the angels who transgressed and became apostates, together

> with the ungodly, and unrighteous, and wicked, and profane
> among men, into everlasting fire; but may, in the exercise of
> His grace, confer immortality on the righteous, and holy, and
> those who have kept His commandments, and have perse-
> vered in His love, some from the beginning [of their Christian
> course], and others from [the date of] their repentance, and
> may surround them with everlasting glory.[14]

In dramatic contrast to the bankruptcy of proof for the teachings of the heretics, Irenaeus came equipped with an ample supply of proofs, so that the
honest inquirer could see the veracity of Jesus.

> I shall adduce proofs from the Scriptures, so that I may come
> behind in nothing of what thou hast enjoined; yea, that over
> and above what thou didst reckon upon, thou mayest receive
> from me the means of combating and vanquishing those
> who, in whatever manner, are propagating falsehood. For the
> love of God, being rich and ungrudging, confers upon the
> suppliant more than he can ask from.[15]

The heretic Marcion was perhaps the most well-known Gnostic, though in
many ways he was an atypical one and a rather poor spokesman for the sect.
He held on to its dualistic aspects and even advanced them. But unlike popular Gnosticism, which had its own body of writings, he concentrated on revis-
ing the New Testament in his desire to produce a Christianity unalloyed by
Judaism. To him, Christianity was a totally new covenant and represented a
different God from the Yahweh of the Old Testament. By salvation, he meant
possessing the esoteric knowledge of the good God revealed in Jesus and the
rejection of the evil God of the Old Testament. For Marcion, the Old Testament Yahweh was a vengeful, tribal bully who provided the Hebrews with a
national identity while they contended with their national neighbors. Jesus,
on the other hand, revealed a good God without the wrath, judgment and
atonement in the Old Testament.

Quite fittingly, then, Marcion set about to form his own canon of Scripture
and cut any references in the Gospels and Pauline epistles to "the old God."
Anything that portrayed a meek, mild and wrathless Jesus stayed. The result,
of course, was that he totally drained the true gospel of its saving power.

This corrupting and watering-down of the true gospel incensed Irenaeus.
Throughout his career, he reverenced the primacy of the whole scriptural rev-

elation of God and maintained an unwavering commitment to the Bible as the final court of appeal for all matters concerning faith and practice. If he disagreed with some teaching, he appealed immediately to sacred Scripture. The binding authority of the Bible was his recurring theme.

For example, in *Against Heresies,* Irenaeus wrote that "the Scriptures are indeed perfect, since they were spoken by the Word of God and His Spirit."[16] And, "We have learned from *none others* the plan of our salvation, than from those through whom the Gospel has come down to us, which they did at one time proclaim in public, and, at a later period, by the will of God, *handed down to us in the Scriptures, to be the ground and pillar of our faith"* (emphasis added).[17] Finally, "The tradition from the apostles does thus exist in the Church, and is permanent among us, [therefore] let us revert to the *Scriptural proof* furnished by those apostles who did also write the Gospel, in which they recorded the doctrine regarding God, pointing out that our Lord Jesus Christ is the truth"(emphasis added).[18] In response to Marcion, Irenaeus wrote,

> Those . . . who desert the preaching of the Church, call in question the knowledge of the holy presbyters, not taking into consideration of how much greater consequence is a religious man, even in a private station, than a blasphemous and impudent sophist. Now, such are all the heretics, and those who imagine that they have hit upon something more beyond the truth, so that by following those things already mentioned, proceeding on their way variously, inharmoniously, and foolishly, not keeping always to the same opinions with regard to the same things, as blind men are led by the blind, they shall deservedly fall into the ditch of ignorance lying in their path, ever seeking and never finding out the truth.[19]

Irenaeus offered an allegorical contrast between the poisonous doctrines of the Gnostics, as though they were the wicked fruit of the primordial garden, versus the sweetness of the gospel in the paradise of the Lord:

> We must avoid the heretic's doctrines and take careful heed lest we suffer injury from them; but to flee to the Church, and be brought up in her bosom, and be nourished with the Lord's Scriptures. For the Church has been planted as a garden in this world; therefore says the Spirit of God, "Thou mayest freely eat from every tree of the garden," that is, you may eat

from every Scripture of the Lord; but you shall not eat possessing a haughty mind, nor touch any heretical discord. For these men profess that they have in themselves the knowledge of good and evil; and they suppose to set their own impious minds above the God who made them. Therefore they form opinions on what is beyond the limits of understanding. For this cause also the apostle says, "Be not wise beyond what it is fitting to be wise, but be wise prudently," that we be not led astray by eating of the poison "knowledge" of these men. Go rather into the Lord's paradise that He has introduced to those who obey His call.[20]

Besides Marcion, other more mainstream Gnostics included Valentinus and Basilides whom Irenaeus also opposed at length in *Against Heresies*. Some major Gnostic texts besides the Gospel of Thomas include the *Gospel of Truth,* the *Acts of Peter,* the *Acts of Thomas, Treatise on the Three Natures,* the *Apocalypse of Adam,* the *Gospel of Matthias* and the *Gospel of Philip.* All such writings were sternly rejected by the fathers of the Church.

Irenaeus summed up his own arguments against the Gnostics by saying:

Such, then, is their system, which neither the prophets announced, nor the Lord taught, nor the apostles delivered, but of which they boast that beyond all others they have a perfect knowledge. They gather their views from other sources than the Scriptures; and to use a common proverb, they strive to weave ropes of sand, while they endeavor to adapt with an air of probability to their own peculiar assertions the parables of the Lord, the sayings of the prophets, and the words of the apostles, in order that their scheme may not seem altogether without support. In doing so, however, they disregard the order and the connection of the Scriptures, and so far as in them lie, dismember and destroy the truth. By transferring passages, and dressing them up anew, and making one thing out of another, they succeed in deluding many through their wicked art in adapting the oracles of the Lord to their opinions. Their manner of acting is just as if one, when a beautiful image of a king has been constructed by some skillful artist out of precious jewels, should then take this likeness of the man all to pieces, should rearrange the gems, and so fit them together as to make them into the form of a dog or of a fox, and even that but poorly executed; and should then maintain and declare that this was the beautiful image of the king which the skilful artist constructed, pointing to the jewels which had been admirably fitted together by the first artist to form the image of the king, but have been with bad effect transferred by the latter one to the shape of a dog, and by thus exhibiting the jewels, should deceive the ignorant who had no conception what a king's form was like, and persuade them that that miserable likeness of the fox was, in fact, the beautiful image of the king. In like manner do these persons patch together old wives' fables, and then endeavour, by violently drawing away from their proper connection, words, expressions, and parables whenever found, to adapt the oracles of God to their baseless fictions.[21]

The *Demonstration*

The second work we shall consider is Irenaeus' important *Demonstration of the Apostolic Preaching.* A distinguishing characteristic of this treatise is that whereas *Against Heresies* was negative apologetics to confute error, the *Demonstration* was more positive. It boldly proclaimed the truths of the Christian faith to a wider audience.

The *Demonstration* consisted of two parts. Following the introduction, the first part delineated the fundamentals of the Christian and "Catholic" faith. The author gave special attention to the centrality of the Triunity of the Godhead. The Trinitarian formula is ever present, evidencing the work of redemption as a "Three-in-One" endeavor. This emphasis is also seen in the *Fragments* of Irenaeus:

> Christ, who was called the Son of God before the ages, was manifested in the fullness of time, in order that He might cleanse us through His blood, who were under the power of sin, presenting us as pure sons to His Father, if we yield ourselves obediently to the chastisement of the Holy Spirit. And in the end of time He shall come to do away with all evil, and to reconcile all things, in order that there may be an end of all impurities.[22]

Irenaeus also treated the fall of humanity and Christ's Incarnation. Fallen humankind cannot see God except the Holy Spirit regenerates them. When this truly happens, however, their eternal life is irrevocable because they are "sealed" by baptism in the Savior's name. In the *Demonstration,* we see the recurrence of the Trinitarian formula and its significance:

> We have received baptism for the remission of sins, in the name of God the Father, and in the name of Jesus Christ, the Son of God, who was incarnate and died and rose again, and in the Holy Spirit of God. And that this baptism is the seal of eternal life, and is the new birth unto God, that we should no longer be the sons of mortal men, but of the eternal and perpetual God; and that what is everlasting and continuing is made God and is over all things that are made, and all things are put under Him; and all the things that are put under Him are made His own; for God is not ruler and Lord over the things of another, but over His own; and all things are God's; and therefore God is Almighty, and all things are of God."[23]

The second part of the *Demonstration* provides the apologetical defense of these teachings. Irenaeus appealed again to the manifold evidence of predictive prophecy in the Old Testament. He summarized this powerful apologetic by arguing that:

> If the prophets thus predicted that the Son of God would appear on earth, if they announced where on earth, how and in what manner he would manifest himself, and if the Lord took upon himself all that had been foretold of him, our belief in him is firmly established and the tradition of our preaching must be true, that is, true is the testimony of the Apostles who were sent by God, and who preached all over the world about the sacrifice which the Son of God made by suffering death and resurrection.[24]

In the closing section, Irenaeus exhorted his readers to live in accord with the historic Christian faith, and he warned them to steer away from heretics and their godlessness.[25]

The Easter Controversy

We lastly turn to another great apologetical outreach of Irenaeus' ministry, the Easter controversy. Irenaeus was not only the "Champion of Orthodoxy," but he could also be called the "Mediator" due to his efforts to bring peace amid the Church's turmoil. Like other Christian apologists Irenaeus picked his battles wisely, leveling his apologetical guns only at worthy issues. He strove for unity in the Church so long as essential Christian doctrine was not at stake. This apologetical ethos was evident particularly in his efforts to mediate between the churches concerning when they celebrated Easter. Some churches in Asia Minor did so on the fourteenth day of Nisan, when the Jews celebrated the Passover. The Western churches celebrated on Sunday.

In spite of the external controversies facing the Christian Church in the second century, it struggled internally during this time of expansion and polemicism. Irenaeus, a true master of the art of polemical apologetics, became a capable mediator. Whatever doubts anyone might have had about his ability to bring unity to the Church in the midst of this controversy, they were soon snuffed out. Eusebius gave us a primer on these events:

> A question of no small importance arose at that time. For the parishes of all Asia, as from an older tradition, held that the fourteenth day of the moon, on which day the Jews were commanded to sacrifice the lamb, should be observed as the feast of the Saviour's passover. It was therefore necessary to end their fast on that day, whatever day of the week it should happen to be. But it was not the custom of the churches in the rest of the world to end it at this time, as they observed the practice which, from apostolic tradition, has prevailed to the present time, of terminating the fast on no other day than on that of the resurrection of our Saviour. Synods and assemblies of bishops were held on this account, and all, with one consent, through mutual correspondence drew up an ecclesiastical decree, that the mystery of the resurrection of the Lord should be celebrated on no other but the Lord's day, and that we should observe the close of the paschal fast on this day only. There is still extant a writing of those who were then assembled in Palestine, over whom Theophilus, bishop of Caesarea, and Narcissus, bishop of Jerusalem, presided. And there is also another writing extant of those who were assembled at Rome to consider the same question, which bears the name of Bishop Victor; also of the bishops in Pontus over whom Palmas, as the oldest, presided; and of the parishes in Gaul of which Irenaeus was bishop, and of those in Osrhoene and the cities there; and a personal letter of Bacchylus, bishop of the church at Corinth, and of a great many others,

> who uttered the same opinion and judgment, and cast the same
> vote. And that which has been given above was their unani-
> mous decision.[26]

An Irenaean letter was among the writings that Eusebius mentioned here. Moreover, Irenaeus said that his beloved mentor, Polycarp, in tune with his fellow churchmen in Asia Minor, also kept Easter on the fourteenth day of the moon, on whatever day of the week that might fall, instead of on the prescribed Sunday. The Roman bishop at the time hastily and foolishly excommunicated the churches of Asia Minor for not staying in sync with the others. Irenaeus, despite the fact that he agreed with celebrating Easter on Sunday, found this act precipitous and distasteful. He saw no need to quibble about such issues of marginal consequence but believed that the churches should bend a little over nonessentials lest they break under the weight of senseless hairsplitting. He thus rebuked Victor for this action and pleaded with him to reconsider his actions, stressing the unity of the Church as taking precedence over nonessential matters. The churches, Irenaeus insisted, had the right to maintain their own practices. Unity should not be confused with uniformity. In regard to the issue, Irenaeus, in his *Epistle to Blastus,* wrote,

> The apostles ordained, that "we should not judge any one in
> respect to meat or drink, or in regard to a feast day, or the new
> moons, or the sabbaths." Whence then these contentions?
> Whence these schisms? We keep the feast, but in the leaven
> of malice and wickedness, cutting in pieces the Church of
> God; and we preserve what belongs to its exterior, that we
> may cast away these better things, faith and love.[27]

Though this issue emerged again in the mid-fourth century, the controversy eventually died down, in large part due to Irenaeus' efforts. We can learn from Irenaeus to pick our battles well and to "stop judging by mere appearances, and make a right judgment" (John 7:24). We should concern ourselves with spiritual meat, not ecclesiological parsley.

Conclusion

We live in an age of so-called tolerance. Now, if this meant that we are to tolerate one another in loving-kindness and thoughtful understanding, this wouldn't be a problem for Christians but an imperative. Yet the tolerance being touted today suggests that we ignore destructive false beliefs. Ideas have consequences. Anyone who doubts this simply doesn't know history. The gas chambers of Auschwitz began with philosophical papers shuffled around in academic lecture halls that sought to redefine humanity in the image of Nazi ideology. If tolerating what may be serious error in someone's thinking means never saying anything, we may also be tolerating their own personal destruction.

Irenaeus saw this and acted on it, not out of an imperialistic orthodoxy but out of genuine concern for people's souls. Irenaeus took what people believed seriously. He also recognized the spiritual polarity at work in our world. Jesus said to the individuals who rejected Him, "If God were your Father, you would love me," but they could not hear Him. He added, "You belong to your father, the devil, and you want to carry out your father's desire" (John 8:42, 44). This means that we have one of two fathers in the world, God or the devil.

Irenaeus reminds us that our situation on earth really is as stark as this. He saw the false teachings of his day as "poison knowledge" but the knowledge of the Lord a "paradise that He has introduced to those who obey His call." Poison versus paradise—that is what we truly face in life. We do not like to think this way. We would much rather consider spiritual error to be a transient matter that will work itself out without any exertion on our part. But Irenaeus knew better. He knew that God calls us and raises us up as instruments of truth and light in a spiritually dead world. He wanted to see people freed by the power of the gospel and the living God. To use tolerance as an excuse to do nothing would have been construed by Irenaeus not as an example of Christian love but of malice that cares nothing for the well-being of others.

Yet Irenaeus was not always just focused on correction and polemicism. He was also a healer and a mediator. He knew that unity was important and wanted to realize it in the Church. But he also understood the proper formula for unity: Truth + Liberty = Unity. It was most likely Augustine who later said, "In essentials, unity; in non-essentials, liberty; in all things, charity." The problem with much of today's ecumenism is that it focuses more on liberty than truth. Without truth, there is no real unity—only a veneer of it under the guise of tolerance. It may look like unity, but it is brittle. When unity is built on a core foundation of essential truths, however, a nearly impermeable edifice can be constructed. If we settle on matters of salvific importance (e.g.,

Jesus is God incarnate and died for the sins of the world), then we are in a position to allow for disagreement in other matters, such as when a particular church should celebrate Easter, what kind of music to have in the church, and so on. Irenaeus knew that the date of the Easter celebration did not matter as long as the celebrants followed the biblical axiom that "whatever you do, do it all for the glory of God" (1 Corinthians 10:31).

Irenaeus knew that unity cannot come through ignoring truth, but it also cannot come by confusing unity with uniformity. We must not "major in the minors," for the time for doing battle will come soon enough. We should not hasten it with issues that needlessly divide the Church and that the apostles and Church fathers would have considered but pittance. However, when serious issues do arise that slander God or threaten to steal the true gospel away from people's hearts, we must give it everything we have with persistence and great zeal to the glory of God.

This was Irenaeus' manner, and he remains an enduring gift to the Church. His theology and apologetics were thoroughly grounded in Scripture, he helped defend the Church against the ever-present "ravenous wolves" at her door, and he helped bring stability amid her internal tensions. As church historian Ward Gasque also emphasizes, "He wrote of the cosmic implications of the work of Christ and God's plan in history, and paved the way for the later Christian interpretations of [redemptive] history."[28] He was a skilled apologist, a master theologian, a deft and consoling mediator, a champion of orthodoxy.

Origen
The Prodigal Scholar

The Gospel has a demonstration of its own, more divine than any established by Grecian dialectics. And this diviner method is called by the apostle the "manifestation of the Spirit and of power" . . . on account of the prophecies, which are sufficient to produce faith in any one who reads them.
—Against Celsus, *1.2*

Events in the Life of Origen

185   Born in Alexandria to devout Christian parents.

203   Revived the catechetical school in Alexandria.

231   Fled Alexandria after Demetrius banished him.

232   Began a catechetical school in Caesarea.

248   Wrote *Against Celsus*.

254   Died in Tyre after suffering torture under the emperor Decius.

*B*rowsing the aisles at Barnes & Noble, warm Starbucks coffee in hand, has become a tradition in my family on many wintery Minnesota evenings. The coupling of these two companies provides a welcome respite from other nightlife options in any major city. Yet a strange thing dawns on anyone who has availed themselves of this: A veritable war is taking place on those shelves. It is a battle of words or, more specifically, worldviews. One book refutes another, and another refutes that one and another that one, while yet a fourth tells you in 2,500 pages why the other three are all wasting their time talking about it anyway. If the books on those well-stocked shelves were to suddenly come alive dressed in battle gear, no one would be left when the war was over, save the books on orchids and potting in the gardening section, what I call the "Switzerland" of Barnes & Noble. Thus, if books had weapons, B&N would have to pack its bags, abandon its partnership with Starbucks and start one with local florists.

On my last visit there, as I perused the religion aisle, I came across a volume entitled *Deceptions and Myths of the Bible.* The author begins with the first verse of the Bible, "In the beginning . . .", and launches into an attack, suggesting these words were penned out of sheer ignorance. The biblical author was not able to avail himself of modern cosmological discoveries that would immediately dispel such a notion. The rest of the book was filled with similar arguments, anecdotes and quotes bereft of a firm theological, philosophical or evidential grasp. Fearing that such a book was having an impact on readers, I logged on to Amazon.com to see what people were saying. Thankfully, the book was not garnering much positive attention. One reviewer summed it up well: "This [book] may be a good weapon to infuriate your Christian friends . . . until they read it for themselves." Well said. What is unfortunate, however, is that for those unschooled in Christian theology, this book could be the coffin nail in their decision to cast aside the biblical witness.

A Third-Century Attack

A similar tome was written in the early third century by a statesman and pagan philosopher named Celsus. Celsus gained attention toward the end of the second century as a result of his writings. Not much is known of his life except that he lived during the persecutory reign of Marcus Aurelius and was likely a native Roman. Celsus issued his own version of *Deceptions and Myths of the Bible* under the more general title, *The True Discourse*. In it, he opposed the Christian faith from the standpoint of Platonism, stressing the primacy of reason and its supposed enmity with Christian claims. The work may be divided into roughly five sections.

The first attacked Christianity from the viewpoint of Judaism. Celsus drew an unsavory continuity of Judeo-Christian separatism, insubordinationism and barbarism. He wrote that "Judaism, upon which Christianity depends, was barbarous in its origin."[1] Christians considered they had a superior wisdom when, in reality, their ideas concerning cosmogony and anthropology were common knowledge based on Greek wisdom. Celsus said, "The Greeks are more skilful than any others in judging, establishing, and reducing to practice the discoveries of barbarous nations."[2]

The second section attacked Christianity from the Jewish Scriptures, the Old Testament. Celsus contended that Jesus did not fulfill the messianic predictive prophecies, such as being born of a virgin. Instead, he said, Jesus made the story up Himself, knowing He was the son of a Jewish village woman, the wife of a lowly carpenter. Jesus apparently suffered from megalomania and invented stories about Himself, which His unlearned followers believed and augmented with their own ideas. The presence of a true "god" behind the events of His life was also absent. Jesus' flight into Egypt with His parents in the absence of any divine intervention to guide and protect them was one supposed line of evidence. Similarly, Jesus' miracles were either inventions of His followers or the fruit of magic arts Jesus picked up while sojourning in Egypt. Interestingly, Jewish writers of the Talmud made this same accusation, calling Jesus a "sorcerer and apostate."[3] Jesus' prediction of His own death and resurrection, as well as other statements about His divinity, were also inventions of His devotees. The resurrection narrative was simply borrowed from pagan mythology. Recently, members of the infamous Jesus Seminar made these same arguments.

The third section of *The True Discourse* attacked Christianity directly from philosophy. Celsus castigated Jews and Christians for quibbling over matters of dogma. He argued that since they were both founded on the same moral and philosophical principles, they should stop arguing and get along. One may say that Celsus was the first "comparative religionist" in his attempt to draw common threads between two opposing religions and then passing them off as teaching the same thing. Never mind, as the poet Steve Turner once wrote, that while they both agree on "love and goodness," they merely differ on matters of "sin, heaven, hell, God, and salvation!"[4]

In the fourth section, Celsus exhibited a poor understanding of Christian claims in his criticism of various Christian tenets. He found the incarnation and crucifixion silly, as though God could not accomplish the ends He desired by more direct and more sophisticated means. He argued that Christians invented the stories of Jesus' virgin birth, resurrection and other teachings.

> They continue to heap together one thing after another, discourses of prophets, and circles upon circles, and effluents from an earthly church, and from circumcision; and a power flowing from one Prunicos, a virgin and a living soul; and a heaven slain in order to live, and an earth slaughtered by the sword, and many put to death that they may live, and death ceasing in the world, when the sin of the world is dead; and, again, a narrow way, and gates that open spontaneously. And in all their writings (is mention made) of the tree of life, and a resurrection of the flesh by means of the "tree," because, I imagine, their teacher was nailed to a cross, and was a carpenter by craft; so that if he had chanced to have been cast from a precipice, or thrust into a pit, or suffocated by hanging, or had been a leather-cutter, or stone-cutter, or worker in iron, there would have been (invented) a precipice of life beyond the heavens, or a pit of resurrection, or a cord of immortality, or a blessed stone, or an iron of love, or a sacred leather! Now what old woman would not be ashamed to utter such things in a whisper, even when making stories to lull an infant to sleep.[5]

Celsus also misunderstood Christian teaching concerning God's sovereignty, providence, goodness and justice. He filtered everything through the lens of a nebulous Platonism in which he negated God's direct, physical involvement in the world. Pagan gods would never frequent with lowly fishermen and peasants. Lastly, Celsus argued that Christians plagiarized their eschatology from Grecian philosophy and mythology and derived their idea of a future resurrection of the body from metempsychosis or the transmigration of souls.

The fifth and final section of the work urged Christians to abandon their "cult" and unite with the majority state religion. Christians ought to render their gratitude and allegiance to the Roman gods who had blessed their society. To do less was to invite division in the empire. In their erroneous mono-theistic beliefs, Christians drove a wedge between God and the empire He blessed. "He who, when speaking of God, asserts that there is only one who may be called Lord, speaks impiously, for he divides the kingdom of God, and raises a sedition therein, implying that there are separate factions in the divine kingdom, and that there exists one who is His enemy."[6] Interestingly, Celsus even admonished Christians to "take office in the government of the country, if that is required for the maintenance of the laws and the support of the religion."[7] In addition, idols were good, pagan feasts even better, and the Roman religion was just plain superior. Christians wasted time trying to spread their doctrines, which never stood a chance of attaining global recognition, much less adherence.

Celsus' *True Discourse*, rife with error, demanded an answer from someone thoroughly committed to the Christian way of life, someone schooled in Platonism and attuned with pagan thought in general.

Enter Origen, the "Prodigal Scholar."

The Origin of Origen

Unlike most of his apologetic predecessors, Origen was born to devoutly Christian parents in 185 and apparently adopted their faith early on. So fervent was his faith that when rampant persecution broke out in Alexandria during the reign of Septimius Severus, he wanted to be martyred with his father, Leonides. But his mother hid his clothes, forcing him to stay home. Thus, instead, he wrote a treatise on martyrdom commemorating his father's noble sacrifice and encouraging him to persevere. His father did so up until the day of his martyrdom.

Origen became a teacher and composed educational books on secular subjects that he sold to support his mother and six younger brothers. Later, when Clement of Alexandria, the headmaster of the catechetical school, fled because of persecution, Origen took his post at the age of eighteen. The school under Origen's tutelage attained renown as the finest pedagogical institution of its day. Many Christian neophytes were transformed there into expositors, exegetes and martyrs.

Origen took his studies very seriously, especially theology, considering it the queen of all the sciences under which the rest become unified. Being an expert in many fields, especially philosophy, he at first taught everything from philosophy to astronomy, geometry and the life sciences. Later, however, he asked his associates to teach those subjects so he could devote his time to the exposition of biblical and Christian theology.

Origen became known not only for his incredible genius but also for his virtuous life, even to the point of self-flagellations and other extremes. Church historian Eusebius, who devoted almost the entire sixth chapter of his *Ecclesiastical History* to the life of Origen, had a deep respect for him. Here, Eusebius wrote of Origen's practices and the effect they had on many who knew him:

> He restrained himself as much as possible by a most philosophic life; sometimes by the discipline of fasting, again by limited time for sleep. And in his zeal he never lay upon a bed, but upon the ground. Most of all, he thought that the words of the Saviour in the Gospel should be observed, in which he exhorts not to have two coats nor to use shoes, nor to occupy oneself with cares for the future. With a zeal beyond his age he continued in cold and nakedness; and, going to the very extreme of poverty, he greatly astonished those about him. And indeed he grieved many of his friends who desired to share their possessions with him, on account of the wearisome toil which they saw him enduring in the teaching of divine things. But he did not relax his perseverance. He is said to have walked for a number of years never wearing shoes, and, for a great many years, to have abstained from the use of wine, and of all other things beyond his necessary food; so that he was in danger of breaking down and destroying his constitution.
>
> By giving such evidences of a philosophic life to those who saw him, he aroused many of his pupils to similar zeal; so that prominent men even of the unbelieving heathen and men that followed learning and philosophy were led to his instruction. Some of them having received from him into the depth of their souls faith in the Divine Word, became prominent in the persecution then prevailing; and some of them were seized and suffered martyrdom.[8]

Eusebius' account of Origen's life remains the best biography of the great apologist.

Origen did everything in his power to follow God's path and to purge himself of sinful impurities. This actually led Origen to castrate himself. Since he taught many young females at his school in Alexandria, he took the Lord's admonition in Matthew 19:12 to the utmost extreme. He felt it wise to preclude the possibility of scandal before it ever took form.

Unfortunately, after many years of faithful service at his school, Origen fled his native Alexandria due to his bishop's hostility. The problems between the two, which may have stemmed from Demetrius' jealousy of his underling's talents, began earlier when Origen was ordained on one of his journeys so he could preach the gospel. Theoctistus, the bishop of Caesarea, together with Alexander, bishop of Jerusalem, ordained him. Although Demetrius respected Origen and had issued letters of recommendation on his behalf, he was angry that this took place without his knowledge and, as he thought, in derogation of his rights.[9] Demetrius then claimed that Origen should be disqualified because of emasculating himself, a highly questionable technicality. So Origen was ignominiously excommunicated from Alexandria.

In 232, Origen settled in Caesarea and, under the protection of his friend and admirer Theoctistus, began a new school, which attracted many eager students. Such students were drawn not only by his giant intellect and abilities in biblical exposition but also his godly character. Here, he composed biblical commentaries (most notably on John) and scholarly works, including his renowned *Hexapla*, an edition of the Old Testament in six columns: the Hebrew text, a Greek transliteration, and then four Greek translations. Origen had a high respect for the authority and inspiration of the Bible and wanted to provide only the finest tools for its study. Besides this ambitious work, he also composed his two most well-known theological and apologetic works: *de Principiis*, a treatise on doctrinal theology, and the text with which we are here chiefly concerned, *Against Celsus*.

Origen Responds to *The True Discourse*

In about the year 250, Ambrose, a friend of Origen's, introduced him to *The True Discourse* of Celsus. Ambrose was concerned that, should Celsus' book get a wide circulation and remain unchallenged, it would do damage to the Church. Origen was at first skeptical as to what good a response would do. It would not likely convince those sympathetic to it and conversely would not sway anyone truly committed to Christ's teachings. Thus, he wrote:

> When false witnesses testified against our Lord and Saviour Jesus Christ, He remained silent; and when unfounded charges were brought against Him, He returned no answer, believing that His whole life and conduct among the Jews were a better refutation than any answer to the false testimony, or than any formal defence against the accusations. And I know not, my pious Ambrosius, why you wished me to write a reply to the false charges brought by Celsus against the Christians, and to his accusations directed against the faith of the Churches in his treatise; as if the facts themselves did not furnish a manifest refutation, and the doctrine a better answer than any writing, seeing it both disposes of the false statements, and does not leave to the accusations any credibility or validity.[10]

Origen believed that those who have been truly regenerated by the Holy Spirit would not be led astray by the philosophic wonderings of a harsh pagan critic. What is interesting, then, is the reason why Origen ultimately did choose to take the time to provide a reply:

> I do not congratulate that believer in Christ whose faith can be shaken by Celsus—who no longer shares the common life of men, but has long since departed—or by any apparent plausibility of argument. For I do not know in what rank to place him who has need of arguments written in books in answer to the charges of Celsus against the Christians, in order to prevent him from being shaken in his faith, and confirm him in it. But nevertheless, since in the multitude of those who are considered believers some such persons might be found as would have their faith shaken and overthrown by the writings of Celsus, but who might be *preserved* by a reply to them of such a nature as to refute his statements and to exhibit the truth, we have deemed it right to yield to your injunction, and to furnish an answer to the treatise which you sent us, but which I do not think that any one, although only a short way advanced in philosophy, will allow to be a "True Discourse," as Celsus has entitled it.[11]

Contemporary apologist William Lane Craig, who has debated numerous skeptics, atheists and agnostics, says that when he engages in such exchanges, it is never with the object of merely convincing his opponents. Rather, it is to impact those who hear the truth of the gospel and to edify and preserve his fellow Christians. Thoroughly grounded believers do not need such argumentation, but seekers and honest skeptics can benefit greatly. Moreover, solid believers can become further equipped in their biblical charge to "always being ready to make a defense to everyone who asks you to give an account for the hope that is in you" (1 Peter 3:15, NASB). Thus, Origen writes,

> After proceeding with this work as far as the place where Celsus introduces the Jew disputing with Jesus, I resolved to prefix this preface to the beginning (of the treatise), in order that the reader of our reply to Celsus might fall in with it first, and see that this book has been composed not for those who are thorough believers, but for such as are either wholly unacquainted with the Christian faith, or for those who, as the apostle terms them, are "weak in the faith"; regarding whom he says, "Him that is weak in the faith receive ye." And this preface must be my apology for beginning my answer to Celsus on one plan, and carrying it on another. For my first intention was to indicate his principal objections, and then briefly the answers that were returned to them, and subsequently to make a systematic treatise of the whole discourse. But afterwards, circumstances themselves suggested to me that I should be economical of my time, and that, satisfied with what I had already stated at the commencement, I should in the following part grapple closely, to the best of my ability, with the charges of Celsus. I have therefore to ask indulgence for those portions which follow the preface towards the beginning of the book. And if you are not impressed by the powerful arguments which succeed, then, asking similar indulgence also with respect to them, I refer you, if you still desire an argumentative solution of the objections of Celsus, to those men who are wiser than myself, and who are able by words and treatises to overthrow the charges which he brings against us. But better is the man who, although meeting with the work of Celsus, needs no answer to it at all, but who despises all its contents, since they are contemned, and with good reason, by every believer in Christ, through the Spirit that is in him.[12]

Origen embarked on his task of refuting Celsus point by point. We do not possess a full extant copy of Celsus' discourse but are able to reconstruct it almost in full from Origen's response, three-fourths of which consists of what

Celsus wrote. The work is not only thorough, but the tone is calm and dignified, which soon puts Celsus' accusations in the shadow, shamed almost under the weight of his own invective. Origen also argued against Celsus' insistence on the superiority of Greek thought and his subsequent use of it.

> Celsus [says] that the system of doctrine, viz., Judaism, upon which Christianity depends, was barbarous in its origin. And with an *appearance* of fairness, he does not reproach Christianity because of its origin among barbarians, but gives the latter credit for their ability in discovering such doctrines. To this, however, he adds the statement, that the Greeks are more skilful than any others in judging, establishing, and reducing to practice the discoveries of barbarous nations. Now this is our answer to his allegations, and our defence of the truths contained in Christianity, that if any one were to come from the study of Grecian opinions and usages to the Gospel, he would not only decide that its doctrines were true, but would by practice establish their truth, and supply whatever seemed wanting, from a Grecian point of view, to their demonstration, and thus confirm the truth of Christianity. We have to say, moreover, that the Gospel has a demonstration of its own, more divine than any established by Grecian dialectics. And this diviner method is called by the apostle the "manifestation of the Spirit and of power": of "the Spirit," on account of the prophecies, which are sufficient to produce faith in any one who reads them, especially in those things which relate to Christ; and of "power," because of the signs and wonders which we must believe to have been performed, both on many other grounds, and on this, that traces of them are still preserved among those who regulate their lives by the precepts of the Gospel.[13]

Origen's apologetic approach was the classical method of dealing with Christianity's antagonists. Elements of what professional apologists often refer to as evidentialism and presuppositionalism were also present, making his apologetic approach somewhat integrative. The evidence for Christ's divinity was overwhelming. His birth, life, death and resurrection were foretold in irrefutable detail such that faith in Him is the inevitable fruit of a clear mind. On the presuppositional end, however, Origen was convinced that the negative effects of sin blind the unregenerate soul to these truths so that only the Holy Spirit's quickening power can liberate it from intellectual darkness.

For the law and the prophets are full of marvels similar to those recorded of Jesus at His baptism, viz., regarding the dove and the voice from heaven. And I think the wonders wrought by Jesus are a proof of the Holy Spirit's having then appeared in the form of a dove, although Celsus, from a desire to cast discredit upon them, alleges that He performed only what He had learned among the Egyptians. And I shall refer not only to His miracles, but, as is proper, to those also of the apostles of Jesus. For they could not without the help of miracles and wonders have prevailed on those who heard their new doctrines and new teachings to abandon their national usages, and to accept their instructions at the danger to themselves even of death. And there are still preserved among Christians traces of that Holy Spirit which appeared in the form of a dove. They expel evil spirits, and perform many cures, and foresee certain events, according to the will of the Logos. And although Celsus, or the Jew whom he has introduced, may treat with mockery what I am going to say, I shall say it nevertheless, that many have been converted to Christianity as if against their will, some sort of spirit having suddenly transformed their minds from a hatred of the doctrine to a readiness to die in its defence, and having appeared to them either in a waking vision or a dream of the night. Many such instances have we known, which, if we were to commit to writing, although they were seen and witnessed by ourselves, we should afford great occasion for ridicule to unbelievers, who would imagine that we, like those whom they suppose to have invented such things, had ourselves also done the same. But God is witness of our conscientious desire, not by false statements, but by testimonies of different kinds, to establish the divinity of the doctrine of Jesus. And as it is a Jew who is perplexed about the account of the Holy Spirit having descended upon Jesus in the form of a dove, we would say to him, "Sir, who is it that says in Isaiah, 'And now the Lord hath sent me and His Spirit'?" In which sentence, as the meaning is doubtful—viz., whether the Father and the Holy Spirit sent Jesus, or the Father sent both Christ and the Holy Spirit—the latter is correct. For, because the Saviour was sent, afterwards the Holy Spirit was sent also, that the prediction of the prophet might be fulfilled; and as it was necessary that the fulfillment of the prophecy should be known to posterity, the disciples of Jesus for that reason committed the result to writing.[14]

The belief of Christians, then, is faith at work in evidence. Nevertheless, it presupposes a prevening and effectual grace:

> For the word of God declares that the preaching (although in itself true and most worthy of belief) is not sufficient to reach the human heart, unless a certain power be imparted to the speaker from God, and a grace appear upon his words; and it is only by the divine agency that this takes place in those who speak effectually. The prophet says in the Psalms, that "the Lord will give a word with great power to them who preach." If, then, it should be granted with respect to certain points, that the same doctrines are found among the Greeks as in our own Scriptures, yet they do not possess the same power of attracting and disposing the souls of men to follow them.[15]

Celsus also contended that Christianity would destroy civil virtue and obedience to the state and its religion. Christians during this time kept to themselves since paganism was intertwined with the political system. This suggested a tendency toward insurrection.

Origen responded to this attack ingeniously. As Celsus made himself out to be a zealous patriot, Origen appealed to his readers as a cosmopolitan who understood that the history of nations, kingdoms and empires is the history of God's providence. He appealed to something higher than Celsus' ostensive patriotism and sounded a clarion call to the rulers to seek a higher purpose than mere worldly gain. Origen thus turned Celsus' arguments around once again:

> [Celsus says] what harm is there in gaining the favour of the rulers of the earth, whether of a nature different from ours, or human princes and kings? For these have gained their dignity through the instrumentality of [the gods].[16]
>
> [But] there is [only] One whose favour we should seek, and to whom we ought to pray that He would be gracious to us—the Most High God, whose favour is gained by piety and the practice of every virtue. And if he would have us to seek the favour of others after the Most High God, let him consider that, as the motion of the shadow follows that of the body which casts it, so in like manner it follows, that when we have the favour of God, we have also the good-will of all angels and spirits who are

friends of God. For they know who are worthy of the divine approval, and they are not only well disposed to them, but they co-operate with them in their endeavours to please God: they seek His favour on their behalf; with their prayers they join their own prayers and intercessions for them. We may indeed boldly say, that men who aspire after better things have, when they pray to God, tens of thousands of sacred powers upon their side. These, even when not asked, pray with them, they bring succour to our mortal race, and if I may so say, take up arms alongside of it: for they see demons warring and fighting most keenly against the salvation of those who devote themselves to God, and despise the hostility of demons; they see them savage in their hatred of the man who refuses to serve them with the blood and fumes of sacrifices, but rather strives in every way, by word and deed, to be in peace and union with the Most High through Jesus, who put to flight multitudes of demons when He went about "healing," and delivering "all who were oppressed by the devil." Moreover, we are to despise ingratiating ourselves with kings or any other men, not only if their favour is to be won by murders, licentiousness, or deeds of cruelty, but even if it involves impiety towards God, or any servile expressions of flattery and obsequiousness, which things are unworthy of brave and high-principled men, who aim at joining with their other virtues that highest of virtues, patience and fortitude. But whilst we do nothing which is contrary to the law and word of God, we are not so mad as to stir up against us the wrath of kings and princes, which will bring upon us sufferings and tortures, or even death. For we read: "Let every soul be subject unto the higher powers. For there is no power but of God: the powers that be are ordained of God. Whosoever therefore resisteth the power, resisteth the ordinance of God."[17]

Origen and Biblical Authority

Though Origen used logic and reason, the Bible was his principal guide for all matters pertaining to faith and doctrine. For example, before entering into a christological discussion in his *de Principiis*, he wrote that we must first "ascertain how statements which we have advanced are supported by the authority of Holy Scripture."[18] Later, in the same work, he wrote that "if any one should desire to discuss these matters more fully, it will be necessary, with all reverence and fear of God, to examine the sacred Scriptures with greater attention and diligence."[19] Finally, in *Against Celsus*, he stated that "the sacred Scriptures teach us to think."[20] To him, reason and philosophy were tools, but the manner in which he used them should never be at odds with what is contained in Holy Writ.

Of course, the extent to which Origen always followed this modus is debatable. In the centuries to follow, despite his defending the faith, his teachings became the subject of much controversy, his name was maligned and his contribution upbraided. In matters outside the biblical witness or the settled teachings of the Church, Origen had felt free to philosophize sometimes on a flawed path. As a defender of the veracity of Scripture, he warned his students about the dangers of overphilosophizing the faith and using Plato as an intellectual filter. He seemed, however, to forget his own admonition at times. In fact, later Church councils charged him with heresy. For these reasons, along with the incredible scope of his works, I chose for him the name, the "Prodigal Scholar." By *prodigal* I do not mean immoral like the prodigal son. Rather, I mean "abundant" and "extravagant." Though he was determined to remain orthodox and biblical, Origen was insatiably curious and examined undecided doctrines, which often led him into trouble. Origen's apologetical hammer was constantly raised. But for every dozen nails he pounded in for the Church, he pounded one into the wrong building.

Despite his confidence in the authority and inspiration of the Bible, Origen advocated an allegorical interpretation of historical narratives or outlines of actual events, such as the creation stories. He also believed in the preexistence of souls, the impermanent nature of the physical resurrection and universalism (the doctrine that all people, angels and Satan himself will eventually be saved). He may also have had a subordinationist tendency in his view of Christ (that is, he may have believed that Jesus is subordinate to the Father).

We must remember, though, that vocabulary plays an important part in these issues. The words used to shape the orthodox understandings of later centuries were more precise through historical discussions as opposed to what Origen employed. Origen's critics may have read into his expressions meanings they themselves brought with them but which did not belong to Origen. This is especially true with his possible subordination-ism.

Nevertheless, Origen did get it wrong from time to time. That he advocated his own form of universalism, for example, is virtually uncontested. Church historian Bruce Shelley comments on this issue:

> That doctrine above all others caused him no end of trouble. Many humane souls in the history of the church have dreamed that God's love would someday triumph over all sinful rebellion. Origen's error lay in turning a dream into a doctrine. Orthodox Christians felt that they could not turn the dream into a doctrine because such an idea almost always tends to deny man's free will and its eternal consequences.[21]

These speculations on undeveloped Church dogma have led some Christian apologists to avoid Origen. They think that his theological wanderings and the negatives issuing from them outweigh the positives. While I understand this sentiment and deny these marginal teachings of Origen's, I think to cast him aside too quickly fails to contextualize his contributions to the development of theology and apologetics, as well as his fundamental commitment to matters of the settled orthodoxy of his day. As one commentator writes:

> His [writings] set forth Christian theology on a scale previously unknown to the church. He argued powerfully for the inspiration and authority of Scripture . . . and he affirmed God as Creator of all things, Christ as eternal Son and Word, and the Holy Spirit—each member distinct from the others yet together forming a unity.[22]

Origen wanted to be biblical even if he did, at times, fail to heed his own warnings about overusing secular philosophy. As a testimony to his commitment to the essentials of the faith, when he was finally put to the test, he held firmly to the veracity of Christ's divinity and the truthfulness of the Bible. Shelley agrees, adding that Origen "made no such alterations in the faith" that would blot out the primacy of the gospel message.[23] Indeed, that he suffered dearly at the hands of his persecutors should be remembered in terms of what really mattered to him. He did not endure his trials and tortures for his idle speculations but for the fundamentals of the Church he loved so well.

The Twilight Years

That Origen suffered dearly for this faith in his final years is clear. Eusebius gave us this account of his martyrdom after the Emperor Decius (250) had come to power:

> But how many and how great things came upon Origen in the persecution, and what was their final result—as the demon of evil marshaled all his forces, and fought against the man with his utmost craft and power, assaulting him beyond all others against whom he contended at that time—and what and how many things he endured for the word of Christ, bonds and bodily tortures and torments under the iron collar and in the dungeon; and how for many days with his feet stretched four spaces in the stocks he bore patiently the threats of fire and whatever other things were inflicted by his enemies; and how his sufferings terminated, as his judge strove eagerly with all his might not to end his life; and what words he left after these things, full of comfort to those needing aid, a great many of his epistles show with truth and accuracy.[24]

After these tortures, Origen lingered on a few years and died at the age of sixty-nine. His last days were spent at Tyre in Lebanon, though his reason for going there is unknown. He was buried with great honors as a confessor of the faith and indeed, for a long time his tomb, placed behind the altar of the cathedral there, was visited by faithful Christians from around the world. To-day, all that remains of this cathedral is a mass of ruins, and the exact location of his tomb remains unknown.

We end our look at the life of Origen with his own conclusion from *Against Celsus*, where he urged readers to judge for themselves who spoke by the Spirit of Truth and who did not. He also uttered his intentions should Celsus (or anyone else) decide on a rejoinder:

> You have here, reverend Ambrose, the conclusion of what we have been enabled to accomplish by the power given to us in obedience to your command. In eight books we have embraced all that we considered it proper to say in reply to that book of Celsus which he entitles *A True Discourse*. And now it remains for the readers of his discourse and of my reply to judge which of the two breathes most of the Spirit of the true God, of piety to-

wards Him, and of that truth which leads men by sound doctrines to the noblest life. You must know, however, that Celsus
had promised another treatise as a sequel to this one, in which
he engaged to supply practical rules of living to those who felt
disposed to embrace his opinions. If, then, he has not fulfilled
his promise of writing a second book, we may well be contented
with these eight books which we have written in answer to his
discourse. But if he has begun and finished that second book,
pray obtain it and send it to us, that we may answer it as the Father of truth may give us ability, and either overthrow the false
teaching that may be in it, or, laying aside all jealousy, we may
testify our approval of whatever truth it may contain. Glory be
to Thee, our God; glory be to Thee.[25]

A second book never came.

Conclusion

Like Justin Martyr, Origen illustrates that reason and philosophy can be
powerful tools in the advancement of the gospel. But the manner in which
we use them must never be at odds with what is contained in Holy Scripture.
We do not preach a "god of the philosophers." Rather, we preach the true, living God of the Hebrews. Origen believed this firmly, despite the fact that he
may have failed to heed his own advice at times. His christological speculations may have functioned as a precursor to Arianism a generation later,
which proved to be a thorny issue for the Church.

Origen was an insatiably curious scholar, which probably became his
Achilles' heel. He was like a high-intensity laser beam without an "off"
switch. But the trick for him was knowing where to point it. When he pointed
it at the right issues, it was high-precision and powerfully effective, but it
could do damage when misdirected. Yet Origen was humble and desired to be
biblical. Given the chance of a corrective rebuttal, he may have recanted his
speculatory theology. We must remember that Origen did not have the benefit of centuries of reflection on the issues he addressed, and he actually provided a forum for these issues to be rehashed later.

Origen's positive influence on historic Christianity and his continuing usefulness today far outweighs any negative impact he may have had. As a dar-
ing innovator, he attempted one of the earliest systematizations of the

Christian faith, coupled with an integration of other areas of knowledge. In so doing, a powerful apologetic resulted that the Lord used to convert many gifted students of pagan philosophy to the Church. Credit is also due Origen for the intellectual triumph of Christianity over the inroads of paganism and Gnosticism that threaten orthodoxy. Origen shows us that we are not to cloister ourselves in the Church in the face of worldly opposition. We are not to become isolationists. True, we are not to be *of* the world, but we are called to be *in* the world. Jesus told us that we are not to hide the lamp of the gospel under a bowl. Rather, we are to place the light of truth on a stand so it shines forth to everyone (see Matthew 5:15-16). This should encourage us to challenge issues facing us today, such as relativism, atheistic evolution and New Age mysticism.

Origen's life and apologetic also remind us that what we take for granted as solid, doctrinal orthodoxy was forged in the furnace of affliction. We can only imagine what it must have been like for Origen to live through the persecution of his Christian father. But God used this experience to embolden him further in defending and spreading the truth of Christianity.

Origen's character was transparent and his life nearly beyond reproach. Thus, it wasn't only his intellectual arguments that won people over but how he lived his life. This is a model to us today never to subdivide our character and message. Origen shows us how we can manifest two biblical maxims as we carry the message of the gospel. On one hand, we are to "always [be] ready to make a defense [*apologia*] to everyone who asks you to give an account for the hope that is in you" (1 Peter 3:15, NASB). But that is not all. We are also to "live such good lives among the pagans that, though they accuse you of doing wrong, they may see your good deeds and glorify God on the day he visits us" (1 Peter 2:12). Origen came as close to modeling these biblical commands as anyone has after Jesus Himself. May his life and apologetic also be an example to us.

Athanasius
Preserver of the Faith

And thus we preserve One Beginning of Godhead . . . the Word is by nature Son, not as if another beginning, subsisting by Himself, nor having come into being externally to that Beginning . . . and from the One, a Son in nature and truth, is Its own Word, Its Wisdom, Its Power, and inseparable from It.
 —Discourses Against the Arians

Events in the Life of **Athanasius**

298	Born in Alexandria during the persecution of the emperor Diocletian.
313	Emperor Constantine issued the Edict of Milan declaring Christianity legal.
319	Ordained to the diaconate by Bishop Alexander. Wrote *Contra Gentes* and *De Incarnatione*.
325	Accompanied Alexander to the Council of Nicea.
328	Became the bishop of Alexandria.
335	Faced charges before a synod in Tyre and later fled the city.
335–364	Banished five times from his bishopric in Alexandria. Composed many great works, including *Discourses Against the Arians*.
373	Athanasius died among friends and fellow ministers.

G. K. Chesterton once said, "The problem with not believing in God is not that you believe in nothing, but that you will believe in anything."[1] Convictions are important. Without them, we are like waves tossed in a stormy sea or, as Irenaeus preferred, like "ropes of sand." Paul wrote, "Each one should be fully convinced in his own mind. . . . If we live, we live to the Lord; and if we die, we die to the Lord" (Romans 14:5, 8). Have you ever asked yourself what things you're ready to die for or to *live* for? Perhaps it is a conviction of the Lord's good salvation for all who receive Him, or the Trinity, or the promise of eternal felicity with God in heaven. No doubt all these are glorious hills worth living and dying for.

Yet as we have seen in the life of Irenaeus, it is probably not wise to have too many of these hills. In our short lives on earth, we have to pick our battles well; if we spread ourselves too thin, we may give our talents, energies and time to the wrong things. Thus, we can make two equal and opposite errors: One is to have no cause worth living or dying for; the other is to have too many causes of relative insignificance. We have to decide where to place our true stock and then devote our hearts and energies to becoming disciples of timeless truths. We must "rejoice in eternal verities, not earthly vanities," as one Christian leader puts it.[2]

A Worthy Battle

One of the most important theological controversies ever in Church history was not over one chapter of the Bible or even one word but over one *letter*. Around the year 320, a doctrinal dispute arose in Alexandria, Egypt, and pushed north into Asia Minor, most notably in the churches of Antioch. This new doctrine held that Jesus was not coeternal and "consubstantial" with the Father but merely the highest of all created beings. This doctrine was propounded most forcefully by Arius (250?-336). Arius was at first a presbyter and esteemed preacher of the Baucalis church in Alexandria, then considered the intellectual capital of the Roman Empire. The dispute came to a head after Alexander, his bishop, became aware of several theses Arius had written after his study of the Synoptic Gospels (Matthew, Mark and Luke). Among those theses were the following:

- God the Father is eternal, but Jesus Christ is not. He is the created being of the Father.

- The Father and the Son are not essentially the same in substance or essence.
- The *Logos* entered into the human body of Jesus in place of a human mind or soul.
- Jesus was not the *theanthropos*, the "God-man," since He was neither fully God nor fully man.

Following Alexander's lead, Arius was excommunicated from the Alexandrian community in 321 by a synod of one hundred of his peers. He fled to Palestine and found allies, later known as the "Arians." Soon two opposing theological epicenters, one in Antioch, the other in Alexandria, were pitted against one another over the orthodoxy or heterodoxy of Arius' teachings.

And it is here that the entire controversy hinged on a single letter. Those who concurred with the Alexandrian view held that Christ was *homoousios*, that is, "of the same substance" as the Father, fully divine though fully human. Those who concurred with Arius, which included many from the Antiochene school, held rather to the idea of Christ as *homoiousios*, "of a *similar* but not the *same* substance" with the Father. The *i* in the middle of the word (as hard as it is to see!) made all the difference in the world. The great Athanasius, the "Pillar of the Church," as Gregory of Nazianzus called him, spent the rest of his life arguing against it and trying to flush that little *i* from ecclesiastical parlance.

The Early Years

Beyond the apostles themselves, Athanasius was likely the man to whom we owe the preservation of the historic Christian faith. He was born around 298 in that epicenter of theology and learning, Alexandria. During his early years, Athanasius no doubt witnessed the last and most terrible episode of Christian persecution under the brutal reign of the Emperor Diocletian.[3] Diocletian, along with his compatriot Galerius, had resolved to stamp out Christianity altogether throughout the entire empire. Eusebius wrote that an edict was issued commanding the Roman guard to "tear down the churches to the foundations and to destroy the Sacred Scriptures by fire; and commanding also that those who were in honorable stations should be degraded if they persevered in their adherence to Christianity."[4] Three more edicts between 303 and 304 brought successively more violent stages in the severity of the persecution. The first one ordered that all bishops, presbyters and deacons be imprisoned; the second demanded that they be tortured to repudiate their faith; the third broadened the persecution to include the common laity as well as their pastors. Eusebius told of the massacre of almost an entire town's population because they confessed themselves to be followers of Christ.[5]

In 313, however, things took a dramatic turn in favor of the Church. When Athanasius was just fifteen years old, the Emperor Constantine, having ostensibly converted to Christianity, issued his famous Edict of Milan, declaring that Christianity had legal status equal to, if not greater than, paganism. Almost instantaneously, Christianity was transformed from a shunned and persecuted religion to an officially sanctioned one. Christians finally were free of "the torrent of blood" that had flowed so copiously from their fathers.

In 319 Bishop Alexander ordained Athanasius to the diaconate. During this time, he wrote two of his most important works: *Contra Gentes* (*Against the Heathen*) and *De Incarnatione* (*On the Incarnation*). The works were meant as a pair. The first refuted paganism, idol worship and pantheism. Athanasius stated his aim by saying he would begin by "first refuting the ignorance of the unbelieving; so that what is false being refuted, the truth may then shine forth of itself."[6]

The second work served a more positive apologetic function by explaining these truths. Athanasius showed how the *Logos* took on human flesh as a man and provided redemption. This revelation of God was the only preordained way to save fallen humanity.

> It was in order to sacrifice for bodies such as His own that the Word Himself also assumed a body. . . . He also Himself in like manner partook of the same, that through death He might bring to naught him that had the power of death, that is, the devil; and might deliver them who, through fear of death, were all their lifetime subject to bondage. For by the sacrifice of His own body, He both put an end to the law which was against us, and made a new beginning of life for us, by the hope of resurrection which He has given us. For since from man it was that death prevailed over men, for this cause conversely, by the Word of God being made man has come about the destruction of death and the resurrection of life.[7]

He also demonstrated the uniqueness of Christ in all history:

> And to mention one proof of the divinity of the Saviour, which
> is indeed utterly surprising,—what mere man or magician or
> tyrant or king was ever able by himself to engage with so many,
> and to fight the battle against all idolatry and the whole demo-
> niacal host and all magic, and all the wisdom of the Greeks,
> while they were so strong and still flourishing and imposing
> upon all, and at one onset to check them all, as was our Lord,
> the true Word of God, Who, invisibly exposing each man's er-
> ror, is by Himself bearing off all men from them all, so that
> while they who were worshipping idols now trample upon
> them, those in repute for magic burn their books, and the wise
> prefer to all studies the interpretation of the Gospels? [8]

These major formative works provided an ample foundation for Athanasius' future polemical writings against the Arians. Realizing Athanasius' brilliant gifts both as an intellect and a faithful churchman, Alexander shortly
made Athanasius his personal secretary, a lofty and admired post.

During this time, Arius began to spread his teachings among the believers.
Having written against the full divinity of Christ following his study of the
Synoptics, he now distorted John's Gospel as well. He contended that John
1:1, "In the beginning was the Word, and the Word was with God," merely
taught that at the beginning of the world, Jesus "was," but that before that
He simply did not exist, for God the Father had not yet begotten Him.

Against the Arians

In his preliminary apological work against Arius, Athanasius responded to
this charge by saying that God's "begetting" described an eternal relation between the Father and Son. A divine economy has existed between them from
eternity, which demonstrates God's inherent relational nature. This was a far cry
from Arius' obvious Platonic influence and rationalistic notion that the eternal
Logos cannot possibly be anything other than static and singular even with regard to the trinitarian idea of Persons. Arius had also been heavily influenced
during his formative years by the Origenistic flirtations with christological subor-
dinationism. However, where Origen maintained the eternal divinity of Christ by
appropriating the notion of a beginningless filial generation, Arius took Christ's
"subordination" to an essential extreme. Even Gnostic in some ways, Arianism
thought it totally wrong to conceive of deity ever existing bodily. Hence, Christ

was secondary in essence to the Father who created Him. Indeed, He was not the "perfect man" since, in his body, the *Logos* took the place of His intellect or soul.[9]

Athanasius believed this simply killed the faith. The little *i* in *homoiousios* stripped the Lord of His true claim to deity, and this, in effect, placed the atoning sacrifice of the cross on the shoulders of a *created* being. How can a creature take the punishment justly deserved of other creatures for the offenses done to an eternal God? This would have cost God nothing and was insufficient as an atonement. Secondly, and equally as egregious, "In demanding worship for a created Christ, the Arians were in effect asserting the central principle of heathenism and idolatry, the worship of a creature."[10] This little *i* was a letter that mattered!

Yet the word in which this illustrious diphthong belongs and its polar counterpart, *homoousios*, have a strange and intriguing history. Incredibly, the word that Athanasius spent a lifetime defending had actually been condemned as heretical not even sixty years before. In the early third century, a certain Sabelius reduced the Godhead to three separate modes that changed from one form to another, i.e., Father, Son, Spirit, depending on its various dealings with creation. Sabelius appropriated the word *homoousios* to defend this position, saying that Jesus is of the same substance, like the rays of light emanating from the sun, but He is not coequal with the Father, or in the assumed metaphor, the blazing "Sun" itself. The doctrine has since fallen under many names, including modal monarchianism, patripassianism and, fittingly, Sabellianism. Both Origen and Tertullian (160–225) issued writings against Sabelius and, eventually, the word *homoiousios*—Arius' future favorite word—was actually used to reprove him. In fact, *homoiousios* came to be used as a buzzword for orthodoxy, a christological "litmus test" for good versus bad doctrine. Eventually, Dionysius of Alexandria voiced formal opposition, a council was convened in Rome in 263 and Sabellianism was dispatched as heresy. Thus, it is important to recognize that Arius, by using this word, appealed to something that smacked of orthodox theology at the time. But the tables had turned, Arius pulled a Svengalian move, and Athanasius would have to explain the difference.

At the Council of Nicea

The Emperor Constantine finally undertook to resolve the dispute that by now was rending the Church. He called for a high council of bishops from all over the Christian landscape. The famous council, considered the first of the seven ecumenicals, took place in Nicea (modern-day Iznik, Turkey) in the year 325. Some 318 bishops were present, with Bishop Alexander presiding over the council and Athanasius at his side. Soon, his young associate came to be recognized as a chief spokesman against the Arians. Athanasius' style was stern but eloquent. He propounded that the Son is fully God, fully human, co-equal, coeternal and consubstantial with the Father.

Athanasius always appealed to the binding authority of the inspired Word of sacred Scripture—a fact evident in nearly all his works. He wrote, for example, that, "the sacred and inspired Scriptures are sufficient to declare the truth."[11] In his *Festal Letters*, he first named all twenty-seven books of the New Testament canon (an important early canon list known today as "Athanasius' Canonical List of 367"). He said of them, "These are fountains of salvation, that they who thirst may be satisfied with the living words they contain. In these alone is proclaimed the doctrine of godliness. Let no man add to these, neither let him take aught from these. For concerning these the Lord put to shame the Sadducees, and said, 'Ye do err, not knowing the Scriptures.' And He reproved the Jews, saying, 'Search the Scriptures, for these are they that testify of Me.' "[12]

The bishops needed to determine where the Church would stand on the matter and issue a formal statement for clarification. At first, they tried to base a statement on certain passages of Scripture. The problem, however, was that the Arians kept agreeing with them without changing the substance of what they believed. The bishops at Nicea needed to be calculatedly precise.

When *homoousios* was finally offered as a formal concept, its practical usefulness was soon recognized. No matter how the Arians might try, a word meaning nothing other than "same [exact] substance" could not be applied to a created being. Moreover, the bishops firmly believed that the word did no damage to the scriptural portrait of Jesus. Thus, *homoousios* was in, and *homoiousios* was out. The little *i* was defeated—at least as far as the conciliar bishops were concerned—and the famous Nicene Creed was formed. The council even enjoyed an exceptional majority in the vote, no doubt due in large part to the Athanasian influence. Only two bishops refused to sign. They, along with Arius himself, were banished. In its original form, the Creed of 325 read:

> We believe in one God, father almighty, maker of all things,
> both visible and invisible. And in one lord, Jesus Christ, the

son of God, begotten from the father, only-begotten, that is from the being [*ousia*] of the father, God from God, light from light, True God from True God, begotten not made, one in being [*homoousios*] with the father, through whom all things came to be, both those in heaven and those on the earth, who because of us human beings and because of our salvation descended, became enfleshed, became human, suffered and rose on the third day, ascending to the heavens, coming to judge the living and dead.

And in the Holy Spirit. The catholic and apostolic Church anathematizes those who say: there was when he was not; and before being born he was not; or that he came to be from things that are not; or that the Son of God is from a different *hypostasis* or *ousia* or mutable or changeable.[13]

This statement, also called "The Creed of 318 Fathers," underwent several revisions in different parts of the Church over the next several hundred years, but, for the time being, its purpose was served. The Arians were silenced. Or, at least, it was thought so.

Disgusted over this defeat, the Arians ignored the council. Indeed, no sooner had the council dispersed than its consensus began to crumble. The high hopes for unity and peace among the churches that Emperor Constantine had counted on were soon dashed. Many fickle bishops apparently were still willing to let Arianism be propounded from their pulpits. Some even later tried to modify the creed in an attempt to soften it and pass themselves off as orthodox. The bulk of Athanasius' apological work lay ahead of him.

Against the Arians

In 328 Bishop Alexander died, and Athanasius took his post in Alexandria. While many tried to woo him into ongoing renegotiations of the creed and setting up revisionary councils, he refused to budge. The Nicene Creed properly and effectively communicated the true christology of Scripture. The Arians were the belligerent ones, not he, and the Church was too willing to acquiesce to the pressure the Arians were leveling against sound doctrine. Again stressing that Scripture was clear in the matter and that the Nicene formulation reflected its teaching, he wrote in his *de Synodis*,

> Vainly then do they run about with the pretext that they have demanded Councils for the faith's sake; *for divine Scripture is sufficient above all things*; but if a Council be needed on the point, there are the proceedings of the Fathers, for the Nicene Bishops did not neglect this matter, but stated the doctrine so exactly, that persons reading their words honestly, cannot but be reminded by them of the religion towards Christ *announced in divine Scripture* (emphasis added).[14]

Athanasius was thus branded divisive, and enemies sprouted up against him throughout most of the Church. Worse, the Arians garnered support for themselves among the secular powers, including Constantine himself. Over the next thirty years, Athanasius was banished and restored five times from his bishopric in Alexandria. His critics maligned him, and his peers criticized him. His Arian rivals so despised Athanasius that they derisively called him the "Black Dwarf" due to his short stature and dark complexion (being Egyptian). At one point, the bishop of Nicomedia brought charges against him. Athanasius wrote of these in a shorter work against Arianism called *Defense Against the Arians* (the longer work is the *Discourses Against the Arians*, which we will address shortly). The charges accused him of a violation of canonical age requirements, illegal tax liens, profaning the sacraments and even murdering a bishop named Arsenius in order to use his severed hand for magical incantations.[15] Athanasius agreed to face his accusers and attempt to dispel the charges. He thus appeared before a synod in Tyre in 335 with several dozen of his friends and colleagues who attested to his impeccable character and good name.

As the proceedings began, a woman of ill repute declared in a loud and boisterous manner that she had vowed herself to perpetual virginity but Athanasius had violated her. After she made her charge, Athanasius came forward with his friend Timotheus, a presbyter. Athanasius remained silent, but Timotheus said to her, "Have I, O woman, ever conversed with you, or entered your house?" She exploded in rage, pointed her finger at Timotheus and exclaimed, "It was you who robbed me of my virginity. It was you who stripped me of my chastity!" Clearly the woman had been put to the task by Athanasius' enemies. The devisers of the calumny were put to shame and those churchmen who had been privy to it blushed.

But his accusers still had more tricks up their sleeves. They exhibited a box that exposed an embalmed hand. The assembly fired their indictments at Athanasius, saying that the hand belonged to Arsenius whom he had murdered. Near Athanasius, however, stood a man cloaked in a hood. Athanasius asked those in the assembly if anyone personally knew Arsenius. Finding that they did, he unveiled the face of the hooded man. His accusers were astonished to discover that it was Athanasius' supposed victim—alive and well. Athanasius said, "Is this the right Arsenius? Is this the man I murdered? Is this the man those people mutilated after his murder by cutting off his right hand?" Suddenly, then, a member of the assembly demanded that Arsenius' hands be shown to see whether one had been hacked off at the Black Dwarf's bidding to use as a magical prop. Athanasius then uncovered Arsenius' hands and said, "Let no one seek for a *third* hand, for man has received two hands from the Creator and no more." Laughter broke out across the room.

Yet the "trial" raged on. As Theodoret recounts in his *Ecclesiastical History*,

> Even after [these proofs] the calumniators and the judges who were privy to the crime, instead of hiding themselves, or praying that the earth might open and swallow them up, raised an uproar and commotion in the assembly, and declared that Athanasius was a sorcerer, and that he had by his magical incantations bewitched the eyes of men. The very men who a moment before had accused him of murder now strove to tear him in pieces and to murder him.[16]

It was more than evident, now, that the synod was hell-bent on destroying him, and Athanasius fled the court and escaped to a boat. He determined that he should confront the emperor, clear his name and silence his accusers. Catholic scholar Cornelius Clifford tells the story of this historic encounter:

> The circumstances in which the saint and the great catechumen met were dramatic enough. Constantine was returning from a hunt, when Athanasius unexpectedly stepped into the middle of the road and demanded a hearing. The astonished emperor could hardly believe his eyes, and it needed the assurance of one of the attendants to convince him that the petitioner was not an impostor, but none other than the great Bishop of Alexandria himself. "Give me," said [Athanasius] "a just tribunal, or allow me to meet my accusers face to face in your presence." His request was granted. An order was peremptorily sent to the bishops, who had tried Athanasius and, of course, condemned him in his absence, to repair at once to the imperial city. The command reached them while

they were on their way to the great feast of the dedication of Constantine's new church at Jerusalem. It naturally caused some consternation; but the more influential members of [his opposition] never lacked either courage or resourcefulness. The saint was taken at his word; and the old charges were renewed in the hearing of the emperor himself. Athanasius was condemned to go into exile at Treves, where he was received with the utmost kindness by the saintly Bishop Maximinus and the emperor's eldest son, Constantine. He began his journey probably in the month of February, 336, and arrived on the banks of the Moselle in the late autumn of the same year. His exile lasted nearly two years and a half. Public opinion in his own diocese remained loyal to him during all that time. It was not the least eloquent testimony to the essential worth of his character that he could inspire such faith. Constantine's treatment of Athanasius at this crisis in his fortunes has always been difficult to understand. Affecting, on the one hand, a show of indignation, as if he really believed in the political charge brought against the saint, he, on the other hand, refused to appoint a successor to the Alexandrian See, a thing which he might in consistency have been obliged to do had he taken seriously the condemnation proceedings carried through by the Eusebians at Tyre.[17]

Exile after Exile

Controversy continued to rage over Athanasius, and he was not able to enjoy a secure post in his beloved Alexandria for many years. The Arian doctrines flourished, ever dicing up the Church and creating many enemies of orthodoxy.

During the thirty-year span of cyclical exile and reinstatement back and forth between his Alexandrian post, Athanasius composed the bulk of his many great works. In a day with no means of mass communication, the only viable way to communicate one's message was to write with ink and quill. It is mind-boggling to contemplate the extent to which Athanasius engaged in this important task in order to stem the tide of Arianism.

Though he wrote many works during this time, the most important for our discussion to this point is his *Orationes Contra Arianos* (*Discourses Against the Ari-*

ans). The work is usually rendered in four editions. The first sets the stage with an introduction, summarizes the Arian doctrines and then defends the Nicean definition. Athanasius' resolve against the Arian heresy is made clear from the beginning:

> Of all other heresies which have departed from the truth it is acknowledged that they have but devised a madness, and their irreligiousness has long since become notorious to all men. For that their authors went out from us, it plainly follows, as the blessed John has written, that they never thought nor now think with us. Wherefore, as saith the Saviour, in that they gather not with us, they scatter with the devil, and keep an eye on those who slumber, that, by this second sowing of their own mortal poison, they may have companions in death. But, whereas one heresy, and that the last, which has now risen as harbinger of Antichrist, the Arian, as it is called, considering that other heresies, her elder sisters, have been openly proscribed, in her craft and cunning, affects to array herself in Scripture language, like her father the devil, and is forcing her way back into the Church's paradise, that with the pretence of Christianity, her smooth sophistry (for reason she has none) may deceive men into wrong thoughts of Christ, nay, since she has already seduced certain of the foolish, not only to corrupt their ears, but even to take and eat with Eve, till in their ignorance which ensues they think bitter sweet, and admire this loathsome heresy, on this account I have thought it necessary, at your request, to unrip "the folds of its breast-plate," and to shew the ill savour of its folly. So while those who are far from it may continue to shun it, those whom it has deceived may repent; and, opening the eyes of their heart, may understand that darkness is not light, nor falsehood truth, nor Arianism good; nay, that those who call these men Christians are in great and grievous error, as neither having studied Scripture, nor understanding Christianity at all, and the faith which it contains.[18]

The second and third sections deal directly with the "increate Christ," that is, His eternal generation from the Father. Athanasius marshaled much scriptural evidence, especially from the Gospels, Hebrews, Acts and Proverbs. He began by saying,

I did indeed think that enough had been said already against
the hollow professors of Arius's madness, whether for their
refutation or in the truth's behalf, to insure a cessation and
repentance of their evil thoughts and words about the Saviour. They, however, for whatever reason, still do not suc-
cumb; but, as swine and dogs wallow in their own vomit and
their own mire, rather invent new expedients for their irreligion. Thus they misunderstand [the Scriptures].[19]

He then, text by text, tore down the exegesis of Arianism as in this example
dealing with several New Testament passages:

The Ario-maniacs, as it appears, having once made up their
minds to transgress and revolt from the Truth, are strenuous
in appropriating the words of Scripture, "When the impious
cometh into a depth of evils, he despiseth;" for refutation
does not stop them, nor perplexity abash them; but, as having
"a whore's forehead," they "refuse to be ashamed" before all
men in their irreligion. For whereas the passages which they
alleged, "The Lord created me," and "Made better than the
Angel," and "First-born," and "Faithful to Him that made
Him " have a right sense, and inculcate religiousness towards
Christ, so it is that these men still, as if bedewed with the ser-
pent's poison, not seeing what they ought to see, nor understanding what they read, as if in vomit from the depth of their
irreligious heart, have next proceeded to disparage our Lord's
words, "I in the Father and the Father in Me;" saying, "How
can the One be contained in the Other and the Other in the
One?" or "How at all can the Father who is the greater be contained in the Son who is the less?" or "What wonder, if the
Son is in the Father," considering it is written even of us, "In
Him we live and move and have our being?" And this state of
mind is consistent with their perverseness, who think God to
be material, and understand not what is "True Father" and
"True Son," nor "Light Invisible" and "Eternal," and Its "Ra-
diance Invisible," nor "Invisible Subsistence," and "Immaterial Expression" and "Immaterial Image." For did they know,
they would not dishonour and ridicule the Lord of glory, nor
interpret things immaterial after a material manner, or pervert good words. It were sufficient indeed, on hearing only

words which are the Lord's, at once to believe, since the faith of simplicity is better than an elaborate process of persuasion; but since they have endeavoured to profane even this passage to their own heresy, it becomes necessary to expose their perverseness and to shew the mind of the truth, at least for the security of the faithful. For when it is said, "I in the Father and the Father in Me," they are not therefore, as these suppose, discharged into Each Other, filling the One the Other, as in the case of empty vessels, so that the Son fills the emptiness of the Father and the Father that of the Son, and Each of Them by Himself is not complete and perfect (for this is proper to bodies, and therefore the mere assertion of it is full of irreligion), for the Father is full and perfect, and the Son is the Fullness of Godhead. Nor again, as God, by coming into the Saints, strengthens them, thus is He also in the Son. For He is Himself the Father's Power and Wisdom, and by partaking of Him things originate are sanctified in the Spirit; but the Son Himself is not Son by participation, but is the Father's own Offspring. Nor again is the Son in the Father, in the sense of the passage, "In Him we live and move and have our being;" for, He as being from the Fount of the Father is the Life, in which all things are both quickened and consist; for the Life does not live in life, else it would not be Life, but rather He gives life to all things.[20]

The fourth section continues in this work but adds an apologetic against Marcellus, a bishop who had been present at Nicea and a strong opponent of Arianism but who, in his zealous strides against the Arians, fell into the error of a modified Sabellianism. Athanasius compared the Arian errors with his and refuted them both. The section begins with a defense of the "Three-in-Oneness" of the Godhead:

The Word is God from God; for "the Word was God," and again, "Of whom are the Fathers, and of whom Christ, who is God over all, blessed for ever. Amen." And since Christ is God from God, and God's Word, Wisdom, Son, and Power, therefore but One God is declared in the divine Scriptures. For the Word, being Son of the One God, is referred to Him of whom also He is; so that Father and Son are two, yet the Monad of the Godhead is indivisible and inseparable. And thus too we preserve One Beginning of Godhead and not two Beginnings, whence there is strictly a Monarchy. And of this very Beginning the Word is by nature Son, not as if another beginning, subsisting by Himself, nor having come into being externally to that Beginning, lest from that diversity a Dyarchy and Polyarchy should ensue; but of the one Beginning He is own Son, own Wisdom, own Word, existing from It. For, according to John, "in" that "Beginning was the Word, and the Word was with God," for the Beginning was God; and since He is from It, therefore also "the Word was God." And as there is one Beginning and therefore one God, so one is that Essence and Subsistence which indeed and truly and really is, and which said "I am that I am," and not two, that there be not two Beginnings; and from the One, a Son in nature and truth, is Its own Word, Its Wisdom, Its Power, and inseparable from It. And as there is not another essence, lest there be two Beginnings, so the Word which is from that One Essence has no dissolution, nor is a sound significative, but is an essential Word and essential Wisdom, which is the true Son. For were He not essential, God will be speaking into the air, and having a body, in nothing differently from men; but since He is not man, neither is His Word according to the infirmity of man. For as the Beginning is one Essence, so Its Word is one, essential, and subsisting, and Its Wisdom. For as He is God from God, and Wisdom from the Wise, and Word from the Rational, and Son from Father, so is He from Subsistence Subsistent, and from Essence Essential and Substantive, and Being from Being.[21]

Athanasius' arguments are systematic and incredibly thorough. Indeed, it is not hard to see why his enemies became so infuriated whenever he issued one of his powerful missives. By way of summary, Athanasius exhorted his enemies to become anchored in truth and to glorify the great gift of God incarnate:

Idle then is the excuse for stumbling, and petty the notions concerning the Word, of these Ario-maniacs, because it is written, "He was troubled," and "He wept." For they seem not even to have human feeling, if they are thus ignorant of man's nature and properties; which do but make it the greater wonder, that the Word should be in such a suffering flesh, and neither prevented those who were conspiring against Him, nor took vengeance of those who were putting Him to death, though He was able, He who hindered some from dying, and raised others from the dead. And He let His own body suffer, for therefore did He come, as I said before, that in the flesh He might suffer, and thenceforth the flesh might be made impassible and immortal, and that, as we have many times said, contumely and other troubles might determine upon Him and come short of others after Him, being by Him annulled utterly; and that henceforth men might for ever abide incorruptible, as a temple of the Word. Had Christ's enemies thus dwelt on these thoughts, and recognised the ecclesiastical scope as an anchor for the faith, they would not have made shipwreck of the faith, nor been so shameless as to resist those who would fain recover them from their fall, and to deem those as enemies who are admonishing them to be religious.[22]

Therefore God the Word Himself is Christ from Mary, God and Man; not some other Christ but One and the Same; He before ages from the Father, He too in the last times from the Virgin; invisible before even to the holy powers of heaven, visible now because of His being one with the Man who is visible; seen, I say, not in His invisible Godhead but in the operation of the Godhead through the human body and whole Man, which He has renewed by its appropriation to Himself. To Him be the adoration and the worship, who was before, and now is, and ever shall be, even to all ages. Amen.[23]

The Final Years

In 364, foreseeing his fifth and final banishment from Alexandria now that Emperor Valens (328–378), an Arian, had come to power in the East, Athanasius quietly packed his bags. He took up residence in a country house some distance outside the city. Yet with hostility rising and sporadic persecutions breaking out against orthodox Christians, tradition holds that for four months Athanasius actually hid inside his father's tomb.

After this final period of banishment, however, in yet another providential twist, Valens permitted Athanasius to return home and reassume his post. It appears Valens was concerned about the possibility of a popular uprising and wanted to keep order.

Years of exile, incredible stress and strain now behind him, Athanasius finished his tenure as pastor of Alexandria in relative peace. He continued to speak against Arianism and propounded the importance of remaining faithful to the true doctrines of Christ and the incarnation.

On May 2, 373, Athanasius died peacefully in his own bed surrounded by friends and fellow ministers. Knowing the incredible battle he had fought his entire life for the preservation of the faith against seemingly insurmountable obstacles and at great personal cost, his friends assigned the following epitaph to their pastor and great apologist: *Athanasius Contra Mundum*—"Athanasius Against the World."

Conclusion

Metaphors abound in Scripture to describe the gospel and the Christian's calling in the world. The gospel and we, the vessels who bring it, are like lamps, lights, seeds, leaven, wheat and pearls. But one of the most important is salt. Jesus said that Christians "are the salt of the earth; but if the salt has become tasteless, how can it be made salty again?" (Matthew 5:13, NASB). Athanasius demonstrated how to be a "salty" Christian. Salt is a preservative. So too we Christians are to have a preserving effect on sound doctrine and practice. We must strive to keep biblical doctrine fresh and ward off the decay of false teaching. But we must be prepared to accept the cost and give the glory to God.

Whenever I receive Holy Communion on Sunday, I like to give at least a moment's thought to the great Athanasius and the way God used him to preserve the biblical revelation of Christ's full divinity. Why is this so important? Is it not enough simply to affirm Christ as Savior? The simple answer is that, were the affirmations of Christ's divinity that Athanasius defended not true, the gospel is emptied of its power, and our faith and evangelism are futile. If Christ is not fully divine and fully human, He could not have overcome sin and death. He who was absent of sin took on our nature and made it His own. If Christ were merely a man and nothing more, then His sacrificial atonement would be like that of any other man—unable to pay for our sins. The finite injustice of sin is an affront to the infinite justice of holiness. A mere man, a created being, cannot take the punishment on himself for what was done ultimately to God. Only God can condescend to do this out of His own love and mercy for humankind.

Athanasius said, "For by the sacrifice of His own body He did two things: He put an end to the law of death which barred our way; and He made a new beginning of life for us, by giving us the hope of resurrection. By man death has gained its power over men; by the Word made Man death has been destroyed and life raised up anew."[24] There is no salvation in the absence of Christ's divinity, which Athanasius spent his entire life defending. Athanasius' tenacity and commitment should humble and encourage us. As with the other apologists, we are reminded of the high price many Christian saints have paid for the cause of truth. The Christian doctrine of the Trinity has never been defended by any person as vigorously and boldly as the unassuming "Black Dwarf."

Augustine
The Apologetical Swan

I write for the glory of the city of God, that, being placed in comparison with the other, it may shine with a brighter luster.
    —The City of God, *1.35*

Events in the Life of Augustine

354	Born in Thagaste, Numidia, in northern Africa (roughly modern Algeria).
370	Went to Carthage to study rhetoric.
372	Embraced Manichaeism.
376	Became a professor of rhetoric in Carthage.
386	Converted to Christianity.
391	Ordained to the priesthood in Hippo.
393	Participated in an ecclesiastical council in Carthage.
396	Succeeded Valerius as bishop of Hippo.
401	Completed the *Confessions*.
416	Refuted Pelagianism at a council in Numidia.
413–426	Wrote *The City of God*.
430	Died as the Vandals seized Hippo.

*O*n my first day in the seminary, I was daunted to find myself assigned to a course in Church history as the inaugural class for my studies. For me, the word *history* invoked an ill feeling carried over from my undergraduate days when history courses proved my hardest subject. Yet soon the thoughts whirring about in my mind were interrupted by a cacophony of declarations from the professor: "Documents, my friends. Documents are the *sine qua non* of history! In this class, we will read many, many documents!"

Despite my fears, the class turned out to be a positive experience, and I soon learned why the seminary wanted us to begin our studies that way. Church history gives us a context for the later work of theology and ministry. We learned that the doctrines we subscribe to and cherish came at a price. Countless men and women not only labored to explicate and codify them so that scriptural teachings could be summarized, integrated and better understood, but they also were willing to give their very lives for them. Many beliefs and practices that we hold dear today we take for granted by divorcing them from history. Thus, even the dreaded "documents" turned out to be a true joy to read. Reading firsthand material instead of secondary textbooks set a tactile tone for the class. The focus was on remembering thought, not this datum and that, and, ironically, we found that the latter tended to follow in the process. Thus, we read works by Irenaeus, Tertullian, Wesley, Luther and others.

The most fascinating readings of all were those of the great apologist and theologian extraordinaire, Augustine. Where historical Church documents are concerned, the prodigious bishop from Hippo was absolutely unmatched. As scholar Eugène Portalié puts it, "The great St. Augustine's life is unfolded to us in documents of unrivaled richness, and of no great character of ancient times have we information comparable."[1] B.B. Warfield writes that he had "a literary talent . . . second to none in the annals of the Church."[2] Augustine also blessed us with an account of his life and intellectual and spiritual development in his *Confessions* and *Retractions*. These works are treasures and are staples on most theologians' or philosophers' bookshelves.

More importantly, though, was Augustine's impact on Christian thought, theology and philosophy in general. Classical theologian R.C. Sproul says, "He was the greatest Christian philosopher-theologian of the first millennium and arguably of the entire Christian era."[3] Augustine's life and work bridged the transition from the ancient world to the Middle Ages and took it in a new direction. He was the first theologian to synthesize nearly all the ma-

jor Christian writings before him. The aftermath is a contribution to the development of the Occidental world that cannot be overstated. Alfred North
Whitehead once said that nearly all philosophy was but a mere footnote on
Plato. In many respects, the same thing can be said of the task of theological
construction since Augustine. Even those who disagree with him often use
him as the backboard off which to bounce and construct their own theologies.

Wayward Son

Aurelius Augustine was born in Thagaste, Numidia, in North Africa (roughly
modern Algeria) on November 13, 354. His father, Patricius, was an official of the
Roman curia and a pagan. His mother, Monica, however, was a devout Christian
who raised young Augustine in the ways of the faith. She was also what modern
evangelicals like to call a "prayer warrior." She prayed earnestly for Augustine
throughout his entire life, often to the point of tears. In his early years, Augustine
rejected that faith, but he later prayerfully reflected on the seed of truth his
mother and her helpers had planted in his soul even from his infancy. Indeed, in
his *Confessions* he wrote:

> Thou didst by them give me the nourishment of infancy accord-
> ing to Thy ordinance and that bounty of Thine which underlieth
> all things. For Thou didst cause me not to want more than Thou
> gavest, and those who nourished me willingly to give me what
> Thou gavest them. For they, by an instinctive affection, were
> anxious to give me what Thou hadst abundantly supplied. It
> was, in truth, good for them that my good should come from
> them, though, indeed, it was not from them, but by them; for
> from Thee, O God, are all good things.[4]

Oh, the power of a praying mother!

Augustine received a thoroughgoing Christian education, and his brilliance
was recognized early on. But Patricius, his heart belonging to the state and its
fleeting rewards, pushed for young Augustine to go to Carthage to pursue a
law career. A brilliant mind, his father thought, should not be wasted on the
triviality of religious matters. Augustine soon found himself living idly and
becoming ensconced in worldly pleasures. Again in the *Confessions*, he reflected on those days:

> To Carthage I came, where a cauldron of unholy loves bub-
> bled up all around me. I loved not as I yet learned to love; and

with a hidden want, I abhorred myself that I wanted You not. I searched about for something to love, in love with loving, and hating security, and a way not beset with snares. For within me I had a dearth of that inward food, Thyself, my God, though that dearth caused me no hunger; but I remained without all desire for incorruptible food, not because I was already filled thereby, but the more empty I was the more I loathed it. For this reason my soul was far from well, and, full of ulcers, it miserably cast itself forth, craving to be excited by contact with objects of the senses. Yet, had these no soul, they would not surely inspire love. To love and to be loved was sweet to me, and all the more when I succeeded in enjoying the person I loved. I befouled, therefore, the spring of friendship with the filth of concupiscence, and I dimmed its luster with the hell of lustfulness; and yet, foul and dishonorable as I was, I craved, through an excess of vanity, to be thought elegant and urbane. I fell precipitately, then, into the love in which I longed to be ensnared. My God, my mercy, with how much bitterness didst Thou, out of Thy infinite goodness, besprinkle for me that sweetness! For I was both beloved, and secretly arrived at the bond of enjoying; and was joyfully bound with troublesome ties, that I might be scourged with the burning iron rods of jealousy, suspicion, fear, anger, and strife.[5]

Even his education and genius became idols to him. He wrote that he had become "swollen with pride [and] looked upon [him]self as a great one."[6] The life of a respected academician was intoxicating. He also during this time fathered a son, Adeodatus, out of wedlock, a fact that he desperately feared disclosing to Monica, knowing it would break her heart.

Augustine the Manichaean

Such behavior only widened the pit of his folly and debasement. He soon became enticed by the pagan teachings of Mani (215–276), and his followers, the Manichaeans. Mani taught a fundamental metaphysical dualism of good and evil forces represented by gods of his own design. Manichaeism was syncretistic as well, absorbing elements from Buddhism, Zoroastrianism, Gnosticism and Christianity. Yahweh, the God of the Jews and the Christians, was goodness and light; but Satan, equally as eternal and powerful, represented materiality, carnality and darkness. A quasi-animistic cosmogony was added in which the heavenly hosts of sun, moon and stars were the dwelling places of these gods.

According to an evil ploy of Satan, human souls became trapped in the physicality of their bodies. Thus, the chief objective in life was to expurgate oneself of pleasures and passions so the soul could be released into the heavenlies at death. Those who failed to do this would be recycled in a continual transmigration of souls until they got it right. Augustine was drawn into the sect because it provided him with a philosophy unencumbered by the commitment of faith. The belief system was perfectly malleable, providing him with the needed latitude to pursue his own ideas. Moreover, the responsibility-shifting elements in Manichaeism enabled persons to blame their profligacies on the forces of darkness instead of on themselves—a "devil-made-me-do-it" kind of attitude.

Augustine devoted extensive time and energy to the Manichaean program. He read all its books, attended all its sessions and even defended its doctrines. Quite naturally, his mother abhorred these false teachings even to the point where she refused to receive him into her home. Yet she persisted in reaching out to her prodigal son and was encouraged by the kindly words of a pastor, who declared to her that "the son of so many tears could not perish."[7]

Augustine spent nearly a decade immersed in the cult of Mani. In this time, he grew in learning and as a scholar, becoming a professor of rhetoric. Yet he began to question some Manichaean teachings, such as its baseless cosmology. Mani taught the coeternity of dualism and the identification of the human soul as a fragmented particle of the Light.[8] Incapable of answering his questions, Augustine's Manichaean cohorts assured him that when their great instructor, Faustus, came to town, he could explain everything to him. Ironically, though, Faustus' arrival in Carthage brought the death knell of Augustine's term there. Faustus' answers were as equally vacuous as that of his followers, save a bit more eloquent. Augustine told of the occasion:

> For when it became plain to me that [Faustus] was ignorant of those arts in which I had believed him to excel, I began to despair of his clearing up and explaining all the perplexities which harassed me: though ignorant of these, however, he might still have held the truth of piety, had he not been a Manichaean. For

their books are full of lengthy fables concerning the heaven and stars, the sun and moon, and I had ceased to think him able to decide in a satisfactory manner what I ardently desired—whether, on comparing these things with the calculations I had read elsewhere, the explanations contained in the works of Mani were preferable, or at any rate equally sound? But when I proposed that these subjects should be deliberated upon and reasoned out, he very modestly did not dare to endure the burden. For he was aware that he had no knowledge of these things, and was not ashamed to confess it. . . . Thus that Faustus, who had entrapped so many to their death, neither willing nor wilting it, now began to loosen the snare in which I had been taken. For Thy hands, O my God, in the hidden design of Thy Providence, did not desert my soul; and out of the blood of my mother's heart, through the tears that she poured out by day and by night, was a sacrifice offered unto Thee for me; and by marvelous ways didst Thou deal with me. It was Thou, O my God, who didst it, for the steps of a man are ordered by the Lord, and He shall dispose his way. Or how can we procure salvation but from Thy hand, remaking what it hath made?[9]

Augustine the Neoplatonist

Shortly after these events, Augustine left the Manichaeans and headed for Milan, Italy. His soul still aching for the true philosophy, he continued searching for answers while earning his living as a teacher. Here he had his first substantive encounter with the writings of Plotinus and the school of thought known as Neoplatonism.

For Plotinus, all reality was a unified emanation flowing out of his god concept, which he called "the One." Only negative statements could be made of the One. For example, it was immaterial, impersonal and unknowable. Yet out of the One came the *nous,* or mind, as a conscious emanation. The mind was the highest knowable metaphysical principle. The next emanation was the *psyche*, or world soul, the primary mover behind the universe and all things it contains. The final (and lowest) emanation was the *physis*, or nature. Humans were thought to be microcosms of all the declensions of reality. Yet the farther one moved away from the One, the less unity there was. The One was like the pulsating core of reality drawing people back toward it. Matter was the crudest principle of reality, and, thus, the contemplative and abstemious life was the highest virtue for the Neoplatonist and the path to salvation. For this reason, Plotinian philosophy has often been described as "intellectual mysticism."

This new system of thought at first provided Augustine with some relief in his restlessness for a cogent explanation of the universe. But it was short-lived. He soon recognized that, as much as he adored his studies and the pursuit of the contemplative life, his passions still enslaved him. Chained by his own base desires, he knew he was guilty and unworthy. He felt puny when measured on a scale of moral perfection and purity.

Augustine's Conversion to Christ

Augustine continued to struggle. Once again, we see the hand of providence moving in "mysterious ways," as Puritan hymnist and poet William Cowper aptly said. As a professor of rhetoric, Augustine learned of the powerful oratory skill of Ambrose, the bishop of Milan. Curious to witness the great bishop in action, he decided to go hear him speak. Yet unknown to him, his mother's prayers were at work once again. Augustine was captivated not merely by the deftness of Ambrose as an expert orator but by his message of truth as well:

> For although I took no trouble to learn what he spake, but only to hear how he spake (for that empty care alone remained to me, despairing of a way accessible for man to Thee), yet, together with the words which I prized, there came into my mind also the things about which I was careless; for I could not separate them. And whilst I opened my heart to admit "how skillfully he spake," there also entered with it, but gradually, "and how truly he spake!" For first, these things also had begun to appear to me to be defensible; and the Catholic faith, for which I had fancied nothing could be said against the attacks of the Manichaeans, I now conceived might be maintained without presumption; especially after I had heard one or two parts of the Old Testament explained, and often allegorically—which when I accepted literally, I was "killed" spiritually. Many places, then, of those books having been expounded to me, I now blamed my despair in having believed that no reply could be made to those

> who hated and derided the Law and the Prophets. Yet I did
> not then see that for that reason the Catholic way was to be
> held because it had its learned advocates, who could at
> length, and not irrationally, answer objections.[10]

As Augustine continued to hear Ambrose speak, he became more acquainted with Christian doctrine. He began to see the world not through the lens of philosophers, but through the magnificent and rich simplicity of gospel theism. He saw the continuous stream of truth revealed progressively from Moses and the Prophets, culminating in the advent of Christ who summed them all up in Himself.

Though Augustine's Platonic habits still remained in his thinking, they became a vehicle for further understanding Christian tenets. That Augustine retained many Platonic categories of thought even when contemplating the Savior did no damage as long as those categories served merely as a carriage to the truth.

Far from this being a time of mere reflection on these new truths he had learned, it was also a time of heartrending inner conflict. Augustine now believed in the reality of a holy God in heaven who despises sin and punishes people for their wickedness. He had no doubt of his guilt before almighty God and knew he could not hide from Him whom Luther later called the "Hound of Heaven." Yet he also knew of God's merciful grace in paving the way for forgiveness through the atoning sacrifice of the Son. At this point, with his friend and pupil Alypius by his side to comfort him in his desolation, he experienced an incredible conversion experience in a little garden in Milan.

> But when a profound reflection had, from the secret depths
> of my soul, drawn together and heaped up all my misery before the sight of my heart, there arose a mighty storm, accompanied by as mighty a shower of tears. Which, that I might
> pour forth fully, with its natural expressions, I stole away
> from Alypius; for it suggested itself to me that solitude was
> fitter for the business of weeping. So I retired to such a distance that even his presence could not be oppressive to me.
> Thus was it with me at that time, and he perceived it; for
> something, I believe, I had spoken, wherein the sound of my
> voice appeared choked with weeping, and in that state had I
> risen up. He then remained where we had been sitting, most
> completely astonished. I flung myself down, how, I know

not, under a certain fig-tree, giving free course to my tears, and the streams of mine eyes gushed out, an acceptable sacrifice unto Thee. And, not indeed in these words, yet to this effect, spake I much unto Thee,—"But Thou, O Lord, how long? How long, Lord? Wilt Thou be angry for ever? Oh, remember not against us former iniquities"; for I felt that I was enthralled by them. I sent up these sorrowful cries, "How long, how long? Tomorrow, and tomorrow? Why not now? Why is there not this hour an end to my uncleanness?"

I was saying these things and weeping in the most bitter contrition of my heart, when, lo, I heard the voice as of a boy or girl, I know not which, coming from a neighbouring house, chanting, and oft repeating, "Take up and read; take up and read." Immediately my countenance was changed, and I began most earnestly to consider whether it was usual for children in any kind of game to sing such words; nor could I remember ever to have heard the like. So, restraining the torrent of my tears, I rose up, interpreting it no other way than as a command to me from Heaven to open the [Bible]. . . . So quickly I returned to the place where Alypius was sitting; for there had I put down the volume of the apostles, when I rose thence. I grasped, opened, and in silence read that paragraph on which my eyes first fell, "Not in rioting and drunkenness, not in chambering and wantonness, not in strife and envying; but put ye on the Lord Jesus Christ, and make not provision for the flesh, to fulfil the lusts thereof." No further would I read, nor did I need; for instantly, as the sentence ended,—by a light, as it were, of security infused into my heart, all the gloom of doubt vanished away.[11]

The next step for Augustine was to be baptized by his new and beloved pastor, Ambrose, in 387 along with Alypius and his son, Adeodatus (who sadly died just a year later at only eighteen years of age). He tells us of this glorious occasion:

Thence, when the time had arrived at which I was to give in my name, having left the country, we returned to Milan. Alypius also was pleased to be born again with me in Thee, being now clothed with the humility appropriate to Thy sacraments, and being so brave a tamer of the body, as with unusual fortitude to tread the frozen soil of Italy with his naked feet. We took into our company the boy Adeodatus, born of me carnally, of my sin. Well hadst Thou made him. He was barely fifteen years, yet in wit excelled many grave and learned men. I confess unto Thee Thy gifts, O Lord my God, Creator of all, and of exceeding power to reform our deformities; for of me was there naught in that boy but the sin. For that we fostered him in Thy discipline, Thou inspiredst us, none other,—Thy gifts I confess unto Thee. There is a book of ours, which is entitled The Master. It is a dialogue between him and me. Thou knowest that all things there put into the mouth of the person in argument with me were his thoughts in his sixteenth year. Many others more wonderful did I find in him. That talent was a source of awe to me. And who but Thou could be the worker of such marvels? Quickly didst Thou remove his life from the earth; and now I recall him to mind with a sense of security, in that I fear nothing for his childhood or youth, or for his whole self. We took him coeval with us in Thy grace, to be educated in Thy discipline; and we were baptized, and solicitude about our past life left us. Nor was I satiated in those days with the wondrous sweetness of considering the depth of Thy counsels concerning the salvation of the human race. How greatly did I weep in Thy hymns and canticles, deeply moved by the voices of Thy sweet-speaking Church! The voices flowed into mine ears, and the truth was poured forth into my heart, whence the agitation of my piety overflowed, and my tears ran over, and blessed was I therein.[12]

Augustine continued his growth in the Church like a desert wanderer slowly revived by successive cups of cool water on a weary throat. He penned several masterful writings concerning the faith, such as *On the Value of Believing, On Music, De Fide et Symbolo* and *On the True Religion*. Augustine rapidly gained a reputation as an adroit Christian thinker and apologist.

Augustine's Apologetic

Augustine never gave the idea of entering the priesthood much thought. Yet one day, someone invited him to go to Hippo in North Africa to attend to a friend in spiritual need. While there, he went into a church to pray. To his great surprise, a number of people gathered around him cheering. They soon begged Valerius, the Hipponian bishop, to raise him to the priesthood. Moved to tears, Augustine declined such an offer. Yet he soon yielded to their request and was ordained a priest in 391.[13]

In the years to follow, Augustine's work covered many grounds. He preached, founded a monastery and militated strenuously against heresy, including Manichaeism against which he had great success. Fortunatus, a notable Manichaean instructor, fled Hippo in humiliation over his defeat in a public debate with Augustine.[14] In 393, Augustine also took part in an ecclesiastical council in Carthage, presided over by Bishop Aurelius, and delivered a discourse called *On Faith and Creed*. An exposition of the Apostles' Creed, it dealt with the Three-in-Oneness of the Trinity. This discourse was notable for its analogy of the Triunity of God as represented in being, knowledge and love—themes that Augustine carried over into his later works, including *The City of God* and *On the Holy Trinity*.

In 396, Valerius, riddled by old age, requested that Augustine be his coadjutor, a position that meant logical succession to the bishopric, which in 396 became a reality. Augustine, now forty-two years old, occupied the episcopate in Hippo for thirty-four years. During this time, he wrote a large number of works on various subjects—doxological, theological, axiological, exegetical and apologetical. He proved himself both a highly capable defender of the faith, yet also a tender shepherd of his flock, whom he wished to lead from the darkness of heresy into the brightness of the Lord's Scripture. Indeed, he often preached every day of the week and addressed various problems in his correspondence.

Three major heretical contentions occupied much of Augustine's apologetical energies during his tenure as head pastor. The Donatists taught that pastors had to be holy and doctrinally orthodox in order for Church ordinances to be valid. Pelagianism denied original sin and stressed human effort in "attaining" salvation. (Later, Augustine dealt, primarily in letters, with Arianism. But his efforts were comparatively minor in this regard compared to these other heterodoxies. He also continued to confute Manichaeism.) He composed many polemical writings against these groups, including respectively: *On the Morals of the Manichaeans; On Two Souls—Against the Manichaeans; Concerning the Nature of Good—Against the Manichaeans; On Baptism—Against the Donatists; The Correction of the Donatists; On the Proceedings of Pelagius*; and *Against Two Letters of the Pelagians*.

His most notable apologetical works, however, are positive works concerning the veracity of the apostolic faith. They dealt with theological issues such as the

Trinity, the problem of evil, the manner in which faith and reason cohere, cosmogony and cosmology, the doctrine of God, miracles, ethics, eschatology and biblical anthropology.

Augustine's Confessions

The nonautobiographical sections of his *Confessions* provide a wonderful apologetic for the Christian understanding of God and cosmogony. He stressed the *ex nihilo* (out of nothing) creation of the world, its primordial goodness (contra Plotinus, Mani, et al.), its relation to God, its finitude, purpose, changeableness and temporality:

> Behold, the heaven and earth are; they proclaim that they were made, for they are changed and varied. Whereas whatsoever hath not been made, and yet hath being, hath nothing in it which there was not before; this is what it is to be changed and varied. They also proclaim that they made not themselves; "therefore we are, because we have been made; we were not therefore before we were, so that we could have made ourselves." And the voice of those that speak is in itself an evidence. Thou, therefore, Lord, didst make these things; Thou who art beautiful, for they are beautiful; Thou who art good, for they are good; Thou who art, for they are. Nor even so are they beautiful, nor good, nor are they, as Thou their Creator art; compared with whom they are neither beautiful, nor good, nor are at all. These things we know, thanks be to Thee. And our knowledge, compared with Thy knowledge, is ignorance.[15]
>
> . . . In this Beginning, O God, hast Thou made heaven and earth,—in Thy Word, in Thy Son, in Thy Power, in Thy Wisdom, in Thy Truth, wondrously speaking and wondrously making. Who shall comprehend? who shall relate it? What is that which shines through me, and strikes my heart without injury, and I both shudder and burn? I shudder inasmuch as I am unlike it; and I burn inasmuch as I am like it. It is Wisdom itself that shines through me, clearing my cloudiness, which again overwhelms me, fainting from it, in the darkness and amount of my punishment. For my strength is brought down in need, so that I cannot endure my blessings, until Thou, O Lord, who hast been gracious to all mine iniquities, heal also all mine infirmities; be-

cause Thou shalt also redeem my life from corruption, and crown me with Thy loving-kindness and mercy, and shalt satisfy my desire with good things, because my youth shall be renewed like the eagle's. For by hope we are saved; and through patience we await Thy promises. Let him that is able hear Thee discoursing within. I will with confidence cry out from Thy oracle, How wonderful are Thy works, O Lord, in Wisdom hast Thou made them all. And this Wisdom is the Beginning, and in that Beginning hast Thou made heaven and earth.[16]

Augustine also dealt with the question of the manner in which God occupied Himself before the creation of the world. He considered the question rash and defended a view of divine atemporality, or timelessness, which suggests that this is simply not in the province of humans to know:

Behold, I answer to him who asks, "What was God doing before He made heaven and earth?" I answer not, as a certain person is reported to have done facetiously (avoiding the pressure of the question), "He was preparing hell," saith he, "for those who pry into mysteries." It is one thing to perceive, another to laugh,—these things I answer not. For more willingly would I have answered, "I know not what I know not," than that I should make him a laughing-stock who asketh deep things, and gain praise as one who answereth false things. But I say that Thou, our God, art the Creator of every creature; and if by the term "heaven and earth" every creature is understood, I boldly say, "That before God made heaven and earth, He made not anything. For if He did, what did He make unless the creature?" And would that I knew whatever I desire to know to my advantage, as I know that no creature was made before any creature was made.[17]

On Faith and Reason

Concerning faith and reason, Augustine was an advocate of what would later become important axioms for Anslem, *fides quarens intellectum*, that is, "faith seeking understanding," and *credo ut intelligem*, meaning "to believe in order to understand." For example, in *On Faith and the Creed*, he wrote:

We have, however, the catholic faith in the Creed, known to the faithful and committed to memory, contained in a form of expression as concise as has been rendered admissible by

> the circumstances of the case; the purpose of which [compilation] was, that individuals who are but beginners and sucklings among those who have been born again in Christ, and who have not yet been strengthened by most diligent and spiritual handling and understanding of the divine Scriptures, should be furnished with a summary, expressed in few words, of those matters of necessary belief which were subsequently to be explained to them in many words, as they made progress and rose to [the height of] divine doctrine, on the assured and steadfast basis of humility and charity. It is underneath these few words, therefore, which are thus set in order in the Creed, that most heretics have endeavored to conceal their poisons; whom divine mercy has withstood, and still withstands, by the instrumentality of spiritual men, who have been counted worthy not only to accept and believe the catholic faith as expounded in those terms, but also thoroughly to understand and apprehend it by the enlightenment imparted by the Lord. For it is written, "Unless ye believe, ye shall not understand."[18]

For Augustine, faith is the gift of God. It is not earned but is given unilaterally by the Holy Spirit and, unless it is, the truths of Scripture remain locked to a mind possessed by an unregenerate soul. This does not mean, however, that the mind does not play an integral role in one's coming to a saving knowledge of the Word. Quite the contrary. Augustine said that whatever is believed in the heart must first pass through the nexus of the mind, the God-given faculty of reason and understanding.[19] The difference is that these truths have no substantive heart connection until God liberates the soul from its bondage to sin.

Augustine's belief in the necessity of God liberating the soul and "giving eyes" to the believer does not nullify the unregenerate man's responsibility to acknowledge the existence of God. His understanding of faith and reason working in tandem applies to the application of and trust in God's Word. This cannot happen unless God regenerates the soul. But reason alone can nevertheless impart the intellectual knowledge that God does in fact exist. For this, all men are accountable. Modern apologists Kenneth Boa and Robert Bowman observe that

> Augustine cited Romans 1:20 to show that some philosophers, especially Platonists, have been able from the creation

to recognize the fact of a Creator God. The line of reasoning by which even pagans can be made to admit a Creator is essentially what philosophers would later call a cosmological argument, reasoning from the changeableness of all things in the world (Greek *cosmos*) to the existence of an unmade Maker of all things. This was one of a number of arguments by which Augustine reasoned that knowledge of God was available to pagans. But this knowledge cannot prevent them from falling into idolatry and polytheism. The true worship of God can be found only by placing faith in Jesus Christ.[20]

The City of God

Augustine's *City of God* is a masterpiece and usually first thought of in regard to his apologetics. It has also been considered among the ten books carrying the greatest literary influence on Western civilization. Although Augustine conceded that the composition of this voluminous book was "arduous," nevertheless, "God was [his] helper."[21]

Augustine wrote the book in response to historical events and the Roman contention that Christianity was ruining their civilization. Following the sack of Rome in 410, many people blamed Christians for the weaknesses that brought about its demise. Marcellinus, a Christian official in the court of the Emperor Honorius, invited Augustine to write the book. Augustine worked on it for nearly thirteen years (413–426) and published it in several installments. Augustine gave us the trajectory of this gigantic work in the preface:

> The glorious city of God is my theme in this work, which you, my dearest son Marcellinus, suggested, and which is due to you by my promise. I have undertaken its defence against those who prefer their own gods to the Founder of this city, a city surpassingly glorious, whether we view it as it still lives by faith in this fleeting course of time, and sojourns as a stranger in the midst of the ungodly, or as it shall dwell in the fixed stability of its eternal seat, which it now with patience waits for, expecting until "righteousness shall return unto judgment," and it obtain, by virtue of its excellence, final victory and perfect peace. A great work is this, and an arduous; but God is my helper. For I am aware what ability is requisite to persuade the proud how great is the virtue of humility,

which raises us, not by a quite human arrogance, but by a divine grace, above all earthly dignities that totter on this shifting scene. For the King and Founder of this city of which we speak, has in Scripture uttered to His people a dictum of the divine law in these words: "God resisteth the proud, but giveth grace unto the humble." But this, which is God's prerogative, the inflated ambition of a proud spirit also affects, and dearly loves that this be numbered among its attributes, to "Show pity to the humbled soul, And crush the sons of pride." And therefore, as the plan of this work we have undertaken requires, and as occasion offers, we must speak also of the earthly city, which, though it be mistress of the nations, is itself ruled by its lust of rule.[22]

After this, the book can be divided into two essential parts: the first (books 1-10) refutes faulty pagan contentions. Topics in this section include the social and spiritual bankruptcy of paganism. This way of thinking, not Christianity, brought inevitable doom and trouble. Blessing and blight were in the hand of God alone. The second major section (books 11-22) explicates and defends Christian doctrine and puts it in a comprehensive historical context. The backdrop for this history was the analogy of the two cities, the city of God and the city of man. Those who dwell in the former city love God; the latter love self and are citizens of a city that will eventually come to destruction. The city of God, however, is indestructible, eternal and glorious. Five "acts" unfold the drama of Augustine's history: creation, the sin of the angels and humankind and the subsequent fall, the preparation for the coming of Christ, the incarnation and institution of the Church and the final destiny.[23] Believing Christians, already citizens of a heavenly kingdom, are for now foreign pilgrims in the city of man:

Let these and similar answers (if any fuller and fitter answers can be found) be given to their enemies by the redeemed family of the Lord Christ, and by the pilgrim city of King Christ. But let this city bear in mind, that among her enemies lie hid those who are destined to be fellow-citizens, that she may not think it a fruitless labor to bear what they inflict as enemies until they become confessors of the faith. So, too, as long as she is a stranger in the world, the city of God has in her communion, and bound to her by the sacraments, some who shall not eternally dwell in the lot of the saints. Of these, some are not now recognized; others declare themselves, and do not hesitate to make common cause with our enemies in murmuring against God, whose sacramental badge they wear. These men you may to-day see thronging the churches with us, to-morrow crowding the theatres with the godless. But we have the less reason to despair of the reclamation even of such persons, if among our most declared enemies there are now some, unknown to themselves, who are destined to become our friends. In truth, these two cities are entangled together in this world, and intermixed until the last judgment effects their separation. I now proceed to speak, as God shall help me, of the rise, progress, and end of these two cities; and what I write, I write for the glory of the city of God, that, being placed in comparison with the other, it may shine with a brighter lustre.[24]

For Augustine, history is *His*-story, in which God progressively unfolds His plan of redemption for those who are called by His Name.[25] Sin and evil are a part of this progressive work:

Almighty God, the supreme and supremely good Creator of all natures, who aids and rewards good wills, while He abandons and condemns the bad, and rules both, was not destitute of a plan by which He might [populate] His city with the fixed number of citizens which His wisdom had foreordained even out of the condemned human race, discriminating them not by merits, since the whole mass was condemned as if in a vitiated root, but by grace, and showing, not only in the case of the redeemed, but also in those who were not delivered, how much grace He has bestowed upon them. For every one acknowledges that he has been rescued from evil, not by deserved, but by gratuitous goodness, when he is singled out from the company of those with whom he might justly have borne a common punishment, and is allowed to go scathless. Why, then, should God not have created those whom He foresaw would sin, since He was able to show in and by them both what their guilt merited, and what His grace bestowed, and since, under His creating and disposing hand, even the perverse disorder of the wicked could not pervert the right order of things?[26]

Augustine's contribution toward resolving the problem of evil was highly influential. He realized that the first priority in reaching a resolution was in examining precisely the nature of evil. Is it a substance we can hold in our hands like some gushy, smelly thing that pollutes the human will? Is it an independent force emerging from somewhere? Is it even a *thing*?

In his examination of the issue, he granted that evidence was solid enough to first confidently posit God's existence. In other words, the reality of evil itself was an insufficient basis on which to disprove God even if we consider it an anomaly to His existence. But if God exists and is the source of everything, then does that not make Him the author of evil? Augustine's ingenious solution to this problem has held tremendous currency in the development of philosophical theology. Primarily, he argued that God was the author of everything good. This led to the conclusion that God did not create evil per se, but rather caused good things that could in turn create evil. But since nothing could create things in the sense that God could, then evil must not be a thing. He thus moved on to the next question:

> Where, then, is evil, and whence, and how crept it hither? What is its root, and what its seed? Or hath it no being at all? Why, then, do we fear and shun that which hath no being? Or if we fear it needlessly, then surely: is that fear evil whereby the heart is unnecessarily pricked and tormented, and so much a greater evil, as we have naught to fear, and yet do fear. Therefore either that is evil which we fear, or the act of fearing is in itself evil. Whence, therefore, is it, seeing that God, who is good, hath made all these things good?[27]

His famous answer to this was embodied in the Latin phrase: *Mali enim nula natura est: sed amissio boni, mall nomen accepit*, "Evil has no positive nature; but the loss of good has received the name 'evil.'"[28] The relation of good to an evil being is such that evil has "vitiated and corrupted it, and injured it, and consequently deprived it of good."[29] "Consequently he who inordinately loves the good which any nature possesses, even though he obtain it, himself becomes evil in the good, and wretched because deprived of a greater good."[30]

Evil, then, is the privation of the good (*privatio bonum*). The neglect or misuse of good properties created by God is what engenders evil. It is good that God created volitional beings who choose their course in life for good or ill. It is evil when human beings use the good faculties given them for uses contrary to the will of God and the end to which they were created (i.e., to glorify Him). The further we move away from the purpose to which we are created, the greater evil is the result. Adam's sin in the garden was to think that he could find fulfillment apart from God, to be his own god and make his own happiness. But this is like designing a car to run on high-octane fuel and then depriving the car of that fuel, opting for tar instead or letting the car sit and rust. Evil results in our push away from the good things of God.

Augustine did not deny, of course, that God knew full well that such would be the case in our fallen world. Yet in His providence and wisdom, He ordained that such events would take place so that He could redeem the world and bring glory to His name both from the angelic world and from among people.

> It is He who, when He foreknew that certain angels would in their pride desire to suffice for their own blessedness, and would forsake their great good, did not deprive them of this power, deeming it to be more befitting His power and goodness to bring good out of evil than to prevent the evil from coming into existence. And indeed evil had never been, had not the mutable nature—mutable, though good, and created by the most high God and immutable Good, who created all things good, brought evil upon itself by sin. And this its sin is itself proof that its nature was originally good. For had it not been very good, though not equal to its Creator, the desertion of God as its light could not have been an evil to it. For as blindness is a vice of the eye, and this very fact indicates that the eye was created to see the light, and as, consequently, vice itself proves that the eye is more excellent than the other members, because it is capable of light (for on no other supposition would it be a vice of the eye to want light), so the nature which once enjoyed God teaches, even by its very vice, that it was created the best of all, since it is now miserable because it does not enjoy God. It is he who with very just punishment doomed the angels who voluntarily fell to everlasting misery, and rewarded those who continued in their attachment to the supreme good with the assurance of endless stability as the meed of their fidelity. It is He who made also man himself upright, with the same freedom of will, an earthly animal, indeed, but fit for heaven if he remained

faithful to his Creator, but destined to the misery appropriate
to such a nature if he forsook Him. It is He who when He
foreknew that man would in his turn sin by abandoning God
and breaking His law, did not deprive him of the power of
free-will, because He at the same time foresaw what good He
Himself would bring out of the evil, and how from this mortal
race, deservedly and justly condemned, He would by His
grace collect, as now He does, a people so numerous, that He
thus fills up and repairs the blank made by the fallen angels,
and that thus that beloved and heavenly city is not defrauded
of the full number of its citizens, but perhaps may even rejoice in a still more overflowing population.[31]

Further, in the divine eschaton, the possibility of committing evil will be re-
moved. People's freedom will no longer be encumbered by the ravages of sin.
Rather, they will be liberated, their wills desiring only the divine presence and
His glory.

Toward the end of *The City of God*, Augustine concluded with a vision of the
eternal happiness the citizens of God's great city will enjoy forever in His presence:

How great shall be that felicity, which shall be tainted with
no evil, which shall lack no good, and which shall afford lei-
sure for the praises of God, who shall be all in all! For I know
not what other employment there can be where no lassitude
shall slacken activity, nor any want stimulate to labor. I am
admonished also by the sacred song, in which I read or hear
the words, "Blessed are they that dwell in Thy house, O Lord;
they will be still praising Thee." All the members and organs
of the incorruptible body, which now we see to be suited to
various necessary uses, shall contribute to the praises of God;
for in that life necessity shall have no place, but full, certain,
secure, everlasting felicity. For all those parts of the bodily
harmony, which are distributed through the whole body,
within and without, and of which I have just been saying that
they at present elude our observation, shall then be dis-
cerned; and, along with the other great and marvellous discoveries which shall then kindle rational minds in praise of
the great Artificer, there shall be the enjoyment of a beauty
which appeals to the reason. What power of movement such

bodies shall possess, I have not the audacity rashly to define, as I have not the ability to conceive. Nevertheless I will say that in any case, both in motion and at rest, they shall be, as in their appearance, seemly; for into that state nothing which is unseemly shall be admitted. One thing is certain, the body shall forthwith be wherever the spirit wills, and the spirit shall will nothing which is unbecoming either to the spirit or to the body. True honor shall be there, for it shall be denied to none who is worthy, nor yielded to any unworthy; neither shall any unworthy person so much as sue for it, for none but the worthy shall be there. True peace shall be there, where no one shall suffer opposition either from himself or any other. God Himself, who is the Author of virtue, shall there be its reward; for, as there is nothing greater or better, He has promised Himself. What else was meant by His word through the prophet, "I will be your God, and ye shall be my people," than, I shall be their satisfaction, I shall be all that men honorably desire—life, and health, and nourishment, and plenty, and glory, and honor, and peace, and all good things? This, too, is the right interpretation of the saying of the apostle, "That God may be all in all." He shall be the end of our desires who shall be seen without end, loved without cloy, praised without weariness. This outgoing of affection, this employment, shall certainly be, like eternal life itself, common to all.[32]

In all his works, Augustine appealed to Scripture to encourage his readers, correct error and foster right thinking. This crucial *modus operandi* is evident early on and then throughout his career. Scripture is our guide and source for all faith and practice. He wrote, for example, in *The City of God* that the citizens of Christ's kingdom "believe the Holy Scriptures, old and new, which we call canonical, and which are the source of the faith by which the just lives and by which we walk without doubting whilst we are absent from the Lord."[33] He wrote toward the end of his *Confessions* of the "sublime authority" of "divine Scripture."[34] In his letters, he summed this all up saying, "Let our arguments appeal to reason and to the authoritative teaching of the Divine Scriptures."[35] By constantly appealing to Scripture, Augustine found the grounding he needed to persevere through his life's work.

The Final Years

In 426 Augustine, now seventy-two, named his assistant Eraclius as his auxiliary and successor. Theologian John Piper recounts the momentous occasion on which Eraclius assumed Augustine's preaching duties:

> At the ceremony Eraclius stood to preach, as the old man sat on his bishop's throne behind him. Overwhelmed by a sense of inadequacy in Augustine's presence, Eraclius said, "The cricket chirps, the swan is silent."[36]

Yet, as Piper observes, the apologetical swan is anything but silent today. Indeed, he has not been silent for over 1,600 years.

Augustine died on August 28, 430, just as the Vandals rushed into the city. By another incredible act of divine providence, the vast library of his writings was spared while most others went up in flames. An entire civilization was relegated to an ash heap, while the words of the graceful swan helped spark a new age.

During the Middle Ages, probably no theologian was quoted more often than Augustine. Even the later sixteenth-century Reformers considered their work in many ways to be a conscious revival of Augustinianism. Both Calvin and Luther used Augustine's work to point out the errors of the Roman blur on gospel salvation. Augustine continues to fight battles of which he couldn't even have conceived in his lifetime. The work of this great apologist provides defenders of the faith with the apologetical armor they need to weather the storms in the city of man.

Conclusion

Augustine is an archetypal example of an apologist grounded firmly in the classical tradition. He used reason to defend historic Christianity and to satisfy people's need for fulfilled intellects as opposed to asking people to believe something in their hearts that their minds could not accept as true. Augustine's apologetic is much needed in our day where the idea of maintaining "double truth" is forcefully advocated. The double-truth approach suggests that we can actually believe something in our hearts (the nonrational self) that our minds (the rational self) know to be false. Since heart and mind are separate spheres, reason and faith are separate functions. Reason belongs to the mind; faith belongs to the heart; and never the two shall meet.

But Augustine knew that this was not only a false approach to Christ (who commands us to love Him with all our hearts, souls, strength and minds) but was manifestly impossible. If human beings are created in the *imago Dei*, then they cannot believe something in their hearts that their minds reject. We must be fully convinced in our minds in order to give our hearts to something truly.

We might ask ourselves, for example, what Augustine would do if he were alive today and presented with incontrovertible evidence that God did not exist. Do you suppose Augustine would have said, "I do not care, for I have faith"? Would he say, "Incontrovertible or not, your evidence means nothing to me"? I believe that Augustine, in the face of such evidence, would declare himself an atheist. Should he continue to "believe" something in his heart—knowing rationally that it was not true—for whatever benefits this false belief might provide him with? It is hard to see how any knowingly false belief could benefit someone.

Of course, we know that no incontrovertible evidence can ever be presented in favor of atheism. Indeed, if Christianity is true, then it is impossible for such evidence to exist. The point, however, is that truth and faith are two sides of the same coin in Christianity.

Of course, Augustine knew that being convinced intellectually did not mean that we can attain a full comprehension of the Godhead. Our knowledge of God will always be limited. But we need not have total knowledge of something in order to know that it is a proper object of truth.

Augustine also shows us that our knowledge and reason are bankrupt without a reasonable trust in some authority. When Augustine joined the Manichaeans, he thought this group would allow him to be a total freethinker. He could simply let his reason take him wherever it would go. He later realized that the Manichaean program required him to uncritically place his faith in elaborate claims prior to those claims being established rationally. Thus, while the Manichaeans placed a heavy premium on the use of logic and reason, Augustine saw that they first asked followers to acceptfully the authority of Mani and his teachers. This led Augustine to his formulation of how reason and faith juxtapose: Belief in some form of authority must precede reason. In his *Confessions*, he remarked, "Unless we should believe, we should do nothing at all in this life."[37] Later, these discoveries formulated the basis of Augustine's now famous statement that, "I believe in order that I may understand."[38]

Such statements have led many to believe that Augustine was a fideist (i.e., a person who believes faith and religious devotion are not supported by reason). When we examine his other writings, however, we find this to be erroneous. Augustine reserved an important role for the function of reason. He contended that no one believed anything unless he first processed it intellectually. In Augustine's apologetic, it was necessary to believe something only after careful thought has led the way. Anything else was dangerous and foolish.

The valid function of reason and apologetics, according to Augustine, does not end once we believe in Christ. We also use them to grow in faith and to share the tenets of the faith with others. Augustine was a strong advocate of the use of human reason before, during and after conversion—to the glory of God.

Anselm
Apologist for Greatness

Man was created to see God. . . .
Without God it is ill with us.
— Proslogium, *chapter 1*

Events in the Life of **Anselm**

1033	Born in Aosta, Piedmont (northwestern Italy).
1060	Became a full-time monk at the monastery in Bec.
1070–1078	Wrote the *Monologium* and *Proslogium*.
1078	Became abbot of Bec.
1093	Became the archbishop of Canterbury. Was later exiled.
1109	Died of natural causes.

Anselm was one of the greatest geniuses in the history of Christian thought. He stands as the father of orthodox scholasticism and has even been called "the second Augustine." His mind was sharp and logical, and his writings display profundity, originality and a masterly grasp of intellect.[1]

A Christian Upbringing

Anselm was born in 1033 in Aosta, Piedmont—a breathtaking alpine region in northwestern Italy bordering France (what was then Lombardy on the cusp of Burgundy). His parents were fairly well-to-do financially. His father, Gundulf, was a Lombard; his mother, Ermenberga, a Burgundian. Gundulf was grumpy, harsh and treated young Anselm with disdain. Moreover, he hindered his efforts in becoming a monk and pursuing his Christian studies. As was common among saintly scholars, however, Anselm had a mother who cared deeply about him and raised him in the ways of the Church. She inspired in him a love for learning and for pondering the wonders and mysteries of life. Ermenberga often spoke to young Anselm of God, describing Him as "the One Who dwells on high" and "rules all things."[2] We can only imagine what a majestic image Anselm must have conceived in his mind as he pondered his mother's words amid the beautiful snowcapped mountains of the Italian Alps. Indeed, Anselm's biographer and close companion, Eadmer, writes in his *Life of St. Anselm* this touching story from Anselm's youth:

> He often revolved [such] matters in his mind, [and] it chanced that one night he saw in a [dream] that he must go up to the summit of the mountain and hasten to the court of God, the great King. But before he began to ascend the mountain, he saw in the plain through which he had passed to its foot, women, who were the King's handmaidens, reaping the corn; but they were doing this very negligently and slothfully. Then, grieving for their sloth, and rebuking them, he bethought him that he would accuse them before their Lord and King. Thereafter, having climbed the mountain he entered the royal court. There he found the King with only his cupbearer. For it seemed that, as it was now Autumn, the King had sent his household to gather the harvest. As the boy entered he was called by the Master, and drawing nigh he sat at

his feet. Then with cheery kindliness he was asked who and
whence he was and what he was seeking. To these questions
he made answer as well as he knew. Then at the Master's
command some moist white bread was brought him by the
cupbearer and he feasted thereon in his presence, wherefore
when morning came and he brought to mind the things he
had seen, as a simpler and innocent child he believed that he
had truly been fed in heaven with the bread of the Lord, and
this he publicly affirmed in the presence of others.[3]

Eadmer adds that young Anselm was loved by everyone who knew him and
made rapid progress in his learning.[4] In his midteens, Anselm desired to enter
the monastery. The abbot, however, refused him entry, fearing Gundulf's dis-
pleasure. Biographer W.H. Kent tells us of the curious events that followed:

The boy then made a strange prayer. He asked for an illness,
thinking this would move the monks to yield to his wishes.
The illness came but his admission to the monastery was still
denied him. Nonetheless he determined to gain his end at
some future date. But [before] long he was drawn away by
the pleasures of youth and lost his first ardour and his love of
learning. His love for his mother in some measure restrained
him. But on her death it seemed that his anchor was lost, and
he was at the mercy of the waves.[5]

Kent tells us that following Ermenberga's death, the attitude of Anselm's
father toward him only grew worse, and he treated him with terrible malice,
so much so that the young man finally resolved to leave home.[6]

Now twenty-three years old, Anselm lived a few years in Burgundy and
France. Eventually, though, he was attracted to the Abbey of Bec in Normandy where his countryman Lanfranc was prior. Renowned for his great
learning, Lanfranc left a successful law practice to devote himself to the pursuit of learning and eventually became a professor in Normandy. After several
years, however, he was drawn to the ascetic life of a monk and scholar and
traveled to Bec where the abbot, Herluin, was building a monastery. Herluin
graciously received him, and Lanfranc applied himself to the study of Scripture. Anselm could not have found a better mentor. Lanfranc was smart, car-
ing and devoted to the truth of God's Word. Kent adds that, "Anselm profited
so well by the lessons of this master that he became his most familiar disciple
and shared in the work of teaching."[7]

As a side note, it is interesting to observe here the commonality of both a praying mother and a nurturing mentor in the lives of many of the great apologists. For Irenaeus it was the bold Polycarp; for Origen it was his martyred father, Leonides; for Athanasius it was his intrepid pastor, Alexander; and for Augustine it was his beloved pastor, Ambrose. It is not by accident that the locus of Jesus' own pedagogical approach was one modeled on discipleship.

Anselm at Bec

In 1060 Anselm at last became a full-time monk at Bec. As a testimony to his great learning and superb character, only three years later he succeeded Lanfranc as the prior of Bec after the latter assumed the post of abbot at the Caen monastery in northern France (Lanfranc became the archbishop of Canterbury in 1070). Although some monks took offense at such an early appointment, Anselm's winsome character and gentle manner soon won them over.

Anselm spent the next thirty years at Bec and eventually succeeded Herluin as abbot in 1078. He reluctantly accepted this post, not wanting his studies to be derailed by administrative concerns. During those years, he also opened a school that became famous and attracted some of the brightest students from all over Europe. As his fame spread, many great men prized his friendship and sought his counsel.[8] Anselm also quickly won the hearts of the people.

At Bec, Anselm wrote some of his finest philosophical, theological and apologetical works, especially the *Monologium* and *Proslogium*. Both of these works aimed to prove the existence and nature of God. They have been the topic of much discussion among philosophers and theologians over the last millennium.

Monologium

The *Monologium* was originally titled *An Example of Meditating about the Rational Basis of Faith*. In the form of a meditation, Anselm discussed the being of God, basing his argument on reason alone. It was consistent with the writings of the fathers, especially Augustine, whose influence is clear. After the preface, Anselm began the first chapter by speaking of the necessity of positing a supreme being:

> *There is a being which is best, and greatest, and highest of all existing beings.*

If any man, either from ignorance or unbelief, has no knowledge of the existence of one Nature which is highest of all existing beings, which is also sufficient to itself in its eternal blessedness, and which confers upon and effects in all other beings, through its omnipotent goodness, the very fact of their existence, and the fact that in any way their existence is good; and if he has no knowledge of many other things, which we necessarily believe regarding God and his creatures, he still believes that he can at least convince himself of these truths in great part, even if his mental powers are very ordinary, by the force of reason alone . . .

. . . It is easy, then, for one to say to himself: Since there are goods so innumerable, whose great diversity we experience by the bodily senses, and discern by our mental faculties, must we not believe that there is some one thing, through which all goods whatever are good? Or are they certain and clear, for all who are willing to see, that whatsoever things are said to possess any attribute in such a way that in mutual comparison they may be said to possess it in greater, or less, or equal degree, are said to possess it by virtue of some fact, which is not understood to be one thing in one case and another in another, but to be the same in different cases, whether it is regarded as existing in these cases in equal or unequal degree. For, whatsoever things are said to be *just*, when compared one with another, whether equally, or more, or less, cannot be understood as just, except through the quality of *justness*, which is not one thing in one instance, and another in another.

Since it is certain, then, that all goods, if mutually compared, would prove either equally or unequally good, necessarily they are all good by virtue of something which is conceived of as the same in different goods, although sometimes they seem to be called good, the one by virtue of one thing, the other by virtue of another. For, apparently it is by virtue of one quality, that a horse is called *good*, because he is strong, and by virtue of another, that he is called *good*, because he is swift. For, though he seems to be called good by virtue of his strength, and good by virtue of his swiftness, yet swiftness and strength do not appear to be the same thing.

But if a horse, because he is strong and swift, is therefore good, how is it that a strong, swift robber is bad? Rather, then, just as a strong, swift robber is bad, because he is harmful, so a strong, swift horse is good, because he is useful. And, indeed, nothing is ordinarily regarded as good, except either for some utility—as, for instance, safety is called good, and those things which promote safety—or for some honorable character—as, for instance, beauty is reckoned to be good, and what promotes beauty.

But, since the reasoning which we have observed is in no wise refutable, necessarily, again, all things, whether useful or honorable, if they are truly good, are good through that same being through which all goods exist, whatever that being is. But who can doubt this very being, through which all goods exist, to be a great good? This must be, then, a good through itself, since every other good is through it.

It follows, therefore, that all other goods are good through another being than that which they themselves are, and this being alone is good through itself. Hence, this alone is supremely good, which is alone good through itself. For it is supreme, in that it so surpasses other beings, that it is neither equaled nor excelled. But that which is supremely good is also supremely great. There is, therefore, some one being which is supremely good, and supremely great, that is, the highest of all existing beings.[9]

Anselm's argument from the objectivity of good in the world pointed to a necessary being from which all other beings derive their existence and attributes. Modern apologist Norman Geisler summarizes Anselm's argument for us syllogistically:

1. Good things exist.
2. The cause of this goodness is either one or many.
3. But it can't be many, for then there would be no way to compare their goodness, for all things would be equally good. But some things are better than others.
4. Therefore, one Supreme Good (God) causes the goodness in all good things.[10]

Anselm did not stop with the example of goodness, however, but extended the argument to *being* itself.

There is a certain Nature through which whatever is exists, and which exists through itself, and is the highest of all existing being.

Therefore, not only are all good things such through something that is one and the same, and all great things such through something that is one and the same; but whatever is, apparently exists through something that is one and the same. For, everything that is, exists either through something, or through nothing. But nothing exists through nothing. For it is altogether inconceivable that anything should not exist by virtue of something.

Whatever is, then, does not exist except through something. Since this is true, either there is one being, or there are more than one, through which all things that are exist. But if there are more than one, either these are themselves to be referred to some one being, through which they exist, or they exist separately, each through itself, or they exist mutually through one another.

But, if these beings exist through one being, then all things do not exist through more than one, but rather through that one being through which these exist.

If, however, these exist separately, each through itself, there is, at any rate, some power or property of existing through self (*existendi per se*), by which they are able to exist each through itself. But, there can be no doubt that, in that case, they exist through this very power, which is one, and through which they are able to exist, each through itself. More truly, then, do all things exist through this very being, which is one, than through these, which are more than one, which, without this one, cannot exist.

But that these beings exist mutually through one another, no reason can admit; since it is an irrational conception that anything should exist through a being on which it confers existence. For not even beings of a relative nature exist thus mutually, the one through the other. For, though the terms master and servant are used with mutual reference, and the men thus designated are mentioned as having mutual relations, yet they do not at all exist mutually, the one through the other, since these relations exist through the subjects to which they are referred.

Therefore, since truth altogether excludes the supposition that there are more beings than one, through which all things exist, that being, through which all exist, must be one. Since, then, all things that are exist through this one being, doubtless this one being exists through itself. Whatever things there are else then, exist through something other than themselves, and this alone through itself. But whatever exists through another is less than that, through which all things are, and which alone exists through itself. Therefore, that which exists through itself exists in the greatest degree of all things.

There is, then, some one being which alone exists in the greatest and the highest degree of all. But that which is greatest of all, and through which exists whatever is good or great, and, in short, whatever has any existence that must be supremely good, and supremely great, and the highest of all existing beings.[11]

Proslogium

Anselm's following work, the *Proslogium*, was a sequel of sorts and introduced for the first time Anselm's trademark apologetic contribution now commonly known as the "ontological argument." The argument is not easy to grasp, and philosophers and theologians still debate its warrant and efficacy. In many ways, the argument is not so much a rationalistic "proof" for the existence of God intended to convince the ardent skeptic but is an attempt to better understand the God in whom the faithful already believe. Following Anselm's distinct contemplative and worshipful style, the arguments in the *Proslogium* are couched in prayerful meditation. The first chapter introduces Anselm's seminal epistemological approach: *fides quarens intellectum*, that is, "faith seeking understanding":

> Exhortation of the mind to the contemplation of God—It casts aside cares, and excludes all thoughts save that of God, that it may seek Him. Man was created to see God. Man by sin lost the blessedness for which he was made, and found the misery for which he was not made. He did not keep this good when he could keep it easily. Without God it is ill with us. Our labors and attempts are in vain without God. Man cannot seek God, unless God himself teaches him; nor find him, unless he reveals himself. God created man in his image, that he might be mindful of him, think of him, and love him. The believer does not seek to understand, that he may believe, but he believes that he may understand: for unless he believed he would not understand.[12]

Chapter 2 then begins to unpack the thrust of the ontological arguments:

Truly there is a God, although the fool hath said in his heart, There is no God.

And so, Lord, do thou, who dost give understanding to faith, give me, so far as thou knowest it to be profitable, to understand that thou art as we believe; and that thou art that which we believe. And indeed, we believe that thou art a being than which nothing greater can be conceived. Or is there no such nature, since the fool hath said in his heart, there is no God? But, at any rate, this very fool, when he hears of this being of which I speak—a being than which nothing greater can be conceived—understands what he hears, and what he understands is in his understanding; although he does not understand it to exist.

For, it is one thing for an object to be in the understanding, and another to understand that the object exists. When a painter first conceives of what he will afterwards perform, he has it in his understanding, but he does not yet understand it to be, because he has not yet performed it. But after he has made the painting, he both has it in his understanding, and he understands that it exists, because he has made it.

Hence, even the fool is convinced that something exists in the understanding, at least, than which nothing greater can be conceived. For, when he hears of this, he understands it. And whatever is understood, exists in the understanding. And assuredly that, than which nothing greater can be conceived, cannot exist in the understanding alone. For, suppose it exists in the understanding alone: then it can be conceived to exist in reality; which is greater.

Therefore, if that, than which nothing greater can be conceived, exists in the understanding alone, the very being, than which nothing greater can be conceived, is one, than which a greater can be conceived. But obviously this is impossible. Hence, there is no doubt that there exists a being, than which nothing greater can be conceived, and it exists both in the understanding and in reality.[13]

Chapter 3 furthers this argument, saying that not only must God exist, but He cannot be conceived not to.

God cannot be conceived not to exist. God is that, than which nothing greater can be conceived. That which can be conceived not to exist is not God.

And it assuredly exists so truly, that it cannot be conceived not to exist. For, it is possible to conceive of a being which cannot be conceived not to exist; and this is greater than one which can be conceived not to exist. Hence, if that, than which nothing greater can be conceived, can be conceived not to exist, it is not that, than which nothing greater can be conceived. But this is an irreconcilable contradiction. There is, then, so truly a being than which nothing greater can be conceived to exist, that it cannot even be conceived not to exist; and this being thou art, O Lord, our God.

So truly, therefore, dost thou exist, O Lord, my God, that thou canst not be conceived not to exist; and rightly. For, if a mind could conceive of a being better than thee, the creature would rise above the Creator; and this is most absurd. And, indeed, whatever else there is, except thee alone, can be conceived not to exist. To thee alone, therefore, it belongs to exist more truly than all other beings, and hence in a higher degree than all others. For, whatever else exists does not exist so truly, and hence in a less degree it belongs to it to exist. Why, then, has the fool said in his heart, there is no God, since it is so evident, to a rational mind, that thou dost exist in the highest degree of all? Why, except that he is dull and a fool?[14]

Anselm's ontological argument, though enjoying a long and illustrious status among thinkers, has come under much scrutiny. Few doubt its brilliance. But the degree of its success in providing us with a rational approach to the existence of God has provoked much critical discussion. How can we argue from a cognitive concept to an objective reality?

The first to criticize Anselm's argument formally was a fellow monk by the name of Gaunilo who wrote a point-by-point criticism of it to which Anselm, in turn, provided a rejoinder. Guanilo believed that Anselm's reasoning was unsound in that it argued from a mere intellectual concept to its ontological necessity in reality. On this basis, one could use the argument to prove just about anything. He parodied Anselm's argument, saying, if we replaced "an island than which none greater can be conceived" for "something than which nothing greater can be conceived," then we would prove the existence of that island.[15] Anselm's rejoinder to Guanilo counterargued that his example of the perfect island was a false analogy. They were not talking about the best possible thing in any number of categories. Rather, they were talking about the greatest possible Being beyond all categories. Moreover, this Being is a necessary Being. It cannot not exist. The greatest island does not exist necessarily but contingently. Thus, the objection fails.

Though the debate between Guanilo and Anselm was stern, they conducted it with the utmost courtesy. Indeed, Gaunilo acknowledged the merit of Anselm's work, and Anselm not only praised his adversary but thanked him for his criticism.[16]

Needless to say, the debate over the merit of Anselm's argument remains unsettled and the best and brightest have fallen on both sides of the ledger. As one scholar puts it, the ontological argument was

> rejected by Thomas [Aquinas] and his followers, [though] revived in another form by Descartes. After being assailed by Kant, it was defended by Hegel, for whom it had a peculiar fascination—he recurs to it in many parts of his writings. In one place he says that it is generally used by later philosophers, "yet always along with the other proofs, although it alone is the true one."

Quite appropriately, he adds that

> assailants of this argument should remember that all minds are not cast in one mold, and it is easy to understand how some can feel the force of arguments that are not felt by others. But if this proof were indeed, as some consider it, an absurd fallacy, how could it appeal to such minds as those of Anselm, Descartes, and Hegel? It may be well to add that the argument was not rejected by *all* the great Schoolmen.[17]

Anselm Becomes the Archbishop of Canterbury

During the next fifteen years or so, the dialogue over the validity of the ontological argument continued. In 1089, however, things took a dramatic turn for Anselm when his mentor, Lanfranc, then the archbishop of Canterbury, died. Because of their longstanding relationship and the fact that Anselm had made frequent visits to Canterbury, it was widely recognized that he would make a logical successor to Lanfranc. In fact, during one of his visits to Canterbury, people hailed him as their future archbishop. In modesty, Anselm made no more visits there until things could get sorted out. The king, William Rufus, soon stifled the desires of the church and its congregates, for he did not want a new archbishop. He wanted to keep the office vacant and apply its revenues to his own use. For four years, the church at Canterbury was in chaos while Rufus plundered it for his own gain. The church members prayed that the king would have a change of heart. In 1093, when William fell ill and thought his death imminent, he actually demanded that Anselm become archbishop. Yet typical for Anselm, he did not desire the post, preferring the humble life of a scholar and monastic. One biographer records that he actually had to be dragged to the king's bedside and have the bishop's staff thrust into his closed hand, prying open his fingers one by one.[18] Anselm was consecrated to the Canterburian bishopric the following December.

Unfortunately, the next four years witnessed a continual struggle between the king and new bishop. The idea of the separation of Church and state and such matters as the lay investiture of clergy had not yet worked themselves out in ecclesiastical history. Thus, Anselm had to try to settle arguments regarding money, rights, privileges and who controlled what. At one point, he carried his case to Rome (with the king's permission) but obtained little help there.[19]

Anselm stayed in exile from Canterbury as the controversy raged on. He returned to England, however, in 1100 upon hearing of King William's death. Anselm soon met with Henry, the new king, who received him warmly. Yet the difficulty over lay investiture arose again in full force. Anselm believed firmly that in matters of ecclesiastical authority, the Church and state had separate powers. Royalty did not include the power to ordain clergymen. Anselm remained steadfast in this conviction, and the king remained obstinate. Such a concession was an acquiescence of royal power. Henry always treated Anselm with consideration, but the dispute continued. Anselm refused to accept lay investiture and remained absent and abroad from his bishopric for several years.

During this interval, Anselm held a council at Westminster where stringent canons were passed against the evils of the age and regarding the investiture problem. The state still required Anselm to consecrate bishops invested by the king. He firmly refused, however, and his steadfastness began spreading. Other bishops returned the staffs they had received at royal hands, or they refused to be consecrated by any nonecclesial authority.[20]

Cur Deus Homo?

The most significant undertaking during this period of exile was Anselm's composition *Cur Deus Homo?* or *Why the God-Man?* Though the work was primarily theological, it had an apologetical ring to it in that Anselm demonstrated why God became man to provide redemption. Anselm wrote the book as a dialogue between himself and a Christian named Boso.

Anselm argued that divine love opposed by human wickedness necessitated that God take on human flesh and bridge the ontological gap between the two, thus reconciling His creation to Himself through those who trust in Christ. Anselm acknowledged that unbelieving skeptics scoff at such a notion. For example, in chapter 3, Boso observed:

> Infidels ridiculing our simplicity charge upon us that we do injustice and dishonor to God when we affirm that he descended into the womb of a virgin, that he was born of woman, that he grew on the nourishment of milk and the food of men; and, passing over many other things which seem incompatible with Deity, that he endured fatigue, hunger, thirst, stripes and crucifixion among thieves.[21]

Anselm replied:

> We do no injustice or dishonor to God, but give him thanks with all the heart, praising and proclaiming the ineffable height of his compassion. For the more astonishing a thing it is and beyond expectation, that he has restored us from so great and deserved ills in which we were, to so great and unmerited blessings which we had forfeited; by so much the more has he shown his more exceeding love and tenderness towards us. For did they but carefully consider how fitly in this way human redemption is secured, they would not ridicule our simplicity, but would rather join with us in praising the wise beneficence of God. For, as death came upon the human race by the disobedience of man, it was fitting that by man's obedience life should be restored. And, as sin, the cause of our condemnation, had its origin from a woman, so ought the author of our righteousness and salvation to be born of a woman. And so also was it proper that the devil, who, being man's tempter, had conquered him in eating of the tree, should be vanquished by man in the suffering of the

tree which man bore. Many other things also, if we carefully
examine them, give a certain indescribable beauty to our redemption as thus procured.[22]

The most important development in *Cur Deus Homo?*, however, was Anselm's
gleaning a better understanding of the atonement. His theologizing on this matter is known as the "satisfaction theory" of the atonement and has been the orthodox view within classical Christendom ever since (though not to the
exclusion of other aspects).

The word *atonement*, which is almost the only theological term of English
origin and is a contraction of *at* and *one*, has a curious history. Human sin was
an offense to God and had to be atoned for. However, being finite, people
were not able to make the atonement themselves and thus satisfy the wrath
of God. Therefore, the crucifixion was needed as the atoning satisfaction of
Christ, whereby God and His creation were reconciled. As the Apostle Paul
says, "God was reconciling the world to himself in Christ, not counting men's
sins against them" (2 Corinthians 5:19). In chapter 11, Anselm explained the
nature of providing satisfaction:

> One who imperils another's safety does not enough by merely
> restoring his safety, without making some compensation for
> the anguish incurred; so he who violates another's honor
> does not enough by merely rendering honor again, but must,
> according to the extent of the injury done, make restoration
> in some way satisfactory to the person whom he has dishon-
> ored. We must also observe that when any one pays what he
> has unjustly taken away, he ought to give something which
> could not have been demanded of him, had he not stolen
> what belonged to another. So then, every one who sins ought
> to pay back the honor of which he has robbed God; and this is
> the satisfaction which every sinner owes to God.[23]

He later stated that we must "consider it settled that, without satisfaction,
that is, without voluntary payment of the debt, God can neither pass by the
sin unpunished, nor can the sinner attain that happiness, or happiness like
that, which he had before he sinned; for man cannot in this way be restored,
or become such as he was before he sinned."[24] The remaining chapters explicate the manner in which this satisfaction must be proportionate to our guilt.
Considering our finitude sinning against God's infinitude, we are unable to

accomplish this. But God, in His great love, is both able and willing to be our surrogate for punitive satisfaction. Anselm decried, "And do you not think that so great a good in itself so lovely, can avail to pay what is due for the sins of the whole world?"[25]

Toward the conclusion of *Cur Deus Homo?* Anselm summarized the magnificent work God did for us in our place. His summation echoes his earlier works concerning the ontological argument. God's compassion and holiness are "above anything that can be conceived":

> Now we have found the compassion of God which appeared lost to you when we were considering God's holiness and man's sin; we have found it, I say, so great and so consistent with his holiness, as to be incomparably above anything that can be conceived. For what compassion can excel these words of the Father, addressed to the sinner doomed to eternal torments and having no way of escape: "Take my only begotten Son and make him an offering for yourself"; or these words of the Son: "Take me, and ransom your souls." For these are the voices they utter, when inviting and leading us to faith in the Gospel. Or can anything be more just than for him to remit all debt since he has earned a reward greater than all debt, if given with the love which he deserves.[26]

Anselm's doctrine of the atonement remains to this day the majority view within classical Catholic, Orthodox and Protestant theology.

The Final Years

In 1107, with *Cur Deus Homo?* complete and making its way through the Church's thinking, an agreement was finally reached that allowed Anselm to return to his archbishopric in Canterbury. King Henry gave up his claim to invest bishops and abbots, while the Church continued to allow bishops to grant homage to the state for the temporal possessions they enjoyed.[27] The agreement, though imperfect, at least paved the way for Anselm to reassume his post to devote his energies to other matters, and to instigate further negotiations.

In his last two years, Anselm enjoyed a respite from controversy and concentrated his efforts on overseeing his Canterburian flock and issuing his last writings.

Anselm died of natural causes on April 21, 1109. He never feared death. Rather, like Paul, who said he "would prefer to be away from the body and at home with the Lord" (2 Corinthians 5:8), Anselm looked forward to being with the Lord he had followed throughout his life as a great apologist. That Anselm anticipated this day with faith, hope and joy is evident in one of his most famous prayers:

> I pray, O God, to know thee, to love thee, that I may rejoice in thee. And if I cannot attain to full joy in this life may I at least advance from day to day, until that joy shall come to the full. Let the knowledge of thee advance in me here, and there be made full. Let the love of thee increase, and there let it be full, that here my joy may be great in hope, and there full in truth. Lord, through thy Son thou dost command, nay, thou dost counsel us to ask; and thou dost promise that we shall receive, that our joy may be full. I ask, O Lord, as thou dost counsel through our wonderful Counselor. I will receive what thou dost promise by virtue of thy truth, that my joy may be full. Faithful God, I ask. I will receive, that my joy may be full.[28]

Anselm's work grew in popularity and appreciation following his death. A Christian apologist does not often gain the admiration of secular philosophers and historians in addition to his fellow churchmen. Yet he has enjoyed this distinction. Edward Freeman, in his *History of the Norman Conquest*, writes of him:

> Stranger as he was, he has won his place among the noblest worthies of our island. It was something to be the model of all ecclesiastical perfection; it was something to be the creator of the theology of Christendom—but it was something higher still to be the very embodiment of righteousness and mercy.[29]

Conclusion

Anselm is the most important figure in theology and apologetics in the time between Augustine and Aquinas. Indeed, Anselm may have come closer than anyone in the history of theology to providing a working definition of God. God is "that than which none greater can be conceived." There is no thought greater than the thought of God.

The degree to which the ontological argument is successful as a logical apologetic has been debated for centuries. It is curious that an argument written nearly a millennium ago and which consists of a mere four pages has given rise to enough books over the centuries to fill a library. Karl Barth's 1931 book, *Fides Quaerens Intellectum*, devotes an entire 165 pages to the ontological argument.[30] Contemporary Christian philosopher Alvin Plantinga comments that

> the ontological argument for the existence of God has fascinated philosophers ever since it was formulated. . . . What accounts for this fascination? . . . The cause is perhaps twofold. First, the ontological argument offers an enormous return on a pretty slim investment—a definition, and a perplexing but not altogether implausible premise connecting existence and "greatness," yield the theistic conclusion. Second, although the argument certainly looks at first sight as if it ought to be unsound, it is profoundly difficult to say what exactly is wrong with it. Indeed, it is doubtful that any philosopher has given a really convincing and thorough refutation of the ontological argument. Too often philosophers merely remark that Kant refuted the argument by showing that existence is not a predicate and that "one cannot build bridges from the conceptual realm to the real world." But it is very doubtful that Kant specified a sense of "is a predicate" such that, in that sense, it is clear both that existence is not a predicate and that Anselm's argument requires that it be one. Nor are the mere claims that no existential propositions are necessary or the above comment about bridge building impressive as refutations of Anselm—after all, he claims to have an argument for the necessity of at least one existential proposition. So one must either show just where his argument goes wrong, or else produce a solid argument for the claim that no existential (in the appropriate sense) propositions can be necessary— and this, I think, no one has succeeded in doing.[31]

If the ontological argument is not as watertight as the cosmological or teleological arguments, should we still use it? The reason for doing so is that the argument provokes thinking about God. Anselm's formulation makes it impossible to avoid the question of God, and the ontological "proof" sticks in our minds until we make peace with it. In apologetics we want people to face questions about ultimate reality, and we want to prod them into being less blasé about them. The ontological argument is a gem in this regard.

Philosopher Robert Hartman comments on the power of the ontological argument to wake people up from their intellectual slumber and to promote reflection:

> What is the spell [the ontological argument] casts over the reader so that occupation with [it] becomes a passionate enterprise? [Anselm's] pages do not seem to have the completeness and remoteness of a classic; rather, they seem to call on the reader personally to do something about them. They arouse in him an intellectual passion—either for or against them—which makes him feel that the core of his own thinking is being touched. On the one hand, they seem so concise that nothing can be added, on the other, so loose that everything still has to be done. But what? The reader feels puzzled, teased, imposed upon. He feels called to take a personal part in a Herculean intellectual struggle.[32]

The ontological argument is an excellent example of Anselm's motto, "faith seeking understanding," put to service. Anselm firmly believed that whatever is excellent and true—whether secular or sacred—is the property of Christians. Indeed, in this sense, nothing that is actually true is truly secular, but sacred. We therefore have nothing to fear but much to gain by using our God-given intellects to reason on matters of truth. The facts of reality are on the side of Christians and should be used in service to the kingdom.

We can, however, make two equal and opposite mistakes with Anselm's motto. The first is to turn it into rationalism wherein faith is replaced by reason. This we cannot do, for "faith is the substance of things hoped for, the evidence of things not seen" (Hebrews 11:1, NKJV). Our faith is not a process of reasoning but of permitting reason to operate within the faith context. Philosopher Thomas Williams comments that "if one takes 'faith' to mean roughly 'belief on the basis of testimony' and 'understanding' to mean 'belief on the basis of philosophical insight,' one is likely to regard faith as an epistemically substandard position; any self-respecting philosopher would surely want to leave faith behind as quickly as possible."[33] Anselm is not suggesting that reason displace faith. Faith is love for God, which reason alone cannot engender. A purely cerebral faith is not a faith at all. St. James writes that, "Even the demons believe that [God exists]—and shudder" (James 2:19). Intellectual belief in God is enjoined by demons whose problem is not *knowledge* of God but *love* for Him. For Anselm, love of God is the gift of faith, and reason must operate within it.

The second mistake we can make with Anselm's argument is to reduce faith to fideism, the view that reason plays no part in faith and that we should seek only *heart* knowledge, not *head* knowledge. If this were what Anselm advocated in the ontological argument, then it is robbed of apologetic value and becomes a meditative exercise for believers only. Anselm would argue against this position since in his *Monologium* he pointed out that the argument was meant to *convince* people of the truth of God. Thus we conclude that the ontological argument is meant to be both apologetic and meditative.

Anselm expressed this desire in his prayer cited earlier, when he said,

> I pray, O God, to know thee [and] love thee, that I may rejoice
> in thee. And if I cannot attain to full joy in this life may I at
> least advance from day to day, until that joy shall [become]
> full. . . . Let the love of thee increase, and there let it be full,
> that here my joy may be great in hope, and there full in truth
> . . . that my joy may be full.

Anselm's character and work as a great apologist of the Christian faith set an example for those who seek to defend and articulate the truths of God with love and respect as he so ably did.

Thomas Aquinas
The Apologetical Ox

Truth is defined by the conformity of intellect and thing; and hence to know this conformity is to know truth.
— Summa Theologica, *1.16*

Events in the Life of Thomas Aquinas

1225	Born in Rocca Secca, Italy.
c. 1240	Entered the Dominican Order as a friar.
c. 1240–1243	Confined for two years in his family's fortress.
1245	Went to Cologne, Germany, to study under Albertus Magnus.
1252	Went to Paris to serve as the vice principal of a Dominican study center.
1257	Received his doctor of theology degree from the University of Paris.
1264	Finished *Summa Contra Gentiles*.
1273	Finished *Summa Theologica*.

*T*homas Aquinas was the greatest father of scholasticism and the modern classical approach to Christian apologetics. His impact on the Church, indeed on all Western civilization, was mammoth. His philosophy is so all-encompassing, it can be applied to practically every aspect of life. As testimony to his prodigious stature, he is the only Western philosopher to be referred to simply by his first name, Thomas, and his philosophical system is known simply as *Thomism*.

The Early Years

Thomas was born in Rocca Secca, Italy (near Naples), in 1225, of aristocratic parents. His father, Landulph, was the count of Aquino; his mother, Theodora, was the countess of Teano. When Thomas was five years old, he began his education with the Benedictine monks of Monte Cassino. His diligence in study was noticed from the beginning along with his native inquisitiveness. One of his teachers was impressed with young Thomas when he asked such questions as, "What *is* God?"[1] After some time, Thomas repeated his lessons with more depth and acuity than his masters.[2] Early on, he decided to become a religious scholar and lived a morally pure life.

In the early 1240s, he entered the Dominican order as a friar. Those who knew him wondered why such a bright mind (with awesome earning potential) would adopt the life of a friar bound to poverty. His family members were incensed by his commitment to the Church instead of the familial concerns of estate and civil power. His mother had mixed feelings. She traveled to Naples to see Thomas, but when his superiors heard of her impending visit, they sent him to Rome, fearing she would whisk him away. Countess Theodora did not respond well to this subterfuge and ordered her two other sons, both soldiers under the emperor Frederick II, to abduct him and bring him back home. G.K. Chesterton, in his renowned biography of Thomas, tells how "his family flew at him like wild beasts; his brothers pursued him along the public roads, half-rent his friar's frock from his back and finally locked him up in a tower like a lunatic."[3] For two years, Thomas' family held him captive in the fortress of San Giovanni at Rocca Secca where they strove to purge him of his ecclesial aspirations.

On one occasion, his brothers even tried to attack his virtue and spoil his pursuits by setting him up with temptation. Chesterton tells the story best:

His brothers introduced into his room some specially gorgeous and painted courtesan, with the idea of surprising him by a sudden temptation, or at least involving him in a scandal. His anger was justified, even by less strict moral standards than his own; for the meanness was even worse than the foulness of the expedient. Even on the lowest grounds, he knew his brothers knew, and they knew that he knew, that it was an insult to him as a gentleman to suppose that he would break his pledge upon so base a provocation; and he had behind him a far more terrible sensibility; all that huge ambition of humility which was to him the voice of God out of heaven. In this one flash alone we see that huge unwieldy figure in an attitude of activity, or even animation; and he was very animated indeed. He sprang from his seat and snatched a brand out of the fire, and stood brandishing it like a flaming sword. The woman not unnaturally shrieked and fled, which was all that he wanted; but it is quaint to think of what she must have thought of that madman of monstrous stature juggling with flames and apparently threatening to burn down the house. All he did, however, was to stride after her to the door and bang and bar it behind her; and then, with a sort of impulse of violent ritual, he rammed the burning brand into the door, blackening and blistering it with one big black sign of the cross. Then he returned, and dropped it again into the fire; and sat down on that seat of sedentary scholarship, that chair of philosophy, that secret throne of contemplation, from which he never rose again.[4]

Thomas used his time in detention well by studying, meditating and praying. After a while, his mother permitted his fellow Dominicans to provide him with new friar's habits and numerous books, including the Bible, Aristotle's *Metaphysics* and the *Sentences* of Peter Lombard.[5] Why Thomas was eventually permitted his release is not clear, but, after two years, he was lowered in a basket into the arms of his Dominican brethren.

In his newly gained freedom, Thomas immediately pronounced his vows, and his superiors sent him to Rome to be interviewed by the Roman bishop, Innocent IV. The bishop examined him closely concerning his motives in joining the Dominicans and when he found them to be pure, dismissed him with a blessing and an order forbidding any further interference with his vocation.[6] Around 1245 he went to Cologne, Germany, to study under the illustrious Albertus Magnus, the most renowned professor of the order. Once there his humility and silence were mistaken for signs of dimwittedness. His fellow students even named him the "Dumb Ox." Chesterton tells about Thomas' school days and his reputation as a dunce:

> It seems probable that it was Albertus Magnus himself, the lecturer and learned teacher of all these youths, who first suspected something of the kind. He gave Thomas small jobs to do, of annotation or exposition; he persuaded him to banish his bashfulness so as to take part in at least one debate. He was a very shrewd old man and had studied the habits of other animals besides the salamander and the unicorn. He had studied many specimens of the most monstrous of all monstrosities; that is called Man. He knew the signs and marks of the sort of man, who is in an innocent way something of a monster among men. He was too good a schoolmaster not to know that the dunce is not always a dunce. He learned with amusement that this dunce had been nicknamed the Dumb Ox by his school-fellows. All that is natural enough; but it does not take away the savour of something rather strange and symbolic, about the extraordinary emphasis with which he spoke at last. For Aquinas was still generally known only as one obscure and obstinately unresponsive pupil, among many more brilliant and promising pupils, when the great Albert broke silence with his famous cry and prophecy: "You call him a Dumb Ox: I tell you this Dumb Ox shall bellow so loud that his bellowings will fill the world."[7]

Thomas is also reputed to have been somewhat gullible. One story tells of his schoolmates yelling to him from across the room that he should hurry to the window saying, "Thomas! Look! There's a cow flying through the air!" The giant ogre lumbered over to the window and gazed outside as his classmates burst into laughter. Thomas supposedly turned to them and said, "I would rather believe that a cow flies than that my brothers would deceive me." The room fell as silent as a winter frost.

Around 1252 Thomas was sent to Paris to serve as the vice principal of a Dominican study center. Finally having a chance to teach and share his ideas, Thomas began to make a name for himself. The "Dumb Ox" wasn't so dumb after all. He produced a commentary of Lombard's *Sentences* that amazed his colleagues and provided the foundation for much of his philosophical thought that later emerged in *Summa Theologica*.

In 1257, Thomas received his doctor of theology degree from the University of Paris. From this time forward, his life may be summed up in five words: praying, preaching, teaching, writing and journeying.[8] One biographer describes this period in Thomas' life, saying,

> Men were more anxious to hear him than they had been to hear Albert, whom St. Thomas surpassed in accuracy, lucidity, brevity, and power of exposition, if not in universality of knowledge. Paris claimed him as her own; the [bishops] wished to have him near them; the studia of the order were eager to enjoy the benefit of his teaching; hence we find him successively at Anagni, Rome, Bologna, Orvieto, Viterbo, Perugia, in Paris again, and finally in Naples, always teaching and writing, living on earth with one passion, an ardent zeal for the explanation and defence of Christian truth. So devoted was he to his sacred task that with tears he begged to be excused from accepting the Archbishopric of Naples, to which he was appointed by Clement IV in 1265. Had this appointment been accepted, most probably the *Summa Theologica* would not have been written.[9]

The "*Summas*"

Thomas' two great apologetical (and theological) works are his "*Summas*": the *Summa Contra Gentiles* and *Summa Theologica*. The former, though widely recognized as a masterpiece of systematic theology, had an apologetical intent. The spread of Islam was rapidly gaining momentum, and Christian missionaries were in need of a manual summarizing and defending Christian doctrine. Muslim apologists had attempted to appropriate the Greeks, especially Aristotle, to defend and disseminate their religion. Reason and logic, they contended, were on the side of Mohammed. Thomas demonstrated the veracity of the Christian faith, claiming the sword of Aristotelianism for his own defense.

Thomas wanted to show that Christianity was not irrational, that faith in Christ was not a mindless leap into blind credulity. Rather, faith is supported by Jesus' miracles, historical evidences and reason. Thomas has become the *sine qua non* expositor of the relationship between faith and reason. To be sure, Thomas has his opponents in this arena, but none of them would question that an earnest inquiry into this thorny subject must begin with the *Summas*.

Both *Summa Contra Gentiles* and *Summa Theologica* dealt at length with this subject. In them, Thomas distinguished between what can be known through natural reason alone (sometimes also called "natural theology") and what must be given to us through divine (or "special") revelation. In the former instance, certain "preambles" of the Christian faith, such as God's existence, His immutability and His goodness, can be gleaned without the aid of special revelation. In the latter case, however, certain articles of the faith, such as the incarnation, the Trinity and the gospel plan of salvation itself, can only be understood through God's revelation. Those things that can be gleaned through both natural reason and divine revelation Thomas termed as the *articulus mixtus* (mixed articles), such as the existence of God. Because of this distinction between natural and special theology, Thomas could say, "Faith does not destroy reason, but goes beyond it and perfects it."[10]

Christian philosopher Michael Sudduth, in his excellent work *The Thought of St. Thomas Aquinas*, observes several major points in Thomas' distinction between natural theology and special revelation.[11] First, Thomas' distinctions were not about what we believe but the mode in which we come to know divine truth. Thomas considered both the preambles and articles of Christian faith to fall under the genus of revealed truths. What differentiated them were the modes in which we can know them. This annihilates the assertion that some have made that Thomas' thought "separated nature and grace," suggesting that people can autonomously—through unaided reason—know divine truths. Instead, Thomas believed God revealed everything, including things in nature. Thus, nature is a subset of grace and not the reverse.[12]

Second, we can be certain of both the preambles and the articles of faith, though in the case of the former there is a certainty of comprehension of what is known, whereas the certainty of faith is a psycho-spiritual assurance. Thomas thereby distinguished two types of certitude.

Third, although we cannot prove, for example through logical devices, that the articles of faith are true, we cannot prove them false, either; therefore, any argument that leads to such a conclusion must be defective. So we can demonstrate the invalidity or unsoundness of objections to the articles, but we cannot prove them true. We are open to provide evidences and probable arguments for the articles of faith (e.g., miracles), but these do not carry the force of demonstration.

Fourth, doctrine and theology are a science. Although we cannot prove that the articles of faith are true, we can use them to prove that other things are true, like a scientist begins with first principles and then deduces from them further truths. Thus, theology uses a scientific methodology. Truths are built on premises, one truth leading to the next and so on. The availability of the *scientia Dei*, the knowledge of God, was such a starting point for Thomas and one that he showed can bear much fruit.

Finally, the preambles of faith are the logical conclusions of demonstrative arguments premised on self-evident truths, such as the reality of one's existence. The denial of these are self-refuting and therefore reliable starting points; however, the demonstrations gleaned from them differ from those considered above. They do not spring from premises that presume the very essence of God. This is unknowable to humans—*finitum non capax infinitum*, the finite cannot contain the infinite. A syllogistic argument that proceeds from the cause, essence or being of a thing begins by premising the nature of a thing itself and then arriving at its effects. Another sort of demonstration, however, begins with effects and reasons back to their causes. This is an Aristotelian distinction (set forth in his *Posterior Analytics*). The former method is a *demonstratio propter quid*, a "demonstration of the reasoned fact." The latter is a *demonstratio quia*, a "demonstration of the fact" itself. For Aquinas, rational arguments for the existence of God were always cases of *demonstratio quia*. For example, if we wanted to prove that the planets are in closer proximity to the earth than the stars, we might argue as follows:

P1. The planets do not twinkle (effect).
P2. Twinkling is indicative of greater distance, the optical stasis of proximity (reason).
C1. Therefore, the planets are in closer proximity to the earth (cause).

Similarly, Thomas argued that human reason can show, *demonstratio quia*, "from effects," that a first cause must exist—a necessary being from which contingent beings have their beginning and sustenance. This understanding can be useful when explaining to skeptics and unbelievers the trajectory we follow in arguing for God's existence.

In *Summa Contra Gentiles*, Thomas set forth succinct theses about faith and reason, which Sudduth sums up nicely:

1. There can be no genuine conflict between the deliverance of faith and the deliverance of reason.
2. Apparent conflicts are in principle resolvable by us.
3. Philosophical or scientific objections to the faith can and should be answered on their own terms. This is an important task for Christian intellectuals.
4. Reason, while not so corrupted by sin that it yields falsehoods as certitudes, nonetheless needs the guidance of faith to do its best.
5. Philosophical reason is an important tool in spreading and maintaining the faith.[13]

Christian apologist Norman Geisler explains Thomas' stance on faith and reason by drawing attention to his Augustinian influence and motivation to do apologetical work:

> Following Augustine, Aquinas believes faith is based on God's revelation in Scripture. Support for faith, however, is found in miracles and probable arguments. Although God's existence is provable by reason, sin obscures our ability to know and so belief (not proof) that God exists is necessary for most persons. . . . Believers, nonetheless, should reason about and for their faith.[14]

In other words, not only the intelligentsia can become enlightened by truths through the exercise of their reasoning powers. Faith is available to all. Thomas said,

> Owing to the infirmity of our judgment and the perturbing force of imagination, there is some admixture of error in most of the investigations of human reason. This would be a reason to many for continuing to doubt even of the most accurate demonstrations, not perceiving the force of the demonstration, and seeing the diverse judgments of diverse persons who have the name of being wise men. Besides, in the midst of much demonstrated truth there is sometimes an element of error, not demonstrated but asserted on the strength of some plausible and sophistic reasoning that is taken for a demonstration. And therefore it was necessary for the real truth concerning divine things to be presented to men with

fixed certainty by way of faith. Wholesome therefore is the
arrangement of divine clemency, whereby things even that
reason can investigate are commanded to be held on faith, so
that all might easily be partakers of the knowledge of God,
and that without doubt and error.[15]

Yet this was more than just an added insight into the dilemma of the relationship between faith and reason. Thomas' faith-reason model also provided
a valuable methodology for theological investigation. In Thomas' axiom, faith
does not destroy reason but goes beyond it and perfects it. Reason can take us
far but only so far. For those things that remain in God's secret counsel, we
should cast ourselves on the altar of faith, believing in God's sovereignty to
work out His triumphal plan throughout history. Thus, when we encounter
philosophical and theological difficulties, such as God's sovereignty and human freedom or providence and evil, we can go as far as reason can take us,
but we must recognize the limitedness of finite human reason in exhausting
the solutions. On this side of the ontological boundary between God and humankind, the unanswered conundrums are best left to the secret wisdom of
God emanating from His perfect will.

Far from being "too Aristotelian" when dealing with such matters, this
humble approach is manifest in nearly all of Thomas' theological formula-
tions. For example, in the problem of God's providence and the existence of
evil in his *De Veritate* (or *On Truth*), Thomas deals with the philosophical and
logical objections critics have of reconciling providential control with pain,
suffering and evil. He first explained that not only are there no good reasons
to reject God's guidance in the world, but the *best* way to understand this is to
know something of the divine mind. Alternate theories against providence
are logically flawed, and Christianity is the best answer, even though certain
questions remain. In other words, Thomas takes us to the edge of reason,
shows us that the biblical answers to the problem shed the most light but
then acknowledges the inexhaustibility of the problem. Here, then, is where
faith perfects reason. Thomas thus ended the discussion of providence and
evil with this metaphor:

Even though it may seem to us that all things happen equally
to good and to the evil since we are ignorant of the reasons for
God's providence in allotting these things, there is no doubt
that in all these good and evil things happening to the good or

to the evil there is operative a well worked out plan by which God's providence directs all things. It is because we do not know His reasons that we think many things happen without order or plan. We are like a man who enters a carpenter shop and thinks that there is a useless multiplication of tools because we do not know how each one is used; but one who knows the trade will see that this number of tools exists for a very good reason.[16]

Thomas also contended that truth was objective and knowable. True knowledge, then, had to do with one's level of cognitive conformity with reality. He said, "Truth is defined by the conformity of intellect and thing; and hence to know this conformity is to know truth."[17] In other words, knowing the truth involves understanding coupled with the object of that understanding.

In following this program of demonstrating eternal divine truths through the nexus of human reason, no other apologetic attempt is more well-known than Thomas' so-called "five ways" summarized in *Summa Theologica*. For Thomas, this was general revelation. In it, he attempted to show the logical necessity of God's existence through an observation of the physical world. Princeton theologian Ellen Charry points out that Thomas knew the tension existing between science and religion and was aware that a "natural" apologetic was needed:

Thomas Aquinas recognized the importance of scientific claims made ever since Aristotle. He wrote his monumental work, *Summa Theologica*, to synthesize all learning, both sacred and secular, into a great unified, architectonic whole within a Christian theological framework, hoping to head off precisely the conflict between science and religion that has raged throughout modernity. Of course, St. Thomas lived centuries before modern experimental science. In his day modern science was primarily Aristotelian metaphysics. But it presented itself as an extra-Christian truth that had to be recognized, just as modern empirical science later would be.[18]

This natural apologetic is exemplified in Thomas' famous "five ways":

The existence of God can be proved in five ways.

The first and more manifest way is the argument from motion. It is certain, and evident to our senses, that in the world some things are in motion. Now whatever is in motion is put in motion by another, for nothing can be in motion except it is in potentiality to that towards which it is in motion; whereas a thing moves inasmuch as it is in act. For motion is nothing else than the reduction of something from potentiality to actuality. But nothing can be reduced from potentiality to actuality, except by something in a state of actuality. Thus that which is actually hot, as fire, makes wood, which is potentially hot, to be actually hot, and thereby moves and changes it. Now it is not possible that the same thing should be at once in actuality and potentiality in the same respect, but only in different respects. For what is actually hot cannot simultaneously be potentially hot; but it is simultaneously potentially cold. It is therefore impossible that in the same respect and in the same way a thing should be both mover and moved, i.e. that it should move itself. Therefore, whatever is in motion must be put in motion by another. If that by which it is put in motion be itself put in motion, then this also must needs be put in motion by another, and that by another again. But this cannot go on to infinity, because then there would be no first mover, and, consequently, no other mover; seeing that subsequent movers move only inasmuch as they are put in motion by the first mover; as the staff moves only because it is put in motion by the hand. Therefore it is necessary to arrive at a first mover, put in motion by no other; and this everyone understands to be God.

The second way is from the nature of the efficient cause. In the world of sense we find there is an order of efficient causes. There is no case known (neither is it, indeed, possible) in which a thing is found to be the efficient cause of itself; for so it would be prior to itself, which is impossible. Now in efficient causes it is not possible to go on to infinity, because in all efficient causes following in order, the first is the cause of the intermediate cause, and the intermediate is the cause of the ultimate cause, whether the intermediate cause be several, or only one. Now to take away the cause is to take away the effect. Therefore, if there be no first cause among efficient causes, there will be no ultimate, nor any intermediate cause. But if in efficient causes it is possible to go on to infinity, there will be no first efficient cause, neither will there be an ultimate effect, nor any intermediate efficient causes; all of which is plainly false. Therefore it is necessary to admit a first efficient cause, to which everyone gives the name of God.

The third way is taken from possibility and necessity, and runs thus. We find in nature things that are possible to be and not to be, since they are found to be generated, and to corrupt, and consequently, they are possible to be and not to be. But it is impossible for these always to exist, for that which is possible not to be at some time is not. Therefore, if everything is possible not to be, then at one time there could have been nothing in existence. Now if this were true, even now there would be nothing in existence, because that which does not exist only begins to exist by something already existing. Therefore, if at one time nothing was in existence, it would have been impossible for anything to have begun to exist; and thus even now nothing would be in existence—which is absurd. Therefore, not all beings are merely possible, but there must exist something the existence of which is necessary. But every necessary thing either has its necessity caused by another, or not. Now it is impossible to go on to infinity in necessary things which have their necessity caused by another, as has been already proved in regard to efficient causes. Therefore we cannot but postulate the existence of some being having of itself its own necessity, and not receiving it from another, but rather causing in others their necessity. This all men speak of as God.

The fourth way is taken from the gradation to be found in things. Among beings there are some more and some less good, true, noble and the like. But "more" and "less" are predicated of different things, according as they resemble in their different ways something which is the maximum, as a thing is said to be hotter according as it more nearly resembles that which is hottest; so that there is something which is truest, something best, something noblest and, consequently, something which is uttermost being; for those things that are greatest in truth are greatest in being, as it is written in [Aristotle's *Metaphysics*]. Now the maximum in any genus is the cause of all in that genus; as fire, which is the maximum heat, is the cause of all hot things. Therefore there must also be something which is to all beings the cause of their being, goodness, and every other perfection; and this we call God.

The fifth way is taken from the governance of the world. We see that things which lack intelligence, such as natural bodies, act for an end, and this is evident from their acting always, or nearly always, in the same way, so as to obtain the best result. Hence it is plain that not fortuitously, but designedly, do they achieve their end. Now whatever lacks intelligence cannot move towards an end, unless it be directed by some being endowed with knowledge and intelligence; as the arrow is shot to its mark by the archer. Therefore some intelligent being exists by whom all natural things are directed to their end; and this being we call God.[19]

It is an understatement to say that, contra Immanuel Kant, these arguments—now nearly eight hundred years later—still wield tremendous force. Indeed, many modern renditions by current Christian apologists, whether using the cosmological argument or teleological argument, draw at the rootlets of Thomas' work, only dressing it up in modern parlance and scientific evidences. In this sense, Thomas' "five ways" have remained unanswered by skeptics.

The Final Years

After reading Thomas' theological and apologetical works, it is tempting to merely broadbrush him as a dry scholar. But in addition to being the "Apologetical Ox," Thomas had a passion for God's truth and the need for His grace in our spiritually poverty-stricken lives. Thomas' thesis for his doctorate concerned the majesty of Christ, and he held this conviction throughout his career as friar, teacher, theologian and apologist. He was also a great preacher. In fact, his sermons were often so moving, so passionate, so rich and deep that his hearers were often moved to tears.

Thomas also apparently had several "charismatic" experiences. He did not seek them, but they occurred after he engaged in worship or contemplation for his written works. After completing a treatise on Holy Communion, he heard a voice saying, "Thou hast written well of me, Thomas. What reward wilt thou have?" To which Thomas replied, "None other than Thyself, Lord."[20]

On December 6, 1273, when he was still working on *Summa Theologica*, Thomas had a moving experience during the celebration of the Eucharist, which lasted for a long time. He felt God's presence so palpably that he decided he should no longer write. After declaring his intention to set aside his pen for good, a fellow clergyman urged him to continue writing. But Thomas was shaken by his experience. He said to his brother, "I can do no more. Such secrets have been revealed to me that all I have written now appears to be of little value." Thomas left *Summa Theologica* unfinished.

Thomas, the "Apologetical Ox," died on March 7, 1274. That day, his brethren entered his room to administer that Christian rite of which Thomas was always most moved, Holy Communion. During the ceremony, Thomas spoke his last words:

> If in this world there be any knowledge of this sacrament stronger than that of faith, I wish now to use it in affirming that I firmly believe and know as certain that Jesus Christ, True God and True Man, Son of God and Son of the Virgin Mary, is in this Sacrament. . . . I receive Thee, the price of my redemption, for Whose love I have watched, studied, and laboured. Thee have I preached; Thee have I taught. Never have I said anything against Thee: if anything was not well said, that is to be attributed to my ignorance. Neither do I wish to be obstinate in my opinions, but if I have written anything erroneous concerning this sacrament or other matters, I submit all to the judgment and correction of the church in whose obedience I now pass from this life.[21]

Conclusion

Classical apologetics, by which we adduce rational proofs for the truth of Christianity, reached a crescendo in the work of Thomas Aquinas. Indeed, his rational arguments for the existence of God still wield tremendous force in our day. Far from having become obsolete, they are actually experiencing an incredible revival. New theological institutes, dissertations, books and Web sites are expounding on Thomistic apologetics and theology. For example, a spokesperson for the new Center for Thomistic Studies in Houston, Texas, writes,

> At the forefront of the Church's defense of reason is, once again, St. Thomas Aquinas. Aquinas had "the courage of

truth," a courage which allows his thought to exhibit a wonderfully open quality, a quality which discovers more, not less, in the thoughts of others, while at the same time it bears as witness to the objective reality which serves as the measure of all human inquiry. Indeed, it is Aquinas's engagement with the pagan philosophy of Aristotle, as well as with the Arab, Jewish and Christian thought of his own day, which stands as a model for constructive dialogue in the pursuit of truth in our time."[22]

Modern discoveries in cosmology and the emergence of the big bang theory have disinterred the issues raised by Aquinas. We are confronted once again with the conclusion that the effect of the universe's existence must have a cause. This further means that if something exists now, then something exists necessarily. That is, something must have always existed, for nothing comes from nothing. To see how this argument might be drawn on and expanded today, we might begin by conjecturing four possible explanations for the existence of the universe. The universe is either:

1. an illusion,
2. self-created,
3. eternal or
4. created.

The first option merely reduces to self-referential nonsense, for, if the universe is merely an illusion, then who or what is having the illusion? Something must exist to experience the illusion, which takes us back to the fundamental principle of the argument that if something exists now, then something exists necessarily. That something exists is a logical starting point, and to deny this is to confirm it since the denier would have to exist in order to render the denial, which violates the law of noncontradiction.

The second option can also be eliminated on logic alone. What must something do in order to create itself? Quite simply, it must first be. In order for something to create itself, it would have to exist prior to itself, which also violates the law of noncontradiction since it would have to be and not be at the same time in the same relationship. But either something is or it is not. Something that is not cannot begin to make itself be. Something that is not can only begin to be by virtue of something else.

The third option may also be eliminated, though not on the basis of pure logic. There is nothing contradictory in the idea of an eternal universe. There are, however, three reasons why the eternal-universe option is unacceptable:

1. It simply goes against all the latest scientific discoveries regarding the origins of the universe (i.e., big bang cosmology). This is perhaps the biggest reason why Aquinas' arguments are witnessing a revival.

2. It violates the principles of thermodynamics (e.g., if the universe were eternal, it would have already reached its "heat death").

3. The idea of a quantitatively eternal universe leads to inconsistencies that would make it impossible in reality. For example, the universe would have to extend back in time infinitely. But this leads to an infinite regress, which presents serious problems. For example, how would we ever arrive at today if the universe extends infinitely into the past? To look at it another way, consider that time reaches its historical end in the present. But if this were true, it means that an "infinite" universe reaches its "end" right now. But this destroys infinity since, by definition, an infinite sequence has no beginning or end. Therefore, time must have a beginning.

Thus, we arrive at the final option: The universe was created. Now, Aquinas would probably point out that such arguments do not, in and of themselves, prove *Yahweh*, the true living God. What they do accomplish, however, is to demonstrate that recent truths found in science happen to accord with what is revealed in Scripture, namely, that "in the beginning God created . . ." (Genesis 1:1).

We have much to learn from Aquinas and the model he used to communicate the faith to the thinkers of his day. As Aquinas biographer D.J. Kennedy puts it,

> His extraordinary patience and fairness in dealing with erring philosophers, his approbation of all that was true in their writings, his gentleness in condemning what was false, his clear-sightedness in pointing out the direction to true knowledge in all its branches, his aptness and accuracy in expressing the truth—these qualities mark him as a great master not only for the thirteenth century, but for all times. . . . Were St. Thomas living to-day he would gladly adopt and use all the

facts made known by recent scientific and historical investigations, but he would carefully weigh all evidence offered in favour of the facts. Positive theology is more necessary in our days than it was in the thirteenth century.[23]

The "Dumb Ox" is truly the "Apologetical Ox" of Church history.

Blaise Pascal
The Thinking Reed

It is the conduct of God, who disposes all things kindly, to put religion into the mind by reason, and into the heart by grace.
— Pensees, *185*

Events in the Life of Blaise Pascal

1623	Born in Clermont-Ferrand, France.
1631	Moved to Paris with his family where his education began under his father, Etienne.
1639	At only sixteen years old, Pascal wrote a mathematical treatise that gained him much attention. He and his family moved to Rouen where Pascal assisted his father, a tax collector.
1646	Began following the Jansenists.
1654	Converted to Christianity.
c. 1660	Wrote the *Lettres Provinciales*.
1662	Died from a malignancy that spread to his brain.
1670	Pascal's notes were collected into the first edition of *Pensees*.

The ecclesiastical landscape of the last fifty years has been marked by subjective esotericism and experientialism. People's personal feelings, intuitions and experiences are frequently more valued over the careful, disciplined study of Holy Scripture and the classical doctrines derived from it. Some even shun studies in the humanities, philosophy and logic. One Sunday school teacher told his class, "Absolutely no Christian has any business studying secular philosophy whatsoever!"[1]

Anti-intellectualism and even antidoctrinalism are other hallmarks of the Church today. Statements like, "Don't give me doctrine; just give me Jesus!" and "Don't put God in a box" are familiar. The study of Scripture, theology and Church history are often viewed as "unspiritual."

Seemingly forgotten in many churches is Paul's charge to "watch your life and *doctrine* closely . . . because if you do, you will save both yourself and your hearers" (1 Timothy 4:16). Paul also warned that "the time will come when men will not put up with sound doctrine. Instead, to suit their own desires, they will gather around them a great number of teachers to say what their itching ears want to hear" (2 Timothy 4:3).

Christians are charged with the task of knowing what they believe and defending sound, Christian doctrine. More importantly, Paul said we must "encourage others by sound doctrine and refute those who oppose it" (Titus 1:9). These skills are the ones most sorely lacking in the postmodern Church.

It should be no surprise, then, that doubters and skeptics these days often find little respite within church walls. Whatever critical and pressing questions they have about Jesus, life and faith are often met with anti-intellectualism. Some of them say that Christianity necessarily means "to sacrifice the intellect on the altar of faith" or "to park the brain in the narthex of the church."

This is not to say that faith, experience, feelings and intuitions aren't important. Indeed, faith is central to the gospel message next to grace. But Jesus requires that we lay at His feet all our human faculties when He commands us to "love the Lord your God with all your heart and with all your soul and with all your strength and with all your *mind*" (Luke 10:27). As we strive to develop our hearts and souls and live in submission to Christ, so too must we strengthen our minds and "always be prepared to give an answer to everyone who asks you to give the reason for the hope that you have" (1 Peter 3:15).

One of the Church's great apologists was seventeeth-century mathematician, scientist and philosopher Blaise Pascal. Whereas many today see apologetics and evangelism as mutually exclusive endeavors, Pascal saw the two as analogous to a rider and his horse. As one contemporary theologian comments, "Pascal wasn't interested in defending Christianity as a system of belief; his interest was *evangelistic*. He wanted to persuade people to believe in Jesus."[2] Thus, for Pascal, Christian apologetics served as an invaluable tool for carrying out the task of evangelism. Indeed, it is evangelism.[3]

Yet the task of apologetics does not simply end with evangelism. Rather, for Pascal, it also carried over into discipleship of new converts. He felt the Church must be an asylum for both the spiritually and intellectually hungry before, during and after conversion.

A Unique Upbringing

Pascal was born in Clermont-Ferrand, France, on June 19, 1623. His father, Etienne Pascal, was a well-to-do man, a judge at the Court of Aids and a skilled mathematician. His mother, Antoinette Bégon, died when Pascal was only three years old. In 1631, Etienne took young Pascal and his three siblings to live in Paris. There, with a distrust of the school system, Etienne homeschooled his children. Under his father's tutelage, Pascal learned grammar, Latin, Greek, Spanish and other humanities.

Interestingly, Etienne decided to defer on teaching his own first love, mathematics, until his son was older for fear that the study would monopolize all of young Pascal's intellectual interests. He even hid geometry books from him. Yet despite Etienne's efforts, at age twelve Blaise had figured out many principles of Euclidian geometry on his own.[4] He even produced a brilliant essay on the communication of sounds based on mathematical principles. Pascal's incredible precocity was obvious. Etienne finally relented and bought young Blaise a copy of Euclid's *Elements*, which he quickly devoured.[5]

Over the next several years, Etienne and Blaise regularly attended mathematics lectures and were regular guests at other intellectual gatherings in Paris.[6] When Pascal was sixteen, he wrote a treatise on conic sections, which garnered the attention of the academic elite.

In 1639 Pascal accompanied his father to Rouen, where Etienne had been appointed as a tax collector for the upper region of Normandy. Pascal assisted his father in his tax calculations by inventing the first mechanical calculator. In fact, Pascal's contributions to the development of computing machines is so important that a major contemporary computer programming language is named after him.[7] During this time, Pascal continued his research and studies and published more works on mathematical subjects, including the triangle, probabilities and the cycloid. (A cycloid is a geometrical curiosity in which a curve generated by a point on the edge of a circle "rolls" without slipping on a straight line.)

In 1646, though not yet fully converted to the Christian faith, Pascal began to follow the teachings of the Jansenists, a Catholic subgroup led by Cornelius Jansen. It fell into disfavor with the Roman Church hierarchy due to its emphasis on predestination and its opposition to the moral lapses of the Jesuits. Pascal was passionate enough about Jansenism that he convinced his sister Jacqueline and possibly other family members to join him.

The following year, Pascal became seriously ill and returned with Jacqueline to Paris to recover. Poor health was a constant obstacle to Pascal, and he lived most of his adult life in pain. Even from his youth, he suffered from severe migraines. On his physician's advice, Pascal decided to relax while under the care of his sister.

Pascal's Conversion of Fire

After Pascal's father died in 1651, Jacqueline entered a convent, leaving the ailing Blaise alone. Sadly, Pascal forgot his work and sought to placate himself with the pleasures of city life as a successful academician and bachelor. Though not entirely repudiating it, he turned from the dictates of Jansenism.[8] Yet as we know from his later writings, he became dissatisfied inwardly. Regarding this period in his life, one Pascal biographer writes,

> [He] relaxed his labours and mingled in society, with such friends as the Duc de Roannez, the Chevalier Mere, the poet Desbarreaux, and the actor Milton. This was what has been called "the worldly period of his life," during which he must have written the "[Discourse on the Passion of Love]," inspired, it is said, by Mlle de Roannez. But the world soon became distasteful to him, and he felt more and more impelled to abandon it.[9]

Through the despondency and sense of meaninglessness that Pascal experienced in these years, he learned one of the most painful but important lessons in life. As Christian philosopher Ravi Zacharias rightly observes,

> It is purpose that is prior and pleasure that must be in keep-
> ing. And let us be sure that if the purpose is wrong, then plea-
> sure gets wrongheaded too. That is why, we must remember,
> *meaninglessness does not come from being weary of pain; meaning-*
> *lessness comes from being weary of pleasure* [emphasis added].[10]

Pascal's seeking after pleasure did not bring him the satisfaction he hoped
for. Instead, it had precisely the opposite effect. The more pleasure he im-
bibed in, the more empty he felt inside. Each drink, each woman, each night
on the town just aggravated the widening gulf of despair he felt in his soul.
Pascal later echoed Augustine, saying that "a god-shaped vacuum" is in the
heart of every person. Only God is big enough to fill the yearning of the human soul. As Augustine also said, "You have created us for yourself, O God.
Our hearts are restless until they find their rest in Thee."[11]

Adding further poignancy to Pascal's dire circumstances and inner troubles, he narrowly escaped death in 1654 when the horses pulling his carriage
took off in an uncontrollable mad dash. Both horses were killed, but Pascal
emerged from the wreckage unscathed. The accident frightened him and
caused him to evaluate his life and lifestyle.

A few months later, on the night of November 23, 1654, Pascal had a remarkable conversion experience in which an awesome presence of God envel-
oped him. Pascal wrote about this night and kept the writing sewn in a pocket
of the coat he nearly always wore. The writing, often referred to as "Pascal's
talisman," was discovered in his coat lining following his death. The philosopher wrote,

> The year of grace 1654 . . . From about half past ten at night
> until about half past midnight, FIRE. GOD of Abraham, GOD
> of Isaac, GOD of Jacob not of the philosophers and of the
> learned. Certitude. Certitude. Feeling. Joy. Peace. GOD of Je-
> sus Christ. My God and your God. Your GOD will be my God.
> Forgetfulness of the world and of everything, except GOD. He
> is only found by the ways taught in the Gospel. Grandeur of
> the human soul. Righteous Father, the world has not known
> you, but I have known you. Joy, joy, joy, tears of joy. I have
> departed from him: They have forsaken me, the fount of liv-
> ing water. My God, will you leave me? Let me not be sepa-
> rated from him forever. This is eternal life, that they know
> you, the one true God, and the one that you sent, Jesus

> Christ. Jesus Christ. Jesus Christ. I left him; I fled him, re-
> nounced, crucified. Let me never be separated from him. He is
> only kept securely by the ways taught in the Gospel: Renunci-
> ation, total and sweet. Complete submission to Jesus Christ
> and to my director. Eternally in joy for a day's exercise on the
> earth. May I not forget your words. Amen.[12]

After this seminal experience, Pascal became somewhat of a recluse. He took up Jansenism once again, practiced it diligently and even wrote a defense of it called the *Lettres Provinciales* under the pseudonym Louis de Montalte (to avoid repercussions by the Roman Church). The writing also strongly denounced the moral laxity of the Society of Jesus and called Christians to a higher standard and a stronger focus on God's grace.

Pascal's Apologetic Emerges

In terms of Pascal's apologetic output, the years that followed were the most important. He sought to conform himself to Christ's standards, to help reform the Church and to engage in formal defenses of the Christian faith. As Pascal biographer J. Lataste said,

> Thenceforth, although exhausted by illness, Pascal gave him-
> self more and more to God. He multiplied his mortifications,
> wore a cincture of nails which he drove into his flesh at the
> slightest thought of vanity, and to be more like Jesus cruci-
> fied, he left his own house and went to die in that of his
> brother-in-law. He wrote the "Mystère de Jesus," a sublime
> memorial of his transports of faith and love, and he laboured
> to collect the materials for a great apologetic work. He died at
> the age of thirty-nine, after having received in an ecstasy of
> joy the Holy Viaticum, for which he had several times asked,
> crying out as he half rose from his couch: "May God never
> abandon me!"[13]

Pensees

Pascal authored numerous works during this period but his *Pensees* (French for "Thoughts") is the most important. As he entered the twilight of his short life, he began writing a systematic defense of the Christian faith for skeptics, doubters and freethinkers. The work was to be entitled, *An Apology for the*

Christian Religion. But, Pascal's life was cut short at the age of thirty-nine due to his ongoing illnesses, and he left the work in its infant stages. *Pensees*, then, is the posthumously given name to the embryonic stages of this work, but it was a collection of some thousand notes, maxims, aphorisms and philosophical insights.[14]

What is most incredible about *Pensees* is its uncanny relevance for the modern world and its thinkers. Indeed, Pascal is an apologist for our age. As Christian philosopher Peter Kreeft puts it,

> Pascal is three centuries ahead of his time. He addresses his apologetic to modern pagans, sophisticated skeptics, comfortable members of the new secular intelligentsia. He is the first to realize the new de-christianized, de-sacramentalized world and to address it. He belongs to us. . . . Pascal is our prophet. No one after this seventeenth-century man has so accurately described our [modern] mind.[15]

Pascal was a deeply passionate man who took his faith seriously. He also engaged in the search for meaning and purpose and asked life's hard questions. Regarding the human search for meaning, he wrote in *Pensees* that

> there are only three kinds of persons; those who serve God, having found Him; others who are occupied in seeking Him, not having found Him; while the remainder live without seeking Him and without having found Him. The first are reasonable and happy, the last are foolish and unhappy; those between are unhappy and reasonable.[16]

Coupled with his wit and insight, Pascal had great compassion for honest seekers. Yet he also grew angry toward those who ignored the important questions of life, such as finding meaning and truth. For Pascal, there was no middle ground on such important issues, which made him a man of philosophical extremes. This is seen in the first sections of *Pensees* where Pascal said,

> I can have only compassion for those who sincerely bewail their doubt, who regard it as the greatest of misfortunes, and who, sparing no effort to escape it, make of this inquiry their principal and most serious occupation. But as for those who pass their life without thinking of this ultimate end of life, and who, for this sole reason that they do not find within

themselves the lights which convince them of it, neglect to seek them elsewhere, and to examine thoroughly whether this opinion is one of those which people receive with credulous simplicity, or one of those which, although obscure in themselves, have nevertheless a solid and immovable foundation, I look upon them in a manner quite different. This carelessness in a matter which concerns themselves, their eternity, their all, moves me more to anger than pity; it astonishes and shocks me; it is to me monstrous.[17]

To remedy this condition, Pascal urged that Christians must begin "by showing that religion is not contrary to reason; that it is venerable, to inspire respect for it; then we must make it lovable, to make good men hope it is true; finally, we must prove it is true."[18] For Pascal, the only way we can carry out this task is to first understand the natural, spiritually unregenerate person better. For him, using reason and intellect first involved understanding the human heart and how it drives the reasoning process. In order to be effective apologists, we must understand the spiritual nature of the battle we are engaged in and the seriousness of the effects of sin.

Christian philosopher Rick Wade observes that Pascal honed in on two different poles in fallen humanity. People are both the noblest of all creatures and the most wretched. Noble, because they are created in the *imago Dei*. Wretched, because they are fallen and separated from God. Pascal, in his characteristically passionate manner, said,

> What kind of freak is man! What a novelty he is, how absurd he is, how chaotic and what a mass of contradictions, and yet what a prodigy! He is judge of all things, yet a feeble worm. He is repository of truth, and yet sinks into such doubt and error. He is the glory and the scum of the universe! . . . Know then, proud man, what a paradox you are to yourself. Humble yourself, weak reason; be silent, foolish nature . . . learn from your Master your true condition, of which you are ignorant. Hear God![19]

Pascal was also infuriated by people's penchant to exult in themselves and their own achievements. They have an overdeveloped confidence in the ability of human reason to solve life's riddles. Even as a brilliant scientist, he once referred to the totality of human knowledge as "a vast cul-de-sac." Thus, the manner in which scholars, judges and doctors bragged about their wisdom and strutted around town in fancy robes to show off their great achievements often moved Pascal to righteous indignation. Indeed, he wrote,

> The red robes of judges, the ermine in which they wrap themselves like furry cats, the courts in which they administer justice, the fleurs-de-lis, all such august apparel is so necessary. If the physicians had not their cassocks and their horses, if the doctors had not their square caps and their robes four times too wide, they would never have duped the world, which cannot resist so original an appearance. And if magistrates had true justice, and if physicians had the true art of healing, they would have no occasion for square caps; the majesty of these sciences would of itself be venerable enough. But having only imaginary knowledge, they must employ those silly tools that strike the imagination with which they have to deal; and thereby, in fact, they inspire respect. Soldiers alone are not disguised in this manner, because indeed their part is the most essential; they establish themselves by force, the others by show.[20]

The problem with our hearing God, according to Pascal, is that we suffer from an acute case of denial and overconfidence in our own abilities to master our own destinies. Indeed, Pascal contended that at root, "Men despise religion; they hate it and fear it is true."[21] Thus, humans find diversions to avoid thinking about the deeper things of life. We let work, school, drinking, partying, sports and even religion keep us from thinking about death and eternity. But, as one Reformed preacher puts it, "Denial of reality does not change reality, it only temporarily postpones the inevitable."[22]

This kind of blasé attitude incensed Pascal. To wander through life, adopting a "devil-may-care" posture, with barely a thought devoted to ultimate things, was to him the greatest of follies and simply "monstrous." This is against our natures, which were designed to meditate on the things of God. Unless we do so, we will be in agony until we find our rest in Him:

> Nothing is so important to man as his own state, nothing is so formidable to him as eternity; and thus it is not natural that there should be men indifferent to the loss of their existence, and to the perils of everlasting suffering. They are quite different with regard to all other things. They are afraid of mere trifles; they foresee them; they feel them. And this same man who

spends so many days and nights in rage and despair for the loss
of office, or for some imaginary insult to his honour, is the very
one who knows without anxiety and without emotion that he
will lose all by death. It is a monstrous thing to see in the same
heart and at the same time this sensibility to trifles and this
strange insensibility to the greatest objects. It is an incompre-
hensible enchantment, and a supernatural slumber, which in-
dicates as its cause an all-powerful force. . . . On this point,
therefore, we condemn those who live without thought of the
ultimate end of life, who let themselves be guided by their own
inclinations and their own pleasures without reflection and
without concern, and, as if they could annihilate eternity by
turning away their thought from it, think only of making themselves happy for the moment.[23]

As Wade observes, "Pascal is appalled that people think this way, and he
wants to shake people out of their stupor and make them think about eternity."[24] It is this very fury toward those who willingly remain in such a stupor
that impelled Pascal to devise what is now commonly referred to as "Pascal's
Wager." This famous and powerful argument is often misunderstood as suggesting that Pascal advocated a cosmic dice toss in which we "bet" on God's
existence and go with whichever result suits our fancy. Nothing could be further from the truth. Pascal recoiled in horror at those who went languidly
through life, paying little attention to the grave importance of ultimate
things. His wager was meant to illustrate the supreme folly of this behavior.
People who do not explore the truth play a dangerous game with eternal consequences. Thus, when one contemplates the existence of God,

you must wager. It is not optional. You are embarked. Which
will you choose then? Let us see. Since you must choose, let
us see which interests you least. You have two things to lose,
the true and the good; and two things to stake, your reason
and your will, your knowledge and your happiness; and your
nature has two things to shun, error and misery. Your reason
is no more shocked in choosing one rather than the other,
since you must of necessity choose. This is one point settled.
But your happiness? Let us weigh the gain and the loss in
wagering that God is. Let us estimate these two chances. If
you gain, you gain all; if you lose, you lose nothing. Wager,
then, without hesitation that He is.[25]

Lataste sums up Pascal's argument neatly:

> God exists or He does not exist, and we must of necessity lay
> odds for or against Him:
>> If I wager for and God is—Infinite gain;
>> If I wager for and God is not—No loss.
>> If I wager against and God is—Infinite loss;
>> If I wager against and God is not—Neither loss nor gain.
>> In the second case there is an hypothesis wherein I am ex-
> posed to the loss of everything. Wisdom, therefore, counsels
> me to make the wager which insures my winning all or, at
> worst losing nothing.[26]

The point of Pascal's wager was to illustrate the madness of not thinking about God and humanity's ultimate end. Pascal made this point over and over in *Pensees*, as shown in this passage shortly preceding the wager:

> The immortality of the soul is a matter which is of so great
> consequence to us and which touches us so profoundly that
> we must have lost all feeling to be indifferent as to knowing
> what it is. All our actions and thoughts must take such differ-
> ent courses, according as there are or are not eternal joys to
> hope for, that it is impossible to take one step with sense and
> judgment unless we regulate our course by our view of this
> point which ought to be our ultimate end.[27]

Pascal's goal was to bring others to this search. Thus, humanity's condition was his starting point for moving people toward a genuine knowledge of God.[28] Their intellectual faculties were created to behold the divine:

> Man is but a reed, the most feeble thing in nature, but he is a
> thinking reed. The entire universe need not arm itself to
> crush him. A vapor, a drop of water suffices to kill him. But, if
> the universe were to crush him, man would still be more no-
> ble than that which killed him, because he knows that he dies
> and the advantage which the universe has over him, the uni-
> verse knows nothing of this. All our dignity then, consists in
> thought. By it we must elevate ourselves, and not by space
> and time which we cannot fill. Let us endeavor then, to think
> well; this is the principle of morality.[29]

We must use our minds for this higher purpose, for whether it be the intellect, the body or spirit, "God has created all for Himself,"[30] and we are to use

these gifts to glorify Him. Our hearts must desire to glorify God and seek fulfillment only in Him by making Him the center of our attention. God is the only Being who has the right to be "selfish," for He deserves to have all eyes focused on Him. If I demand that humans glorify me, I sin because I do not merit such adulation. I am not eternal, holy, just and righteous. In a sense, God is selfish, and it is altogether holy and beautiful that He be so.

Pascal knew this was revolting to fallen people because of the state of their hearts. His apologetical approach thus stressed the importance of the heart. A heart's disposition drives the trajectory of reason, and Pascal wrote that "the heart has its reasons which reason does not know."[31] Because of his focus on the heart and the necessity of spiritual regeneration, Pascal has often been accused of fideism. Fideism denies "the power of unaided human reason to reach certitude, affirms that the fundamental act of human knowledge consists in an act of faith, and the supreme criterion of certitude is authority."[32] This is a false charge to apply to Pascal. As Wade observes, Pascal "did not deny the true powers of reason; he was, after all, a scientist and mathematician."[33] He did, however, point out the limitations of reason. "Reason's last step," says Pascal, "is the recognition that there are an infinite number of things beyond it." Wade explains that for Pascal, "Our knowledge is somewhere between certainty and complete ignorance. The bottom line is that we need to know when to affirm something as true, when to doubt, and when to submit to authority."[34]

The philosopher Alvin Plantinga has called faith in God, or theism, a "properly basic belief."[35] In other words, it is abnormal not to believe in God. Pascal, no doubt, would have concurred with this thinking and would have pointed to the noetic effects of sin issuing from the heart as the locus of this abnormality. Pascal's goal, then, was to correct bad thinking due to the corruption of the heart in the hope that such correction would stimulate heart change. Addressing a group of young scholars in 1912, Christian apologist and Pascal enthusiast J. Gresham Machen, of the "Old Princeton School," showed how these two seemingly incongruous concepts cohere in the task of apologetics and evangelism:

> It would be a great mistake to suppose that all men are equally well-prepared to receive the gospel. It is true that the decisive thing is the regenerative power in connection with certain prior conditions for the reception of the Gospel. . . . I

> do not mean that the removal of intellectual objections will
> make a man a Christian. No conversion was ever wrought by
> argument. A change of heart is also necessary . . . but because
> the intellectual labor is insufficient, it does not follow that it
> is unnecessary. God may, it is true, overcome all intellectual
> obstacles by an immediate exercise of His regenerative
> power. Sometimes He does. But He does so very seldom.
> Usually He exerts His power in connections with certain con-
> ditions of the human mind. Usually He does not bring into
> the kingdom, entirely without preparation, those whose
> mind and fancy are completely contaminated by ideas which
> make the acceptance of the Gospel logically impossible.[36]

Machen's point is embodied in the words of Pascal that "it is the conduct of God, who disposes all things kindly, to put religion into the mind by reason, and into the heart by grace."[37] This locus of Pascal's approach recognizes God's unilateral grace in working inner change in us. In the evangelistic and apologetical process, knowledge and grace are partners. Yet grace is at the forefront and arguments do not convert. Rather, true Christian conversion is the work of God the Holy Spirit in grace (see 2 Thessalonians 2:13; Titus 3:4-7). Pascal writes, "If you are united to God, it is by grace, not by nature."[38] Further, humans do not control God's grace; indeed, "we do not know in what grace consists, it is the object of poetry."[39]

A Short Life—A Lasting Legacy

On August 19, 1662, Pascal died at the age of thirty-nine from a malignant growth in his stomach that spread to his brain. The last entry in his notes, which would later be published as the *Pensees*, is somewhat garbled and diffi-cult to follow. It nevertheless reflects the deep recesses of a committed Chris-tian soul in the throes of a debilitating illness.

> I am alone against thirty thousand . . . let me protect the
> truth. It is all my strength. If I lose it, I am undone. I shall not
> lack accusations, and persecutions. But I possess the truth,
> and we shall see who will take it away. . . . Let God, out of His
> compassion . . . grant us all grace that truth may not be over-
> come in my hands. . . . Let us see if we seek God sincerely, by
> comparison of the things which we love.[40]

One could read the *Pensees* a thousand times and still find more gems in it. It is a rare work pregnant with powerful insights and words that stir the soul. Since his death, innumerable works have been devoted to Pascal's life and thought, testifying to his stature as a great apologist and minister to the doubter and those searching for meaning. As Lataste says,

> Poets, critics, roman-writers, theologians, philosophers have drawn their inspiration from him or made him the subject of discussion. . . . He is not only one of the princes of style, but he represents the religious soul in its most tragic and terrified aspects. Moreover, the problems which he presents are precisely those which confront us nowadays.[41]

Religion professor Edward Oakes calls Pascal "the first modern Christian."[42] T.S. Eliot perhaps best sums up the great apologist's life and achievement:

> I can think of no Christian writer . . . more to be commended than Pascal to those who doubt, but who have the mind to conceive, and the sensibility to feel, the disorder, the futility, the meaninglessness, the mystery of life and suffering, and who can only find peace through a satisfaction of the whole being.[43]

And that is the apologetical legacy of Blaise Pascal, the "Thinking Reed."

Conclusion

As we look at Pascal's work today, we find insights concerning the role of apologetics in carrying out the Great Commission to evangelize the lost. Pascal knew that Christian faith is not just an intellectual process by which the mind is convinced via rational arguments and then faith inevitably follows. He said that "the heart has it reasons which reason does not know"[44] and that God "put religion into the mind by reason, and into the heart by grace."[45] If evidences and arguments do not convert, why engage in them? From what we've seen in Pascal's approach, I believe the answer is threefold:

1. It is to remove the unbelievers' intellectual stumbling blocks that hinder their faith commitment to Christ.

Paul says in 2 Corinthians 10:5 that we are to "demolish arguments and every pretension that sets itself up against the knowledge of God, and . . . take captive every thought to make it obedient to Christ." Engaging in Christian apologetics, then, is not a biblical suggestion, it is a biblical imperative. Christians have a divine mandate to give unbelievers reasons for the hope that resides within them. Christ does not call on the world to make a mindless blind leap of faith into a dark abyss of unfounded credulity. Rather, He calls people out of the darkness and into the light of His truth. Never in Scripture does God command that people believe apart from offering them reasons to do so. Jesus Himself said, "Believe me when I say that I am in the Father and the Father is in me; or at least believe on the evidence of the miracles themselves" (John 14:11). Peter reminded unbelievers that Christ was "a man accredited by God to you by miracles, wonders and signs" (Acts 2:22). Peter and Paul both argued that Jesus Christ was the Messiah by showing how Old Testament prophecies were fulfilled in His life, ministry, death and resurrection (see Acts 3:18-26; 13:27; 26:22-23; 28:23). Christians must also be prepared to offer such reasons for belief.

The question remains, however, how apologetical arguments fit in with the Holy Spirit's work, which was primal to Pascal. There are at least two ways. The first is a consideration of the various elements of saving faith. The Protestant Reformers of the sixteenth century identified three. They are (in their Latin form):

a. The *notitia* or "knowledge." The *notitia* is the information contained in the gospel message as recorded in the Scriptures. This information may be communicated either through reading the Scriptures or by hearing it preached.

b. The *assensus* or "intellectual assent." The *assensus* refers to one's intellectual assent to what is communicated in the *notitia*. In other words, it is understanding, acknowledging and agreeing with the gospel message.

c. The *fiducia* or "trust/faith." The *fiducia* refers to placing our trust in the object of the *notitia* and *assensus*. For example, we can know intellectually that chairs can support our bodies. It is another thing to put that belief to work by sitting in the chairs, thereby demonstrating our trust in them. In the same way, the Bible makes it clear that we may know, understand and even believe in the things of God but still withhold our faith and trust in Him. Thus, knowledge and belief are nothing in themselves without submission and trust.

We address the *notitia* and *assensus* in apologetics. By stripping away the layers of intellectual objections, we leave people without intellectual excuses before God. But in the end, only the Holy Spirit can turn their hearts so they entrust their lives to Christ.

The second reason we engage in apologetics is that the Holy Spirit often uses apologetical arguments to convict people of the truth. The Holy Spirit uses apologists and evangelists to bring the world to repentance and faith. This same principle also applies discipling new Christians.

2. It is to ground believers in their faith so their witness may be fearless and bold (see Acts 19:8; Ephesians 6:19) and so they themselves are not deceived by worldly philosophies (see Colossians 2:4, 8).

As in Pascal's day, we live in an age that bombards us with ideas in diametrical opposition to the things of God. Christians attending secular colleges and universities often undergo harrowing experiences of professorial antagonism, not to mention hostility from their academic peers. Christians are also caricatured by the media, the scientific community and other public institutions as ignorant and regressive.

Apologetics helps to undergird believers in their faith, knowing that, as Thomas Aquinas put it, "Faith does not destroy reason, but goes beyond it and perfects it." Indeed, the two work in tandem with one another and strengthen each other. Augustine observed that "anything at all that is true ultimately points to God." Thus, Christians need not fear the arguments of a hostile and skeptical world. If the biblical God is real, then nothing that science or philosophy can muster demonstrably precludes His existence. Apologetics, then, strengthens faith and helps train Christians in the discernment of error and the proclamation of the truth.

For Pascal, this includes helping new believers reinterpret the world through a biblical lens. As Christian apologist Hank Hanegraff puts it, we must make them "so familiar with the essentials of the Christian faith that, when a counterfeit looms on the horizon, they will recognize [and repudiate] it immediately."[46]

3. It is to silence the attacks of the unbelieving world, which attempts to place reason and science at enmity with faith.

Pascal's often volatile approach toward nonbelievers and their attacks on the faith echoes John Calvin's admonition that one task of Christian apologetics was to "stop the mouths of the obstreperous."[47] Peter supported this contention by saying that we are to "always be prepared to give an answer to everyone who asks you to give the reason for the hope that you have. But do this with gentleness and respect, keeping a clear conscience, so that those who speak maliciously against your good behavior in Christ *may be ashamed of their slander*" (1 Peter 3:15-16). According to Peter, by giving sound reasons for our faith and living moral lives, we "shame" those who "slander" the faith. This is the silencing aspect of apologetics. It is, in effect, its "negative" task as opposed to the "positive" tasks of convincing unbelievers of the truth and supporting believers in their faith.

But we must not understress the second part of Peter's command to keep clear consciences when engaging the unbelieving world. Apologetics is not merely a call to engage in intellectual argumentation but to live lives of sound Christian character. Pascal took this charge seriously as we've seen, wearing a cincture of nails to remind him to lead a pure life. As Peter also affirmed, "Live such good lives among the pagans that, though they accuse you of doing wrong, they may see your good deeds and glorify God on the day he visits us" (1 Peter 2:12). As we "contend for the faith" (Jude 3) with evidences and reason, we must also live lives beyond moral reproach. By doing both of these, we are able to silence the false teachings and accusations of the unbelieving world to the glory of God.

Joseph Butler and William Paley

Tag Team for the Enlightenment

It is come, I know not how, to be taken for granted, by many persons, that Christianity is not so much as a subject of inquiry; but that it is . . . discovered to be fictitious. . . . It is not, however, so clear a case, that there is nothing in it. There is, I think, strong evidence of its truth.

—*Joseph Butler*, Analogy of Religion

Courtesy of Christian History Institute Archives.

Events in the Life of Joseph Butler

1692	Born in Berkshire, England, to Presbyterian parents.
1718	Received divinity degree from Oxford University and was made preacher at the Chapel of the Rolls, where he remained for eight years.
1720–1726	Wrote the *Fifteen Sermons*.
1726–1736	Wrote *The Analogy of Religion*. Served as priest at several English congregations.
1736	Became chaplain to Queen Caroline.
1737	Became bishop of Bristol.
1750	Became bishop of Durham.
1752	Died of natural causes.

Upon the whole, after all the schemes and struggles of a reluctant philosophy, the necessary resort is to a Deity. The marks of design are too strong to be gotten over. Design must have had a designer. That designer must have been a person. That person is GOD.
—*William Paley*, Natural Theology

Events in the Life of William Paley

1743   Born in Peterborough, England, to Christian parents.

1758   Entered Christ College, Cambridge.

1763   Graduated from Cambridge with a degree in mathematics.

1764   Became a fellow at Cambridge.

1767   Ordained as a priest and assigned to the rectory of Musgrave in Cumberland.

1780   Sent to the diocese of Carlisle as an archdeacon and prebendary.

1785   Became chancellor of the Carlisle diocese. Vocally opposed the slave trade.

1790   Completed *Horae Paulinae*, defending the historicity of the New Testament.

1791   Paley's wife died, leaving four sons and four daughters.

1794   Completed *A View of the Evidences of Christianity*.

1795   Received the doctor of divinity degree.

1802   Completed *Natural Theology*.

1805   Died of natural causes.

The eighteenth century was a time of enormous social and cultural change. One historian remarks that "when Europeans entered the nineteenth century, they lived in a world that barely resembled the beginning of the eighteenth."[1] During that age of the Enlightenment, the Western philosophical climate of Europe became dominated by naturalism and materialism on the heels of Isaac Newton's scientific discoveries and a multitude of philosophical systems. Rene Descartes' rationalism, Pierre Bayle's skepticism, Baruch Spinoza's pantheistic monism and John Locke's and Francis Bacon's empiricism undercut people's reliance on the Church's authority. These teachings fomented the belief in natural law and the ability of human reason to solve the universe's riddles. This was the sociocultural *coup de grace* at the tail end of the intellectual revolution that began with the Protestant Reformation three centuries earlier and gave way to the Renaissance and the rejection of religious scholasticism. Now, the weight of ecclesiastical institutionalism had been lifted and "the wedge of private judgment had been driven into authority."[2] Yet despite the divergence of philosophical opinion, this age was marked by progress and human perfectibility and intellect as the guiding features. Scientists and freethinking philosophers were becoming society's new priests.

The Rise of Deism

The circumstances couldn't have been better for the emergence of deism, "the view that represents the universe as a self-sustained mechanism from which God withdrew as soon as he created it."[3] In a philosophical sense, deism is a form of theism since it also posits the existence of a god or gods who set the universe into motion. Practically, however, it is more akin to atheism in that it allows little or no place for God's involvement in history and dismisses the possibility of miracles and revelation. It is a natural religion, what some have called a "physico-theology," which acknowledges only those truths ascertained through human reason.

The power of the Holy Spirit, however, emerged in the Age of Reason alongside the rise of deism and sparked a new school of apologetics called evidentialism. This remains today perhaps the most popular mode of doing Christian apologetics as seen in the writings of Clark Pinnock, John Hick, Gary Habermas, John Warwick Montgomery, Richard Swinburne, Josh McDowell and others. Evidentialism applies science, history and evidential research to the claims of Christianity, which it believes will be vindicated if their rules are applied without bias. Modern classical apologists such as R.C. Sproul, Norman Geisler, William Lane Craig and J.P. Moreland also make heavy use of some strengths of evidentialism.

Joseph Butler

With great intellectual and philosophical faculties, English apologist Joseph Butler is considered by many to be the "Father of Evidentialism." He employed the same tools used against the Church at the time, turned them around and used them for his defense of it. Concurrently, he also used those tools to show the inadequacy of applying naturalistic methods to explain all phenomena. Given the massive currency of John Locke's empiricism, Butler built an apologetic system using Lockian principles and theories of probability. Probability, he sought to demonstrate, points to a Creator as well as the New Testament. Reason and evidence support faith; therefore, to embrace Christianity is not an act of intellectual suicide but is reasonable.

Yet Butler was not just another ivory-tower intellectual with his guns of criticism ready to shoot down the next argument. Nor was he just another intellectual steeped in philosophical preoccupations. He also had a congenial disposition and bore a pastoral concern for people. Thus, for him, philosophy had to be practical and apologetic in order to serve the people of God. As philosopher David White, an expert on Butler, puts it:

> Butler has become an icon of a highly intellectualized, even rarefied, theology, "wafted in a cloud of metaphysics," as Horace Walpole said. Ironically, Butler refused as a matter of principle to write speculative works or to pursue curiosity. All his writings were directly related to the performance of his duties [as a clergyman] . . . all his works were devoted to pastoral philosophy.[4]

Butler's upbringing was ideal for the tasks that lay ahead of him. Born in 1692, at the start of the Enlightenment tumult, he was raised as a Presbyterian in the town of Wantage in Berkshire, England. His father was a linen draper and a devoted churchman who wanted young Joseph to become a minister. After grammar school, Butler attended a "dissenting academy" in

Gloucester where young men of every religious denomination were present and from whom no confession of faith was required. While at the academy, Butler became disillusioned with Presbyterianism and joined Anglicanism, intent on becoming a priest and theological educator. Now in his early twenties, he also studied philosophy and garnered the attention of the well-known philosopher Samuel Clarke. Butler had written to him, critiquing some ideas found in Clarke's celebrated book, *Demonstration of the Being and Attributes of God*. Rather than being offended by this unsolicited critique, Clarke was so impressed with Butler's philosophical acuity that he contacted him immediately and later included some original correspondence in a later edition of the *Demonstration* as a challenge and refinement of it.

In 1715 Butler entered Oxford University but found it lacking in substance and referred to it later in life as "frivolous" and "unintelligible."[5] People were not thinking for themselves but were rather content in parroting popular theories and uncritically adopting other people's philosophies. Nevertheless, Butler became good friends with one of the resident fellows at Oxford, Edward Talbot, the son of the bishop of Oxford. In 1718 Butler received his divinity degree, was ordained and then—and on the recommendation of Talbot and Clarke—was nominated preacher at the Chapel of Rolls, where he continued on through 1726. Rolls was the first step in Butler's apologetical career, for here he issued the first of his two most important works, the *Fifteen Sermons*.

The *Fifteen Sermons*

The *Fifteen Sermons* were reactions to the intellectual teaching that knowledge was gained only through reason. Echoing Pascal, who had proffered all human knowledge to be little more than "a vast cul-de-sac," Butler also wished to instill a healthy discontent with the reaches of human knowledge without first recognizing the need of a Creator. During his time at Rolls, Butler declared to his congregation:

> Creation is absolutely and entirely out of our depth, and beyond the extent of our utmost reach. And yet it is as certain that God made the world, as it is certain that effects must have a cause. It is indeed in general no more than effects, that the most knowing are acquainted with: for as to causes, they are as entirely in the dark as the most ignorant. What are the

laws by which matter acts upon matter, but certain effects; which some, having observed to be frequently repeated, have reduced to general rules? The real nature and essence of beings likewise is what we are altogether ignorant of. All these things are so entirely out of our reach, that we have not the least glimpse of them. And we know little more of ourselves, than we do of the world about us: how we were made, how our being is continued and preserved, what the faculties of our minds are, and upon what the power of exercising them depends. 'I am fearfully and wonderfully made: marvelous are thy works, and that my soul knoweth right well.' Our own nature, and the objects we are surrounded with, serve to raise our curiosity; but we are quite out of a condition of satisfying it. Every secret which is disclosed, every discovery which is made, every new effect which is brought to view, serves to convince us of numberless more which remain concealed, and which we had before no suspicion of. And what if we were acquainted with the whole creation, in the same way and as thoroughly as we are with any single object in it? What would all this natural knowledge amount to? It must be a low curiosity indeed which such superficial knowledge could satisfy. On the contrary, would it not serve to convince us of our ignorance still, and to raise our desire of knowing the nature of things themselves; the author, the cause and the end of them?[6]

In replying to antagonists of the faith who lamented the mysteries of nature and also the difficulties in interpreting Scripture, Origen wrote, "He who believes the Scripture to have proceeded from him who is the Author of nature, may well expect to find the same sort of difficulties in it, as are found in the constitution of nature."[7] This statement was meaningful in Butler's day, since a growing number of academicians dealt only with the difficulties and paradoxes in the study of nature but then complained that the Bible was difficult and full of paradoxes. In response Butler pointed out that we must study both nature and religion "with the expectation of finding difficulties, and with a disposition to take up and rest satisfied with any evidence whatever which is real."[8] He expanded further:

> [We] should beforehand expect things mysterious, and such as we will not be able thoroughly to comprehend, or go to the

bottom of. To expect a distinct comprehensive view of the whole subject, clear of difficulties and objections, is to forget our nature and condition; neither of which admit of such knowledge, with respect to any science whatever. And to inquire with this expectation, is not to inquire as a man, but as one of another order of creatures.[9]

Just as Newton had observed that his task as a scientist was "to study what God made," Butler propounded the call to humility and faith and the need that

in all lowliness of mind we set lightly by ourselves: that we form our temper to an implicit submission to the Divine Majesty; beget within ourselves an absolute resignation to all the methods of his providence, in his dealings with the children of men: that, in the deepest humility of our souls, we prostrate ourselves before him and join in that celestial song, "Great and marvelous are thy works, Lord God Almighty!"[10]

The Analogy of Religion

After leaving Rolls in 1726, Butler served as a parish priest at several different English churches. During this time he also began his magnum opus, *The Analogy of Religion*. In 1736 he became chaplain to Queen Caroline, the wife of King George II and the same year published the *Analogy* with the full title, *The Analogy of Religion, Natural and Revealed, to the Constitution and Course of Nature*. The work was a defense of the Christian faith against deism, though other important themes are brought up as well. Indeed, Butler appended to the main work a treatise entitled, *Of the Nature of Virtue,* which established him as one of the foremost British writers on ethics and moral philosophy.[11]

The *Analogy* appears to have been a response to the English deist Matthew Tindal's book, *Christianity as Old as the Creation* (1730). Tindal displayed his rationalistic views and reliance on unaided reason in this book, dubbed the "Bible of Deism." Tindal argued that "there is a religion of nature and reason written in the hearts of every one of us from the first creation by which mankind must judge the truth of any instituted religion whatever."[12] For Tindal, reason is the epistemologically preceding factor in all human inquiry. He thus denied that presuppositional faith assertions must be granted before reason is exercised. Human intellect is sufficient in all matters of inquiry and is the judge of all things.

Toward the beginning of the *Analogy*, Butler began by saying,

> It is come, I know not how, to be taken for granted, by many
> persons, that Christianity is not so much as a subject of in-
> quiry; but that it is, now at length, discovered to be fictitious.
> And accordingly they treat it, as if, in the present age, this
> were an agreed point among all people of discernment and
> nothing remained, but to set it up as a principal subject of
> mirth and ridicule, as it were by way of reprisals, for its hav-
> ing so long interrupted the pleasures of the world. On the
> contrary, thus much, at least, will be here found, not taken
> for granted, but proved, that any reasonable man, who will
> thoroughly consider the matter, may be as much assured, as
> he is of his own being, that it is not, however, so clear a case,
> that there is nothing in it. There is, I think, strong evidence of
> its truth.[13]

The deists concluded Christianity and the Bible were untenable because of the
difficulties involved in understanding them. Since paradoxes and mysteries
abound in Scripture, deists thought it was unintelligible and unworthy of rational acceptance. This is where Origen's analogy between nature and religion becomes important. Butler was not attempting to refute atheism but deism. He
pointed out that it was nonsensical for deists, who believed that God was the Author and Designer of nature, to dismiss divine revelation because of difficulties in
Scripture. Nature has just as many difficulties, yet deists do not deny the teleology of God in it. This is a glaring inconsistency.

> He who denies the Scripture to have been from God, upon ac-
> count of these difficulties [from revelation], may for the very
> same reason, deny the world to have been formed by him. On
> the other hand, if there be an analogy, or likeness, between
> that system of things and dispensation of Providence which
> revelation informs us of, and that system of things and dis-
> pensation of Providence which experience, together with rea-
> son, informs us of, i.e., the known course of nature; this is a
> presumption, that they have both the same author and cause;
> at least so far as to answer objections against the former be-
> ing from God, drawn from any thing which is analogical or
> similar to what is in the latter which is acknowledged to be
> from him; for an Author of nature is here supposed.[14]

As Norman Geisler observes, "Since the deists admitted the latter they should not deny the former. As James Rurak notes, 'Both natural and revealed religion will be assessed by the same standard, the constitution and course of nature. Natural religion cannot be used as a standard to judge revelation.' There is an analogy between them."[15]

Butler also devoted significant attention to the deistic disbelief in the possibility of miracles in a chapter in the *Analogy* entitled, "Of the Supposed Presumption Against a Revelation, Considered As Miraculous." He drew an analogy between revelation and nature to argue that no automatic presumption against miracles can be granted. First, human knowledge is so limited in scope that some forces and phenomena remain unknown. Second, the very creation of the world, which the deists grant, should be classified as a miracle itself, perhaps the most important of all. Thus, further miracles should present no additional difficulties. Third, historical testimonial accounts of miracles should be granted unless faced with doubts about the trustworthiness of the source. Miracles are extraordinary, not impossible. After setting forth these points, Butler said,

> Upon all this I conclude, that there certainly is no such presumption against miracles, as to render them in any wise incredible; that, on the contrary, our being able to discern reasons for them, gives a positive credibility to the history of them, in cases where those reasons hold; and that it is by no means certain; that there is any peculiar presumption at all, from analogy, even in the lowest degree, against miracles, as distinguished from other extraordinary phenomena.[16]

Butler did not offer a positive defense of the Christian faith until chapter 7 of part 2 of the *Analogy*, having by then considered the deists' objections. At this point he demonstrated the evidences in favor of Christianity and how nature supported them. Butler marshaled two kinds of evidence for the veracity of scriptural revelation. The first was miracles and prophecy. Second, he examined "the general import of all the circumstances attending revelation from the beginning."[17] Butler commentator B.F. Tefft offers this summation of Butler's evidential work in this chapter:

> The fulfillment of certain known prophecies confirms our confidence, that all of them will be eventually fulfilled. The argument from fulfilled prophecy, though requiring considerable

historical learning to comprehend it, is really conclusive. A person, by comparing the known prophecies of Scripture with the recorded events of history, corresponding to these prophecies, would be naturally inclined to take the one as foretelling the other. All these particulars require separate and critical examination; and, when carefully studied, must be confessed to have great weight in them. The truth of Christianity, like truth in ordinary matters, is to be determined by comparing all the points for and against it; and the duty of making this comparison is enjoined on every reasonable person. It is, nevertheless, easy to talk flippantly against Christianity, and difficult to sum up the vast amount of evidence in its favor. The positive evidence for Christianity is such, that, though it may seem to be lessened, it cannot be destroyed by any sort of opposition.[18]

Butler's Legacy

In 1737 Butler was made the bishop of Bristol, one of the poorest bishoprics in England. George II admired Butler, however, and in 1746 purportedly offered him the archbishopric of Canterbury, which Butler refused. Four years later, on October 16, 1750, Butler was moved to the more affluent bishopric of Durham, a place known for bishops possessing great literary and oratory prowess. Butler served in Durham until his death on June 16, 1752, his sixtieth year. Tefft offers this moving account of Butler's life and ministry:

It need not be said, that such a man, so honored in life, was lamented in death by every friend of religion in the world. The intellectual powers of Bishop Butler were of the highest order, penetrating, profound, and comprehensive. In examining his works, especially the *Analogy*, the reader will be impressed, not with the extent of his researches, or the subtlety of his metaphysics, so much as the depth, the candor, and the comprehensiveness of his reasoning. He seems to see every use, which the most ingenious opposer might make of his expressions; and he everywhere guards his language with a caution indicative of his perfect mastery of his subject. Endowed with a truly wonderful insight into the philosophy of humanity, in its broadest signification, he makes both the knowledge and the ignorance of mankind contribute equally, and with equal facility, to the progress and success of his great argument. His style is always close, correct, and expressive, though never light, easy, or beautiful. The *Analogy*, the greatest of his works, is a perfect chain of conclusive reasonings, every link of which is forged and fitted with a skill ever to be admired. His essays and sermons, though characterized by originality and strength, have received only a less amount of praise. The moral character of Bishop Butler is without a blemish. Though praised, admired, flattered, and promoted, though the associate of every great man of his times, including statesmen, nobles, princes, and even his King and Queen; never did the voice of envy, even, say one word against a moral character so pure.[19]

The following epitaph was written on a marble slab at Butler's tomb in the cathedral church of Bristol:

Beneath this marble, Butler lies entombed, Who, with a soul enflamed by love divine, His life in presence of his God consumed, Like the bright lamps before the holy shrine. His aspect pleasing, mind with learning fraught, His eloquence was like a chain of gold, that the wild passions of mankind controlled; Merit, wherever to be found, he sought. Desire of transient riches he had none; These he, with bounteous hand, did well dispense Bent to fulfil the ends of Providence; His heart still fixed on an immortal crown; His heart a mirror was, of purest kind, Where the bright image of his Maker shined; Reflecting faithful to the throne above, the irradiant glories of the Mystic Dove.[20]

Yet even with such a wonderful epitaph, "the Bishop's best monument is his immortal work, *The Analogy of Religion*, which must continue to be read, and studied, and admired to the very latest age."[21]

William Paley

Butler's passing did not, of course, mark the last chapter in the period of the great Enlightenment apologists. Indeed, his work acted as a catalyst for the next great apologist to assume his mantle and carry the apologetical baton into those tumultuous times when deism began to give way to atheism.

In July 1743, while Butler pastored as the bishop of Bristol, William Paley was born in Peterborough, England. Paley had a mother of keen intellect and faith who was sure to have him baptized and well-instructed. His father was a minor canon and teacher. Paley was an awkward and clumsy youth, which led him to the pursuit of knowledge and study, at which he excelled. In fact, his father thought young William had one of the most lucid and capable minds he had ever seen.

In 1758 Paley entered Christ College at Cambridge. Since he excelled in mathematics at his father's school, he took his degree in the same subject in 1763. Later, he became usher at an academy in Greenwich before being elected a fellow at Cambridge. At the university he became a good friend of John Law, son of Edward Law, the bishop of Carlisle, and lectured in metaphysics, morals, the Bible and Greek. He was also a student and admirer of Samuel Clark and Joseph Butler, especially of Butler's *Analogy*, and was also well-versed in Locke. In 1767, while still at Cambridge, he was ordained a priest and was assigned to the rectory of Musgrave in Cumberland. Later, in 1780, he was sent to the diocese of Carlisle in northwest England as an archdeacon and prebendary entitled to a stipend for performing special services at the collegiate church. Toward the end of 1785, he became the chancellor of the diocese and an active opponent of the rampant slave trade. During this time Paley's apologetical writings began to flourish. Since he was already known as a great writer of academic textbooks, this talent carried over into defending the historic Christian faith.

Four major works stand out for Paley: *The Principles of Moral and Political Philosophy* (1785); *Horae Paulinae* (1790), in which he set out to prove that the New Testament account of Jesus was not "a cunningly devised fable"; *A View of the Evidences of Christianity* (1794); and *Natural Theology* or *Evidences of the Existence and Attributes of the Deity* (1802). Paley is most celebrated for the last two, and both achieved great popularity during his lifetime. In fact, *A View of the Evidences of Christianity* was so astute that it became required reading at Cambridge and remained so until as late as the twentieth century. *Natural Theology*, containing Paley's most influential arguments for theism, was also widely read. So influential were these works that Charles Darwin recounted in his autobiography his days studying at Cambridge and reported that Paley's works

> gave me as much delight as did Euclid. The careful study of
> these works, without attempting to learn any part by rote,
> was the only part of the academical course which, as I then

felt and as I still believe, was of the least use to me in the education of my mind. I did not at that time trouble myself about Paley's premises; and taking these on trust, I was charmed and convinced by the long line of argumentation.[22]

Natural Theology

In *Natural Theology*, Paley contended that God's creation points to Him as a purposive Designer. Then Paley introduced the watchmaker, one of the most powerful metaphors in the history of philosophy and science.

> In crossing a heath, suppose I pitched my foot against a stone, and were asked how the stone came to be there; I might possibly answer, that, for any thing I knew to the contrary, it had lain there for ever: nor would it perhaps be very easy to show the absurdity of this answer. But suppose I had found a watch upon the ground, and it should be inquired how the watch happened to be in that place; I should hardly think of the answer which I had before given, that, for any thing I knew, the watch might have always been there. Yet why should not this answer serve for the watch as well as for the stone? why is it not as admissible in the second case, as in the first? For this reason, and for no other, viz. that, when we come to inspect the watch, we perceive (what we could not discover in the stone) that its several parts are framed and put together for a purpose, e.g., that they are so formed and adjusted as to produce motion, and that motion so regulated as to point out the hour of the day; that, if the different parts had been differently shaped from what they are, of a different size from what they are, or placed after any other manner, or in any other order, than that in which they are placed, either no motion at all would have been carried on in the machine, or none which would have answered the use that is now served by it.[23]

As Geisler observes, "Paley offered what has become the classic formulation of the teleological argument . . . based on the watch analogy: If one found a watch in an empty field, one would rightly conclude that it had a maker because of its obvious design. Likewise, when one looks at the even more complex design of the world in which we live, one cannot but conclude that there is a great Designer behind it."[24] Indeed, Paley maintained that "the inference is inevitable, that the watch must have had a maker: that there must have existed, at some time, and at some place or other, an artificer or artificers who formed it for the purpose which we find it actually to answer; who comprehended its construction, and designed its use."[25] Just as the connection between the watch's parts suggests its purposive teleology for telling time, so too "the marvelous adaptations of means to ends in organisms, whether at the level of whole organisms, or at the level of various subsystems [Paley focused especially on the mammalian eye], ensure that organisms are the product of an intelligence."[26]

For Paley, ignoring the teleological evidence and maintaining a wooden atheism was the height of folly. In the face of facts, it simply stretched credulity beyond the breaking point. He wrote:

> This is atheism: for every indication of contrivance, every manifestation of design, which existed in the watch, exists in the works of nature; with the difference, on the side of nature, of being greater and more, and that in a degree which exceeds all computation. I mean that the contrivances of nature surpass the contrivances of art, in the complexity, subtlety, and curiosity of the mechanism; and still more, if possible, do they go beyond them in number and variety; yet, in a multitude of cases, are not less evidently mechanical, not less evidently contrivances, not less evidently accommodated to their end, or suited to their office, than are the most perfect productions of human ingenuity.[27]

Further,

> Upon the whole, after all the schemes and struggles of a reluctant philosophy, the necessary resort is to a Deity. The marks of design are too strong to be gotten over. Design must have had a designer. That designer must have been a person. That person is GOD.[28]

Of course, many today find Paley's arguments passé. But according to many modern scientists, this is an uncritical rush to judgment. These scientists maintain that Paley's argument is one of the most powerful in favor of a theistic universe. Mathematician and philosopher William Dembski writes of the modern resurgence of Paleyan teleology, saying:

> Though intuitively appealing, Paley's argument had until recently fallen into disuse. This is now changing. In the last five

years design has witnessed an explosive resurgence. Scientists are beginning to realize that design can be rigorously formulated as a scientific theory.[29]

Classical apologist Norman Geisler offers this modern vindication of Paleyan thought:

> Paley's arguments for God and for Christianity still provide the backbone for much of contemporary apologetics. The only major difference is that we now have much more "meat" to put on the skeleton. With the discovery of evidence for an origin of the universe, [David] Hume's infinite time has been scientifically eliminated. With the discovery of the anthropic principle it is evident that there is only one supernatural Mind behind the universe from the moment of its inception. Microbiology, with the incredible complexity of the DNA molecule adds dimensions of specified complexity and intelligent contrivance to Paley's argument that he never could have imagined.[30]

Paley also deduced providentially benevolent aspects of God's natural creation as well. If He had taken such care in designing even the most diminutive organisms, how much more must He care for every human being whom He created in His image. Paley wrote,

> One Being has been concerned in all. Under this stupendous Being we live. Our happiness, our existence, is in his hands. All we expect must come from him. Nor ought we to feel our situation insecure. In every nature, and in every portion of nature, which we can describe, we find attention bestowed upon even the minutest parts. The hinges in the wings of an earwig, and the joints of its antennae, are as highly wrought, as if the Creator had nothing else to finish. We see no signs or diminution of care by multiplicity of objects, or of distraction of thought by variety. We have no reason to fear, therefore, our being forgotten, or overlooked, or neglected.[31]

An interesting and important fact about Paley's writing of *Natural Theology* is that he, like Pascal, completed it while suffering terrible pain. The pain was caused by a condition that would eventually claim his life. About two years before the publication of the book in 1802, Paley was stricken with nephralgia, an excruciating disorder of the kidneys, coupled with melena. This condition often made him sedentary and prevented him from performing his clerical duties. Nevertheless, fearing death, he persisted in writing his book to help stem the growing tide of atheistic naturalism. His determination to finish this great work is nothing short of incredible. Posthumously, Sir Charles Bell and Lord Brougham wrote the following as a testament to his fortitude:

> That truly eminent man was then engaged in finishing his *Natural Theology*; but the completion of that great undertaking was frequently interrupted by severe accessions of a painful disorder, under which he had long labored, and which has since proved fatal. Dr. Clarke often expressed his admiration of the fortitude with which he bore the most painful attacks; and at the readiness, and even cheerfulness, with which, on the first respite from pain, he resumed his literary labors. When it is considered that the twenty-sixth chapter of his work was written under these circumstances, what he has said of the alleviation of pain acquires additional weight. It is not a philosopher, in the full enjoyment of health, who talks lightly of an evil, which he may suppose at a distance. When Dr. Paley speaks of the power which pain has of shedding a satisfaction over intervals of ease, which few enjoyments exceed; and assures us, that a man resting from severe pain is, for the time, in possession of feelings which undisturbed health cannot impart the sentiment flowed from his own feelings. He was, himself, that man; and it is consolatory, amidst the numerous diseases to which the human frame is liable, to find how compatible they are with a certain degree of comfort, and even enjoyment. Something may, indeed, be attributed, in Dr. Paley, to a vigor of intellect, which is allotted to very few; but it cannot be doubted, that resignation in suffering is less the gift of great intellectual powers, than of well regulated religious and moral sentiments.[32]

The *Evidences*

Before concluding this discussion of Paley's life and work, one final item we must consider concerning his apologetic for theism, and Christianity, was his defense of the miraculous against the antisupernaturalism of the Scottish philosophical skeptic David Hume. Dealt with primarily in *A View of the Evidences of*

Christianity, Paley argued that the biblical miracles and historicity are essential certifications of the veracity of Christian revelation. According to Norman Geisler, Paley proceeded along historical lines

> to affirm the truth of Christianity by two propositions; namely, that "there is clear proof that the apostles and their successors underwent the greatest hardships rather than give up the Gospel and cease to obey its precepts" and that "other miracles than those of the Gospel are not satisfactorily attested." To these he appends "auxiliary" arguments drawn from the "morality of the Gospel," "originality of Christ's character," and others.

Geisler discusses his approach in this vein:

> [Paley] accepted David Hume's contention that the credibility of miracles depends on the reliability of witnesses. The witnesses for Christianity, he argued, are known to be reliable since they persisted in their report even under the risk of persecution and the threat of death. He rejected other wonders that could be reduced to false perceptions, exaggeration, or that were important to the self-interest of the one claiming them. [However], Paley rejected Hume's contention that universal experience testified against miracles. This, he held, begged the question, since miracles by definition must be an exception to universal occurrence. The real issue is whether there are reliable witnesses [which the Bible possesses].[33]

Coupling this with Paley's general apologetic for theism, we see an evidential apologetical system that remains one of the most powerful, both substantively and methodically, in the history of the great apologists.

The Final Years

The last days of Paley's life were spent in continued writing and defense of the faith. In 1792, after coming to the vicarage of Aldingham, he was bestowed with another prebend in official recognition for his prodigious apologetical writings. In 1795 he took the degree of doctor of divinity and accompanied it with a powerful sermon on the dangers attendant to the duties of clericalism. During that same year he also remarried. His first wife died in

1791, leaving four sons and four daughters. He was later made subdean of the cathedral in Lincoln by the local bishop there before Paley's death in 1805.
Bell and Brougham write of the circumstances of his death:

> Dr. Paley's constitution was gradually yielding to the encroachments of sickness. . . . In the spring of 1805, he was seized with a violent attack of his disorder, which all art and assiduity were unable to repel. None of his faculties were destroyed during his sickness, except, perhaps, his sight, which, it is believed, failed him a few days before his decease. His sufferings did not overcome his fortitude, nor disturb his composure of mind; but, during the whole scene of his last trials, he maintained the greatest serenity and self-possession. He soothed the distress of his family, with those consolations of religion which supported himself, and, on the evening of the 25th of May, tranquilly expired.[34]

Paley's remains were deposited near those of his first wife, in the cathedral of Carlisle, with this simple inscription:

Here lies interred,
The remains of William Paley, D. D.
Who died May 25, 1805
Aged 62.

One modern historian offers this reflection on Paley's life and contribution:

> The face of the world has changed so greatly since Paley's day that we are apt to do less than justice to his undoubted merits . . . his strong reasoning power, his faculty of clear arrangement and forcible statement, place him in the first rank of expositors and advocates. He masses his arguments, it has been said, with a general's eye. His style is perfectly perspicuous, and its "strong home-touch" compensates for what is lacking in elasticity and grace. Paley displays little or no spirituality of feeling; but this is a matter in which one age is apt to misjudge another, and Paley was at least practically benevolent and conscientiously attentive to his parish duties. The active part he took in advocating the abolition of the slave-trade is evidence of a wider power of sympathy. His unconquerable cheerfulness becomes itself almost religious in the last chap-

ters of the *Natural Theology*, considering that they were written during the intervals of relief from the painful complaint
which finally proved fatal to him.[35]

Paley was one of the great apologists of the late eighteenth and early nineteenth centuries with continuing influence on the defense of the historic
Christian faith. His work, together with Joseph Butler's before him, made
them a powerful apologetical "Tag Team for the Enlightenment." Their arguments put a new and reinforced face on the task of Christian apologetics.

Conclusion

Butler and Paley's arguments continue to wield tremendous force and are witnessing a revival today. Butler's theory of knowledge and revelation had fallen
on hard times during the nineteenth and early twentieth centuries. But toward
the end of the twentieth century and now into the twenty-first, a new wave of
philosophical reasoning in epistemology is throwing light back on Butler's insights.

In opposition to eighteenth-century empiricism, most contemporary episte-
mologists (philosophers of knowledge) realize—following Butler—that even in
empirical matters there is no such thing as absolute demonstration. Rather,
there is probability. This means that where there is an accumulation of various
strands of probable arguments, the evidence for a claim is multiplied exponen-
tially. This, in turn, leads to what we might call "practical certainty." In Christian
apologetics this is sometimes called the "cumulative case method." The idea here
is simple: that no *one* argument for Christianity is best. Rather, when several
strands of argumentation are woven together (such as the cosmological, teleological, moral, and historical arguments), a powerful, cumulative case is made in
favor of the Christian faith. While the unbeliever may have responses in reference to isolated arguments, credulity begins to be stretched beyond the breaking
point when multiple levels of evidence all point to the same conclusion: that
there is a Creator who undergirds the fabric of the universe, superintends it and
governs it for His purpose.

Butler's other great epistemological insight is the analogy between nature
and theology. The *Analogy* shows that special revelation is analogous to natural revelation. For Butler, this is similar to most decisions we make in every-
day life. Revealed religion is much like nature. Here we must press non-

believers to become more consistent in their objections to Christianity. If they are willing to accept both the clear and the unclear in nature, why then do they not accept the clear and unclear in revelation? For example, just as *apparent* contradictions (i.e., paradoxes) exist in the Bible, so do they exist in nature. Why then are natural science and knowledge granted leniency in this regard but not revealed religion? Many ostensible contradictions in the Bible have been resolved over the centuries just as they have in nature. They both stand the test of time and have proven themselves to be experientially valid.

Whereas the Butlerian revival has been primarily within the field of epistemology, Paley's influence has found its resurgence in both science and philosophy. This is especially true in the new intelligent-design movement headed by such thinkers as William Dembski, Michael Behe and Phillip E. Johnson. Critics have derided this movement as a mere repacking of Paley's arguments, as though Paley had long ago been discredited. Nothing could be further from the truth. Like Aquinas, modern scientific discoveries are lending credence to their arguments and bringing them back to the fore. Research in such fields as microbiology, information science and other areas are casting serious doubts on the "received version" of Darwinian theory. For example, the so-called "simple cell" of Darwin's day is now known to be more complex than the biggest man-made supercomputer. Not only this, but the fundamental building blocks of life exhibit what biochemist Behe calls "irreducible complexity." Behe defines this as

> a single system composed of several well-matched, interacting parts that contribute to the basic function, wherein the removal of any one of the parts causes the system to effectively cease functioning. An irreducibly complex system cannot be produced directly (that is, by continuously improving the initial function, which continues to work by the same mechanism) by slight, successive modifications of a precursor system. Any precursor to an irreducibly complex system that is missing a part is by definition nonfunctional. An irreducibly complex biological system, if there is such a thing, would be a powerful challenge to Darwinian evolution.[36]

Such thinking unearths Paley's logical notion that design naturally implies a Designer. Indeed, Dembski adds to this the observation that not only are the building blocks of nature complex, but they also exhibit "specified complexity."[37]

This means that patterns and signs of arrangement are in the complexity we observe in nature. It is one thing for an item to be merely complex, but it is another for that complexity to be arranged. A simple illustration would be little pieces of paper listing the numbers 1 to 10. If these pieces were strewn about the floor haphazardly and out of order, you might conclude that they just fell out of someone's pocket. But if you saw them arranged on the floor consecutively (1, 2, 3 . . .), you would immediately infer that an intelligent being purposely arranged them that way. Now, if this is a common assumption with everything in our daily lives, then why does modern biological science abandon such common sense when looking at life itself?

As we've seen, the most famous argument from design is Paley's in *Natural Theology*, where he used the analogy of a watch and its maker. Dembski applies this argument to today, saying,

> According to Paley, if we find a watch in a field, the watch's adaptation of means to ends (that is, the adaptation of its parts to telling time) ensure that it is the product of an intelligence, and not simply the output of undirected natural processes. So too, the marvelous adaptations of means to ends in organisms, whether at the level of whole organisms, or at the level of various subsystems (Paley focused especially on the mammalian eye), ensure that organisms are the product of an intelligence. . . . Though intuitively appealing, Paley's argument had until recently fallen into disuse. This is now changing. In the last five years design has witnessed an explosive resurgence. Scientists are beginning to realize that design can be rigorously formulated as a scientific theory.[38]

I see these recent events as a vindication of Butler and Paley's primary arguments. What we are witnessing in the recapitulation of them in the context of modern science and philosophy shows that all truth does indeed meet at the top and that "all truth is God's truth." Truth is a force, and, though secular theories will constantly attempt to build levies around it to hold it back, the levies ultimately break. And when they do, truth rolls in like a flood from all directions.

C.S. Lewis
10 The Literary Apologist

Christianity, if false, is of no importance, and, if true, of infinite importance. The one thing it cannot be is moderately important.
—God in the Dock

Events in the Life of C.S. Lewis

1898   Born in Belfast, Northern Ireland.

1908   Lewis' mother, Flora, died of cancer.

1914   Studied literature and philosophy under the private tutelage of W.T. Kirkpatrick.

1916   Kirkpatrick helped Lewis garner a prestigious scholarship at Oxford University.

1918   Wounded on Mount Berenchon during the Battle of Arras.

1924   Graduated with honors earning degrees in English, Greek and Latin literature, philosophy and ancient history.

1925   Became Fellow of Magdalen College, Oxford, where he served as an English and literature tutor for twenty-nine years.

(continued)

Events in the Life of C.S. Lewis (continued)

1929   Converted to Christianity.

1944   Delivered radio talks on the BBC, later to be compiled as *Mere Christianity*.

1954   Became chair of Medieval and Renaissance literature at Cambridge.

1961   Wrote *A Grief Observed* following the death of his wife, Joy, from cancer.

1963   Died on November 22, the same day on which President Kennedy was assassinated.

I came to the Christian faith as a skeptic. Indeed, before I had ever even learned of the field of apologetics, much less the word itself, I already knew the apologetical writings of C.S. Lewis. Few Christian writers have enjoyed the power and ubiquitous appeal that Lewis' books have had on the reading world. His works are loved by all manner of Christians—Protestant, Catholic or Eastern Orthodox—and are stocked in most bookstores. Yet Lewis' influence extends beyond the Christian world into the realm of the skeptic and doubter. Since Lewis' books are often the only ones that skeptics of Christianity are willing to read, I often give them to those interested in hearing a cogent defense of the faith, especially *Mere Christianity*. The impact of Lewis' writings defending the Christian faith cannot be overstated. Many seminaries now offer entire courses on his writings and apologetical methodology.

Lewis was visually imposing and intense, but his personal demeanor was congenial. His biographer and good friend, George Sayer, describes him as

> a heavily built man who looked about forty, with a fleshy oval face and a ruddy complexion. His black hair had retreated from his forehead, which made him especially imposing. I knew nothing about him, except that he was the college English tutor. I did not know that he was the best lecturer in the department, nor had I read the only book that he had published under his own name (hardly anyone had). Even after I had been taught by him for three years, it never entered my mind that he could one day become an author whose books would sell at the rate of about two million copies a year. Since he never spoke of religion while I was his pupil, or until we had become friends 15 years later, it would have seemed incredible that he would become the means of bringing many back to the Christian faith.[1]

The Making of The Literary Apologist

Clive Staples Lewis ("Jack") was born in Belfast, Northern Ireland, on November 29, 1898, to Albert James Lewis, a court attorney, and Flora Augusta Hamilton Lewis, an educator. Flora was an intellectually gifted woman with an honor's degree in mathematics from Queen's University, Belfast. Lewis described her not only as one with "cheerful and tranquil affection" but also as "a voracious reader of novels."[2] Young Jack was the second child after Warren Hamilton Lewis, or "Warnie" as they called him, who was born in 1895. As a young child, following the death of the family dog, Lewis commemorated the hound by appropriating its name, "Jacksie," and demanded that he be addressed as such.[3]

In 1905 the Lewis family moved to a new house on the outskirts of Belfast, which they named "Little Lea." A few years later Lewis' mother, Flora, was stricken with cancer and died. Hoping that her sons would keep God in their hearts, Flora left young Lewis and his brother each their own Bibles and signed them, "from Mommy, with fondest love, August 1908." During this period Lewis' grandfather and great-uncle also passed away. Lewis had desperately prayed for his mother's healing, and when this prayer was not answered, his faith was shaken.

His mother's death spurred young Jack to question life and to search for answers. For this, he turned to books. As one biographer writes,

> Lewis was reared in a peculiarly bookish home, one in which the reality he found on the pages of the books within his parents' extensive library seemed as tangible and meaningful to him as anything that transpired outside their doors. . . . [He was] more at home in the world of ideas and books of the past, than with the material, technological world of the 20th century. When the tranquility and sanctity of the Lewis home was shattered beyond repair by the death of his mother when he was ten, Lewis sought refuge in composing stories and excelling in scholastics. Soon thereafter he became precociously oriented toward the metaphysical and ultimate questions.[4]

With Albert's great learning as a lawyer and later a politician and Flora's own achievements in reading and mathematics, Little Lea was a veritable cavern of literature and thinking that Lewis availed himself of completely. He wrote,

> I am a product of long corridors, empty sunlit rooms, upstairs indoor silences, attics explored in solitude, distant noises of gurgling cisterns and pipes, and the noise of wind under the tiles. Also, of endless books. My father bought all the books he read and never got rid of any of them. There were books in the study, books in the drawing room, books in the cloakroom, books (two deep) in the great bookcase on the landing, books in a bedroom, books piled as high as my shoulder in the cistern attic, books of all kinds reflecting every transient stage of my par-

ents' interest, books readable and unreadable, books suitable for a child and books emphatically not. Nothing was forbidden me. In the seemingly endless rainy afternoons I took volume after volume from the shelves. I had always the same certainty of finding a book that was new to me as a man who walks into a field has of finding a new blade of grass.[5]

In 1908 Lewis began schooling at Wynard School in Hertfordshire, England, along with his older brother. Wynard was a harsh place, employing draconian punishment for even the slightest wrongs, such as a rap on the knuckles for merely erring on a math problem. It was hardly an environment conducive to shaping young Lewis in his search for meaning and lifelong pursuit for inner Joy with capital "J" (a subject he would eventually write extensively on). This was one factor that contributed to a pessimism and cynicism that remained with Lewis for the rest of his life. One Lewis biography sheds further light on this:

> Lewis's boyhood is largely a tale of meeting Joy in a variety of venues. Sometimes it rushed over him on the cool, colorful autumn afternoons of County Down; other times it gripped him through the creative forms of nursery tales, Celtic and Norse mythology; or Wagner's riveting Ride of the Valkyries. Lewis longed for such moments. All of life paled next to the thrall of this mystical experience. . . . [Yet] These romantic moments were offset by a surprisingly sour outlook on life. Lewis's pessimism was largely due to an inherited genetic flaw, a jointless thumb. This abnormal digit excluded Lewis from the typical boyhood pastimes like working a wrench or swinging a bat. Not that he longed for grease under his nails or dirt on his trousers, for engines and athletics were two things for which Lewis lacked both proclivity and interest. What he did long for, however, was the ability to bring his dreams to life. He wanted to build cardboard castles and animals in dashing coats of armor—three-dimensional expressions of his imagination. Yet his attempts at construction yielded nothing but frustration. Unable to build his imaginary world by hand, Lewis settled for the next best thing—constructing it with words.[6]

Later, Lewis attended Campbell College in Belfast as a boarding student, though he was only a mile or so from Little Lea. Lewis' time at Campbell was cut short, however, due to a respiratory illness that forced him to attend a live-in medical facility that specialized in lung disorders. He subsequently entered Malvern College in 1913.

In 1914 Lewis moved to Surrey in southeast England and began intensive studies in literature and philosophy under the private tutelage of W.T. Kirkpatrick, also known as "The Great Knock," apparently due to his intense Socratic abilities. In 1916 Kirkpatrick helped Lewis garner a prestigious scholarship at Oxford University. He began further studies there a short time later. This time was also cut short, however, due to the start of World War I into which Lewis was hurriedly thrown as a second lieutenant in the infantry. After training, he was sent to the front lines in the Somme Valley of France. Over the next two years, he learned the miseries of war, experiencing firsthand the violence of combat, "trench fever" (an infectious disease characterized by chills and fever) and the pain of losing his good friend Paddy Moore, who was killed on the battle lines of France. Lewis himself was wounded on Mount Berenchon during the Battle of Arras by an exploding shell, which left a metal shard in him.

Lewis returned to Oxford in 1919, where he later graduated with honors, earning degrees in English, Greek and Latin literature, philosophy and ancient history. He also published his first book, *Spirits in Bondage*, a collection of lyric poems, under the pseudonym "Clive Hamilton." Lewis then privately tutored for a time before being elected a fellow of Magdalen College at Oxford. He then worked as an instructor of English and literature for twenty-nine years until he left for Cambridge University to become a professor of medieval and Renaissance literature in 1954.

Throughout much of this time, Lewis remained an avowed atheist. He had seen his prayers for his mother go "unanswered," had suffered harsh environments in his youth in so-called Christian schools and had witnessed the horrors of war and death. He also had been schooled in the currents of "right reason" endemic to Renaissance and Enlightenment thought, complete with its skepticism of the supernatural. This combination led Lewis to categorically reject Christianity as a viable system. The world was simply too chaotic for there to be a benevolent Creator. It wasn't until 1929 that Lewis finally embraced God after a vigorous war of ideas had raged in his mind for well over a decade.

As we would expect of Lewis, the circumstances leading up to his conversion began with books. While tutoring at Magdalen College, he continued to devour book after book. Yet it wasn't until he came across the writings of

Christian author George MacDonald that his thinking about theism and Christianity began to change. One volume in particular, *Phantastes*, had a radical effect on him, posing a powerful challenge to his atheism. Lewis later reflected on MacDonald, saying,

> It must be more than thirty years ago that I bought—almost unwittingly, for I had looked at the volume on that bookstall and rejected it on a dozen previous occasions—the Everyman edition of *Phantastes*. A few hours later I knew that I had crossed a great frontier. I had already been waist-deep in Romanticism; and likely enough, at any moment, to flounder into its darker and more evil forms, slithering down the steep descent that leads from the love of strangeness to that of eccentricity and thence to that of perversity. Now *Phantastes* was romantic enough in all conscience; but there was a difference. Nothing at that time was further from my thoughts than Christianity and I therefore had no notion what this difference really was. . . . What [the book] actually did to me was to convert, even to baptize . . . my imagination. . . . I should have been shocked in my teens if anyone had told me that what I learned to love in *Phantastes* was goodness.[7]

C.S. Lewis was also greatly influenced by the writings of G.K. Chesterton, most notably *The Everlasting Man*, which raised further doubts in Lewis' mind about the tenability of atheistic materialism. These writings also helped show Lewis that faith was intelligent. He had to discover for himself that the intellect need not be sacrificed on the altar of faith in order to embrace God but that faith and reason are mutually complementing and intrinsically symbiotic. True faith embraces the intellect and utilizes it to grow deeper spiritually by learning more about reality. Coming to know reality draws one nearer to God, not trying to escape it with faulty ecclesiastical opium. Lewis later wrote that "in reading Chesterton, as in reading MacDonald, I did not know what I was letting myself in for. A young man who wishes to remain a sound atheist cannot be too careful of his reading. . . . God is, if I may say it, very unscrupulous."[8] Yet this wasn't all. Some key friendships in Lewis' life also helped push him in the direction of the Christian faith. *Christianity Today* editor Ted Olsen tells the story:

> While MacDonald and Chesterton were stirring Lewis's thoughts, close friend Owen Barfield pounced on the logic of

Lewis's atheism. Barfield had converted from atheism to theism, then finally to Christianity, and he frequently badgered
Lewis about his materialism. So did Nevill Coghill, a brilliant
fellow student and lifelong friend who, to Lewis's amazement,
was "a Christian and a thoroughgoing supernaturalist." Soon
after joining the English faculty at Oxford's Magdalen College,
Lewis met two more Christians, Hugo Dyson and J.R.R.
Tolkien. These men became close friends of Lewis. He admired
their brilliance and their logic. Soon Lewis recognized that most
of his friends, like his favorite authors—MacDonald, Chesterton, Johnson, Spenser, and Milton—held to this Christianity.[9]

Lewis' atheism was broken, at least in principle. Yet it wasn't as though
Lewis himself was jumping for joy. Quite the contrary, a cognitive dissonance
and emotional despondency crept over him. How could he have been so dead
wrong all these years, missing the most important truth of life, that "God is
God"? Lewis wrote of when he finally broke ties with his atheism:

You must picture me alone in that room in Magdalen, night
after night feeling, whenever my mind lifted even for a second from my work, the steady, unrelenting approach of Him
whom I so earnestly desired not to meet. That which I greatly
feared had at last come upon me. In the Trinity Term of 1929 I
gave in, and admitted that God was God, and knelt and
prayed: perhaps, that night, the most dejected and reluctant
convert in all of England. I did not then see what is now the
most shining and obvious thing, the Divine humility which
will accept a convert even on such terms. The prodigal son at
last walked home on his own feet. But who can duly adore
that Love which will open the high gates to a prodigal who is
brought in kicking, struggling, resentful, and darting his eyes
in every direction for a chance of escape? The words "com-
pelle intrare," compel them to come in, have been so abused
by wicked men that we shudder at them; but properly understood, they plumb the depth of Divine mercy. The hardness of
God is kinder than the softness of men, and His compulsion is
our liberation.[10]

In 1933 Lewis began meeting regularly at a local pub called "The Eagle and
Child" with a now famous inner circle of friends, including J.R.R. Tolkien,

Weville Coghill, Owen Barfield, Lewis' brother Warren, Hugo Dyson, Charles Williams, Robert Havard and various others. "The Inklings," as they called themselves, were united by a common interest in all kinds of literature, the Middle Ages, the antics, fairy tales and myths. They debated, read, discussed and reviewed each other's books and papers.

The Inklings proved to be a good forging ground for Lewis to sharpen his apologetic. Indeed, this point marked the beginning of a mammoth literary and apologetical career that garnered one of the most lasting sociocultural and philosophical impacts on the Western world. His voice remains a prophetic one. In the years following, Lewis not only wrote about the sociocultural and spiritual contours of the twentieth century, but helped shape them. Biographer Bruce Edwards describes the period from Lewis' conversion and beyond, saying,

> The rest of his saga and the particulars of his writing career might be seen as the melancholy search for the security he took for granted during the peace and grace of his childhood. By Lewis's testimony, this recovery was to be had only in the joy he discovered in an adult conversion to Christianity. Long-time friend and literary executor of the Lewis estate, Owen Barfield, has suggested that there were, in fact, three C.S. Lewises. That is to say, during his lifetime Lewis fulfilled three very different vocations—and fulfilled them successfully. There was, first, Lewis the distinguished Oxbridge literary scholar and critic; second, Lewis, the highly acclaimed author of science fiction and children's literature; and thirdly, Lewis, the popular writer and broadcaster of Christian apologetics. The amazing thing, Barfield notes, is that those who may have known of Lewis in any single role may not have known that he performed in the other two. In a varied and comprehensive writing career, Lewis carved out a sterling reputation as a scholar, a novelist, and a theologian for three very different audiences.[11]

Justice can scarcely be done in these short pages to describe the many varied works Lewis produced from 1929 on. Thus our focus must necessarily be directed chiefly to his apologetics. Before turning to this, however, I should mention at least two works that are hallmarks of Lewis' life and career. First, *The Allegory of Love* (reworked by Lewis at a more popular level nearly twenty-five years later in *The Four Loves*) received rave reviews and is recognized as one of the finest commentaries on literature ever produced. The primary thrust of the book is to explore love and romance in medieval literature. Second, Lewis' greatest commercial success was the seven-volume *Chronicles of Narnia*. "These popular children's fantasies began with the 1950 volume, *The Lion, the Witch, and the Wardrobe*, a tale centered on Aslan the lion, a Christ-figure who creates and rules the supernatural land of Narnia, and the improbable adventures of four undaunted British schoolchildren who stumble into Narnia through a clothes closet."[12]

Lewis' Apologetic

Lewis' religious and apologetical books are many. They include *The Pilgrim's Regress*, a parody of John Bunyan's *The Pilgrim's Progress*, in which Lewis surveys his exodus from atheistic materialism and skepticism to Christian faith. *The Great Divorce* (1945) takes readers on a journey through heaven and hell, introducing an array of ethereal beings that challenge the way we think about good and evil. *The Screwtape Letters* (1941) is a short reading featuring the demon "Screwtape," who corresponds with his neophyte, under-devil nephew "Wormwood," mentoring him on how best to tempt and destroy his "patient" (an earthly man) to steal him away from "The Enemy" (God) and bring him to their "Lord below" (the devil). *God in the Dock* (published posthumously in 1970) is a collection of forty-eight essays discussing various theological and ethical questions, such as evil, miracles, politics, current events, animals, science fiction and even the possibility of the existence of aliens. Lewis wrote *A Grief Observed* (1963), following the untimely death of his wife, Joy, from cancer. Lewis reflects on that experience and the problem of God and suffering, saying,

> Your bid—for God or no God, for a good God or a Cosmic Sadist, for eternal life or nonentity—will not be serious if nothing much is staked on it. And you will never discover how serious it was until the stakes are raised horribly high; until you find that you are playing not for counters or for sixpences but for every penny you have in the world. Nothing less will shake a man—or at any rate a man like me—out of his merely verbal thinking and his merely notional beliefs. He has to be knocked silly before he comes to his senses. Only torture will bring out the truth. Only under torture does he discover it himself.[13]

A Grief Observed also inspired the movie about Lewis' life, *Shadowlands*. *Mere Christianity* (1952), perhaps Lewis' most important apologetical work, is a powerful and lucid defense of the basic tenets of the historic Christian faith. It is comprised of three works that had earlier been published separately as *The Case for Christianity*, *Christian Behaviour* and *Beyond Personality*. Most of the book was delivered as a series of BBC radio broadcasts during World War II and had a tremendous impact on many people affected by the war who were stammering for answers and hope. *Miracles: A Preliminary Study* (1947) answered the onslaught of philosophical naturalism and its attending anti-supernaturalism, especially in liberal biblical studies. The work was "aimed at leaving open the possibility of the miraculous by presenting philosophical views which can be applied to observations, rather than giving evidence for any particular miracle as a proof that they are possible. His major aim was to set up a philosophical framework in which one could admit that miracles are, historically speaking, fair game."[14] Lewis wrote:

> If . . . you now turn to study the historical evidence for yourself, begin with the New Testament and not with the books about it. . . . And when you turn from the New Testament to modern scholars, remember that you go among them as a sheep among wolves. Naturalistic assumptions, beggings of the question such as that which I noted on the first page of this book, will meet you on every side—even from the pens of clergymen. . . . In using the books of such people you must be continually on guard. You must develop a nose like a bloodhound for those steps in the argument which depend not on historical and linguistic knowledge but on the concealed assumption that miracles are impossible, improbable, or improper.[15]

The Problem of Pain (1940) answered the aged "Epicurean Dilemma" (revived in Hume and Mill), which asks, "How can an all-loving, all-powerful God allow people to experience pain and suffering?" Lewis argued that God does not permit evil without an entirely good purpose in mind. Even natural evil has an important part to play in God's unfolding redemptive plan. In the end Lewis concludes on the existential level that "God whispers to us in our pleasures, speaks in our conscience, but shouts in our pain: it is His megaphone to rouse a deaf world."[16]

In *Reflections on the Psalms* (1958), Lewis reflected both on the literary form and the meaning of the psalms and offered a hint of his own apologetical curiosity and life search, saying, "Where we find difficulty, we may always expect that a discovery awaits us."[17] In *Surprised by Joy* (1955), Lewis' spiritual autobiography, he traced his journey from the simple faith of his early youth to unbridled atheism, to theism and finally to full-bodied Christianity. *The Weight of Glory* (1941, 1947, published in 1975) is a collection of nine sermons delivered during World War II to offer guidance, hope and inspiration during that time of instability and anxiety. As usual, Lewis provided a passionate, compelling and highly charitable vision of the Christian faith. A common thread was his observation that we desire heaven and eternity because that is the very end to which we were created. *The Abolition of Man* (1943) is a reflection on society and nature with an eye toward inculcating sound morality and refuting the spreading tentacles of relativism. Lewis contended that we must include moral instruction as a staple in the educational process lest we have highly educated children bereft of a moral compass and unfit to lead solid, productive, thoughtful lives.

As Lewis became more and more steeped in Christian apologetics, not everyone approved of his efforts. Even his inner circle, the Inklings, often castigated him for his apologetic zeal. Oxford University also passed him over several times for a professorship due to his apologetical books. Such controversy served only as testimony to the power of Lewis' apologetic. Arguments carrying little intellectual weight tend not to engender the sort of heated denigration that Lewis encountered. Historically, nonsense fades with a whisper but depth and acuity linger with a shout. The power and incisiveness of Lewis' apologetic made people think about Christianity and sometimes made them angry.

Lewis was not a theologian and considered himself a layman. And, although some of his theology may be questioned, he essentially placed himself in the classical lode. As apologist Norman Geisler observes, "Lewis accepted the Augustine-Anselm-Aquinas view of God as eternal, necessary, transcendent, morally perfect, and personal."[18]

Lewis was intent on knowing this God, but even more so on making Him known. In doing so he issued a powerful stream of apologetics that demonstrated the existence of God, the divinity of Christ and the fallaciousness of naturalism, antisupernaturalism and paganism.

Concerning arguments for theism, Lewis employed two of his own renditions of the cosmological and moral arguments for God, while adding a third at the end—what is commonly called "the argument from meaning." Geisler explains the first of these.

> Lewis believed in creation out of nothing. For "What God creates is not God; just as what man makes is not man" (*God in the Dock*, 138). He explained that matter is not coeternal with God: "Entropy by its very character assures us that though it may be the universal rule in the Nature we know, it cannot be universal absolutely. If a man says, 'Humpty Dumpty is falling,' you see at once that this is not a complete story. The bit you have been told implies both a later chapter in which Humpty Dumpty will have reached the ground, and an earlier chapter in which he was still seated on the wall. A Nature which is 'running down' cannot be the whole story. A clock can't run down unless it has been wound up" (*Miracles*, 157). . . . Matter is the product of a cosmic Mind. "But to admit that sort of cosmic mind is to admit a God outside Nature, a transcendent and supernatural God" (*Miracles*, 30). The universe is matter. Matter cannot produce mind; only mind can produce matter. The creation of the world was not from some pre-existing matter or stuff. It was created from nothing. God created this world freely: "The freedom of God consists in the fact that no cause other than Himself produces His acts and no external obstacle impedes them—that His own goodness is the root from which they all grow and His own omnipotence the air in which they all flower" (*Problem of Pain*, 23).[19]

The argument from cosmological causality was not the only approach, however, that Lewis employed in demonstrating the need for a Creator. Indeed, it was the necessity of moral principles finding their ground in a moral lawgiver that drove Lewis to embrace theism and later provided him with his favorite theistic apologetic. In his apologetical magnum opus, *Mere Christianity*, Lewis reflected back on his days as an atheist and identified what he came to see as an insuperable deficiency in the atheistic worldview:

> My argument against God was that the universe seemed so cruel and unjust. But how had I got this idea of just and unjust? A man does not call a line crooked unless he has some idea of a straight line. What was I comparing this universe with when I called it unjust? . . . for the argument depended on saying that the world was really unjust . . . Thus in the very

act of trying to prove that God did not exist . . . I found I was
forced to assume that one part of reality—namely my idea of
justice—was full of sense. Consequently atheism turns out to
be too simple. If the whole universe has no meaning, we
should never have found out that it has no meaning.[20]

As Geisler observes, "Lewis begins *Mere Christianity* with the premise that an
objective moral law, such as even common disagreements presuppose, entails
a Moral Law Giver."[21] There is something directing the universe, a kind of law
that urges us to do right and convicts us of wrongdoing.[22] Over and against
the "herd instinct" theory of morality—still common in our day—Lewis did
not deny that we have something like it. What he did deny was the idea that
this resembles the moral law to which we are all subject in as equal measure
as we are to brute instinct.

Human instincts drive us onward in our desires—things like love, sex or
food. Sometimes an instinctual desire to assist our fellow man wells up. The
desire to help someone, however, is very different from a sense that one *ought*
to help. This is where Lewis contends that the moral law plays a mysterious
but undeniable part. Lewis uses the analogy of hearing a cry for help from a
stranger. Two desires seem to emerge in us. One is to help out. The other is for
self-preservation, that is, to get *ourselves* out of harm's way. Lewis acknowledges both of these as herd instincts. But the strange thing is the *third* impulse that arises, which tells us that we *ought* to heed the impulse to help out
and suppress the desire to run away. This third impulse judges between the
two opposing desires and is distinct from them. It tells us that we should only
obey instincts on *some* occasions but that we should never disobey our consciences. Thus, instincts are like the keys on a piano, and the moral law that
informs the conscience is the sheet music. Different notes are right at different times.[23]

This moral law, then, cannot be explained away through an appeal to naturalistic postulates. In the theory of the "survival of the fittest," nature does
not explain why a person would heed the third impulse—especially when it
does not benefit "the organism." Postulating, then, that morality is nothing
more than a freak of Darwinian evolution does not so much explain objective
morality as it simply denies it. Morality itself is altruistic, selfless, altogether
good and uninterested in whether it benefits the preservation of the self or
species. A moral act is performed because it is the right thing to do.

Geisler summarizes Lewis' argument:

1. There must be an objective, universal moral law, or else no ethical judgments make sense. Nothing could be called evil or wrong, and there would be no reason to keep promises or treaties (*God in the Dock*, chap. 1).
2. This moral law does not originate with us. In fact, we are bound by it.
3. The source of this law is more like mind than matter, and it cannot be part of the universe any more than an architect is part of the building he designs.
4. Therefore, there exists a Moral Law Giver who is the ultimate source and standard of all right and wrong (*God in the Dock*, chap. 7).[24]

Lewis took this a step further, however, and argued that without an ultimate standard of goodness, life is fundamentally bereft of meaning. Herein is embodied his argument from meaning. We find ourselves in a "terrible fix." If the universe is not ruled by an ultimate standard of goodness, then all efforts in this life are hopeless. But, if the world *is* ruled by a standard of goodness, then every day we are making ourselves enemies of that goodness by not making Him the center of our lives. Thus, we cannot do with God, yet we cannot do without God. Lewis calls God "the only comfort," but He is also "the supreme terror." God is what we need most in life, but He is also the very thing we want most to hide from.[25]

Our ignoring God is, for Lewis, the height of folly. The only way we can extract meaning in life is by looking to the ultimate joy offered to us by our Creator. Not to do this is the worst of human blunders and is like refusing a cool glass of water offered to us in the desert.

> If we consider the unblushing promises of reward and the staggering nature of the rewards promised in the Gospels, it would seem that Our Lord finds our desires, not too strong, but too weak. We are halfhearted creatures, fooling about with drink and sex and ambition when infinite joy is offered us, like an ignorant child who wants to go on making mud pies in a slum because he cannot imagine what is meant by the offer of a holiday at the sea.[26]

Lewis' arguments are reminiscent of the writer of Ecclesiastes. We long for something greater and deeper than what we find in this life, but the things of this world elude us in our search for meaning. Lewis wrote:

> Most people, if they had really learned to look into their own hearts, would know that they do want, and want acutely, something that cannot be had in this world. There are all sorts of things in this world that offer to give it to you, but they never quite keep their promise. The longings which arise in us when we first fall in love, or first think of some foreign country, or first take up some subject that excites us, are longings which no marriage, no travel, no learning, can really satisfy. I am not now speaking of what would be ordinarily called unsuccessful marriages, or holidays, or learned careers. I am speaking of the best possible ones. There was something we grasped at, in that first moment of longing, which just fades away in the reality. I think everyone knows what I mean. The wife may be a good wife, and the hotels and the scenery may have been excellent, and chemistry may be a very interesting job: but something has evaded us.[27]

In a more technical apologetic, Lewis' argument for meaning takes on the following form:

1. Human beings have an inherent need for meaning and purpose and expend great energies in search of them.
2. This sense of a need for meaning does not make sense in a naturalistic or materialistic worldview, since meaning implies something beyond mere physicality.
3. Therefore, life must have meaning drawn from a nonphysical reality. The inverse of this argument is enunciated in Lewis' earlier finding as an atheist that if the universe has no meaning, we will never grasp the notion of meaninglessness.

Lewis' manner of delineating the only logical options in examining the deeper questions of life is an important apologetical *modus operandi*. Certain facts are identified, theories examined and then drawn out to their logical conclusions. Lewis employed this same methodology in arguing for the divinity of Christ in what has come to be known as the "Lord, Liar, Lunatic Trilemma." Jesus claimed to be the divine Son of God. If this statement was false, then Jesus was either a liar or a lunatic on the fringes of reality. Lewis unpacked these options while considering the skeptics' objection to Jesus as divine by calling Him merely a great moral teacher (as did Bertrand Russell). Lewis thought it pure folly to call Jesus a great moral teacher but deny His claim to be God. He points out that

> A man who was merely a man and said the sort of things Jesus said would not be a great moral teacher. He would either be a lunatic—on a level with the man who says he is a poached egg—or else he would be the Devil of Hell. You must make your choice. Either this man was, and is the Son of God: or else a madman or something worse. You can shut Him up for a fool, you can spit at Him and kill Him as a demon; or you can fall at His feet and call Him Lord and God. But let us not come with any patronising nonsense about His being a great human teacher. He has not left that open to us. He did not intend to.[28]

Lewis revisited this argument in his 1950 essay, "What Are We to Make of Jesus Christ?" The whole essay was an expansion of the *Mere Christianity* passage. He observed that in dealing with the person of Jesus we must reconcile two things: 1) the generally admitted depth and sanity of His moral teaching; and 2) the appalling nature of this Man's theological remarks about Himself. He then reformed the trilemma, saying:

> There is no halfway house and there is no parallel in other religions. If you had gone to Buddha and said, "Are you the son of Bramah?" he would have said, "My son, you are still in the veil of illusion." If you had gone to Socrates and asked, "Are you Zeus?" he would have laughed at you. If you had gone to Mohammed and asked, "Are you Allah?" he would first have rent his clothes and then cut your head off. If you had asked Confucius, "Are you heaven?" I think he would probably have replied, "Remarks which are not in accordance with nature are in bad taste." The idea of a great moral teacher saying what Christ said is out of the question. In my opinion, the only person who can say that sort of thing is either God or a complete lunatic suffering from that form of delusion which undermines the whole mind of man. If you think you are a poached egg, when you are not looking for a piece of toast to suit you, you may be sane, but if you think you are God, there

is no chance for you. We may note in passing that He was never regarded as a mere moral teacher. He did not produce that effect on any of the people who actually met Him. He produced mainly three effects—Hatred—Terror—Adoration. There was no trace of people expressing mild approval.[29]

We must finally consider Lewis' argument against the prevailing naturalism of his day among his fellow academicians. Lewis explained:

What the Naturalist believes is the ultimate Fact, the thing you can't go behind, is a vast process in space and time which is going on of its own accord. Inside that total system every particular event (such as your sitting reading this book) happens because some other event has happened. All things and events are so completely interlocked that no one of them can claim the slightest independence from "the whole show."[30]

In other words, if naturalism is in fact true, then every occurrence in nature must be explainable in terms of the total system of nature. But, as Geisler explains, Lewis argued that

human (inferential) reason, such as even naturalists assume and exercise, cannot be explained strictly in terms of non-rational natural causes. Moreover, "the Naturalist cannot condemn other people's thoughts because they have irrational causes and continue to believe his own, which have (if Naturalism is true) equally irrational causes." Furthermore, argues Lewis, if naturalism is right then there is no reason that the thoughts of a lunatic or drug addict should not be valued by a naturalist as much as his or her own thoughts. This is the self-contradiction of naturalism. There is more than nature; there is mind which cannot be reduced to matter. And there is value (ought), which cannot be reduced to nature (what is). In fact, there is an absolute moral Mind behind nature who gives the moral law.[31]

Ultimately, for Lewis, the whole of human history could be summed up as "the proving ground for eternity. . . . At the end of life and history, Lewis finds two kinds of people: those who say to God, 'Thy will be done,' and those to whom God says, in the end, 'Thy will be done.' All that are in hell, choose it."[32] This is the vision that he sought to explicate and defend . . . and, indeed, did so lastingly.

A Quiet Death—A Lasting Influence

During the autumn of 1963 Lewis' health took a turn for the worse. He died in his sleep on November 22, precisely the same day that JFK was assassinated and renowned litterateur Aldous Huxley died. Neither the death of Lewis nor Huxley saw much fanfare in the shadow of the president's death, which shocked the entire world. Lewis barely made the newspapers, and his quiet funeral was attended mainly by close friends and family. Nevertheless, as one biographer puts it, "Lewis may have been buried without fanfare, but his impact on hearts and lives has never stopped growing."[33] And, as J.I. Packer has rightly said, "The combination within him of insight with vitality, wisdom with wit, and imaginative power with analytical precision made Lewis a sparkling communicator of the everlasting gospel."[34]

Conclusion

The number of Christians whom C.S. Lewis has helped in their journeys to know God better is staggering. It is also fascinating that, while many Christian apologists are known almost exclusively in Christian circles alone, Lewis is almost universally known to inquiring seekers of all stripes—secular and sectarian. Since his death in 1963, the sales of his books have risen to an amazing two million copies a year. A 1980 issue of *Time* magazine called him "this century's most-read apologist for God,"[35] while a recently polled cross-section of *Christianity Today* readers rated him the most influential writer in their lives.[36] As Packer says:

> Not just evangelicals, but all Christians, should celebrate Lewis, "the brilliant, quietly saintly, slightly rumpled Oxford don" as James Patrick describes him. He was a Christcentered, great-tradition mainstream Christian whose stature a generation after his death seems greater than anyone ever thought while he was alive, and whose Christian writings are now seen as having classic status.
>
> Long may we learn from the contents of his marvelous, indeed magical, mind! I doubt whether the full measure of him has been taken by anyone.[37]

Part of the genius of C.S. Lewis' apologetic is that it spanned many genres and made excellent use of his literary talents. He used not only rational arguments but also allegory, fable, fantasy, myth, romance and philosophy as vehicles for illustrating Christian truth. As writers Kenneth Boa and Robert Bowman observe, "Lewis explained his apologetic purpose by noting that 'any amount of theology can now be smuggled into people's minds under the cover of romance without their knowing it.' By stripping Christian truths 'of their stained-glass and Sunday school associations,' one could sneak past the 'watchful dragons' that keep unbelievers from seriously considering those truths."[38]

The lasting influence of Lewis' apologetic should indicate the efficacy of his style. He communicated profound truths in relatively simple language that pulled at readers' heartstrings. He expressed the reality of human sin, its effrontery to God and the need of placing faith in Jesus Christ for salvation—in a palatable way. Lewis never played the judge but guided people to reach conclusions for themselves. He offered a blueprint for right thinking, a map that steered clear of complicated and esoteric theories and philosophies. Lewis' apologetical style was winsome; he made readers *want* to agree with him. He also brought truths together and found unifying principles in knowledge. Edwards comments that "those who try to read through the entire Lewis corpus confess that they receive an education in history, philology, sociology, philosophy, and theology so extensive and exhilarating that others seem thin and frivolous in comparison. While Lewis caricatured himself as a dinosaur, the last of the Old Western Men, many today see him as a forerunner of what may still be the triumph of men and women of Biblical faith in an age that derides the pursuit of truth and righteousness."[39]

Few writers in the history of literature, much less apologetics, have possessed this unique gift. Contemporary apologist Norman Geisler writes that these considerations make Lewis "arguably the most influential twentieth-century Christian theist and apologist."[40]

Appendix 1:
Great Apologists and Their Works

Historical Epoch, Time Period, Apologetical Issues	Apologists and Their Works
The Early Postapostolic Apologists *(70–200)* • Judaism • Paganism • Mystery Religions • Emperor Cultism • Heresies • Gnosticism • Stoicism, Epicureanism, Neoplatonism, etc. • False Religions	Quadratus (c. 75–140), *Apologia to Hadrian* Aristides (100–150), *Apologeticum* Justin Martyr (100–165), *Dialogue with Trypho; First and Second Apology; Discourse in Favor of the Faith* Melito of Sardis (165?), *An Apology for the Christian Faith* Tatian (170), *Pros Hellenas; Diatesseron* Theophilus of Antioch (180?), *Ad Autolychum* Apollinaris of Hierapolis (180?), *Apology for the Christian Religion* (addressed to Emperor Marcus Aurelius) Athenagoras (150?–200), *Apology; Treatise on the Resurrection* Irenaeus (125?–202), *Against Heresies; Proof of the Apostolic Preaching*
The Pre-Nicene Period *(200–325)* • Paganism • Judaism • Antitrinitarianism • Stoicism, Epicureanism, Neoplatonism, etc. • False Religions	Clement of Alexandria (155–220), *Hortatory Discourse to the Greeks; Exhortation to the Heathen; The Instructor; Miscellanies;* Fragments Tertullian (160–230), *Against the Jews; Apologeticus; Ad Nationes; Against Praxeas* Origen (185?–254), *Against Celsus; de Principiis; Hexalpla* Cyprian (200?–258), *Three Books of Evidence Against the Jews*

Historical Epoch, Time Period, Apologetical Issues	Apologists and Their Works
Nicene and Post-Nicene Period (325–475) • Neoplatonism • Arianism • Manichaeism • Donatism • Pelagianism • Paganism • False Religions	Athanasius (298?–373), *Discourses Against the Arians; Defense Against the Arians; Contra Gentes; De Incarnatione* Gregory Nazianzen (c. 330–390), *Orations; Letters* Gregory of Nyssa (c. 330–395?), *Against Eunomius; Oratio Catechetica; On the Holy Spirit, Against the Followers of Macedonius; On Not Three Gods; On the Faith* Jerome (c. 340–420), *Against John of Jerusalem; The Dialogue Against the Luciferians; Against Jovinianus; Against Vigilantius; Against the Pelagians* Augustine (354–430), *The City of God; Confessions; On the Holy Trinity; On Heresies; Against Faustus; On the Correction of the Donatists;* the Anti-Pelagian Writings John Cassian (c. 360–c. 435), *Against Nestorius*
The Middle Ages (476–1500) (Fall of the Roman Empire in 476 to the fall of Constantinople in 1453 and the discovery of America in 1492) • Antitrinitarianism • Pagan philosophy • Mohammedanism • False Religions	Anselm (1033?–1109), *Proslogium; Monologium; De Fide Trinitatis; Cur Deus Homo?* Thomas Aquinas (1225–1274), *Summa Contra Gentiles; Summa Theologica* John Duns Scotus (1266–1308), *Opus Oxoniense; Quæstiones Quodlibetales; On the First Principle; Collationes* William of Occam (1280–1349), *Dialogus; Expositio aurea et admodum utilis super totam artem veterem; Quoestiones et decisiones in quatuor libros sententiarum; Centiloquium theologicum; Quodlibeta septem; De Sacramento altaris; De corpore Christi, De prcedestinatione et futuris contingentibus*

Historical Epoch, Time Period, Apologetical Issues	Apologists and Their Works
The Reformation Age *(1517–1700)* • Romanism • Nomianism/Antinomianism • False Religions	Martin Luther (1483–1546), *The Babylonian Captivity of the Church; Christian Liberty; On the Bondage of the Will* John Calvin (1509–1564), *Institutes of the Christian Religion*; Letters; Biblical Commentaries Blaise Pascal (1623–1662), *Pensees; Provincial Letters*
The Enlightenment Age *(1700–1900)* • Rationalism • Deism • Pantheism • Naturalism • Agnosticism • False Religions	Joseph Butler (1692–1752), *Analogy of Religion; Fifteen Sermons* Thomas Reid (1710–1796), *An Inquiry into the Human Mind on the Principles of Common Sense; Essays on the Intellectual Powers of Man; Essays on the Active Powers of Man* William Paley (1743–1805), *A View of the Evidences of Christianity; Evidences of the Existence and Attributes of the Deity; Horae Paulinae; The Principles of Moral and Political Philosophy* Soren Kierkegaard (1818–1855), *Either/Or; Fear and Trembling; Stages On Life's Way; Concluding Unscientific Postscript; On Authority and Revelation* Charles Hodge (1797–1878), *Systematic Theology; Princeton Sermons*
Modernity *(1900–1970)* • Logical Positivism • Skepticism • Cynicism • Rationalism • Religious Liberalism • False Religions	James Orr (1844–1913), *The Christian View of God and the World; The Faith of a Modern Christian; The Resurrection of Jesus; The Virgin Birth of Christ* B.B. Warfield (1851–1921), *Studies in Theology; The Works of Benjamin Warfield; Biblical and Theological Studies; Studies in Tertullian and Augustine*

Historical Epoch, Time Period, Apologetical Issues	Apologists and Their Works
Modernity (continued)	C.S. Lewis (1898–1963), *Mere Christianity; The Problem of Pain; Miracles; The Great Divorce; The Abolition of Man; The Weight of Glory* E.J. Carnell (1919–1967), *An Introduction to Christian Apologetics: A Philosophic Defense of the Trinitarian-Theistic Faith; Philosophy of the Christian Religion; Christian Commitment and Apologetic; The Case for Orthodox Christianity* Gordon H. Clark (1902–1985), *A Christian View of Men and Things; God's Hammer: The Bible and Its Critics; In Defense of Theology; The Philosophy of Science and Belief in God; Religion, Reason, and Revelation* Cornelius Van Til (1895–1987), *Apologetics; A Christian Theory of Knowledge; Christianity in Conflict; Christianity and Barthianism; The Defense of the Faith* Bernard Ramm (1916–1992), *A Christian Appeal to Reason; After Fundamentalism; The Christian View of Science and Scripture; Protestant Christian Evidences; Varieties of Christian Apologetics* Greg L. Bahnsen (1948–1995), *Always Ready: Directions for Defending the Faith* Abraham Kuyper (1837–1920), *De Gemeene Gratie; Principles of Sacred Theology* Herman Dooyeweerd (1894–1977), *In the Twilight of Western Thought; A New Critique of Theoretical Thought; Roots of Western Culture: Pagan, Secular, and Christian Options*

Historical Epoch, Time Period, Apologetical Issues	Apologists and Their Works
Postmodernity *(1970–Present)* • Postmodernism • Relativism • Pluralism • Obscurantism • Religious Liberalism • New Age Philosophies • False Religions	Francis Beckwith, *Relativism: Feet Firmly Planted in Mid-Air*; *Law, Darwinism & Public Education*; *The New Mormon Challenge*; *See the Gods Fall: Four Rivals to Christianity*; *David Hume's Argument Against Miracles* Michael Behe, *Darwin's Black Box*; *Intelligent Design: The Bridge Between Science & Theology* Kelly James Clark, *Return to Reason* William Lane Craig, *Reasonable Faith*; *Assessing the New Testament Evidence for the Historicity of the Resurrection of Jesus*; *The Existence of God and the Beginning of the Universe*; *The Kalam Cosmological Argument*; *Knowing the Truth about the Resurrection*; *No Easy Answers* William A. Dembski, *The Design Inference*; *No Free Lunch: Why Specified Complexity Cannot Be Purchased Without Intelligence*; *Intelligent Design: The Bridge Between Science & Theology*; *Signs of Intelligence: Understanding Intelligent Design*; *Unapologetic Apologetics*; *The Design Revolution: Answering the Toughest Questions about Intelligent Design*; *Mere Creation*; *Science, Faith & Intelligent Design* C. Stephen Evans, *Despair: A Moment or a Way of Life*; *Existentialism: The Philosophy of Despair and the Quest For Hope*; *Faith Beyond Reason: A Kierkegaardian Account*; *The Historical Christ and the Jesus of Faith*; *Philosophy of Religion*; *The Quest for Faith*; *Why Believe?* John M. Frame, *Apologetics to the Glory of God*; *Cornelius Van Til: An Analysis of His Thought*; *Doctrine of the Knowledge of God*

Historical Epoch, Time Period, Apologetical Issues	Apologists and Their Works
Postmodernity (continued)	Norman Geisler, *Baker Encyclopedia of Christian Apologetics*; *Christian Apologetics*; *Miracles and Modern Thought*; *The Roots of Evil*; *When Skeptics Ask*; *When Critics Ask*; *Roman Catholics and Evangelicals: Agreements and Differences* Gary Habermas, *Dealing with Doubt*; *The Historical Jesus*; *Paradigm Shift: A Challenge to Naturalism*; *Resurrection Claims in Other Religions*; *The Resurrection of Jesus: An Apologetic* Philip E. Johnson, *Darwin on Trial*; *The Right Questions: Truth, Meaning & Public Debate*; *The Wedge of Truth: Splitting the Foundations of Naturalism*; *Reason in the Balance: The Case Against Naturalism in Science, Law & Education*; *Objections Sustained: Subversive Essays on Evolution, Law & Culture* Peter Kreeft, *Handbook of Christian Apologetics*; *Between Heaven and Hell*; *C.S. Lewis for the Third Millennium*; *Making Sense Out of Suffering*; *Socrates Meets Jesus*; *A Refutation of Moral Relativism: Interviews with an Absolutist* Gordon Lewis, *Testing Christianity's Truth Claims: Approaches to Christian Apologetics* John Warwick Montgomery, *Tractatus Logico-Theologicus*; *Faith Founded on Fact: Essays in Evidential Apologetics*; *History and Christianity*; *How Do We Know There Is a God? Evidence For Faith*; *The Shape of the Past: A Christian Response to Secular Philosophies of History*; *Where Is History Going? Essays in Support of the Historical Truth of the Christian Revelation*; *Christianity for the Tough-Minded*; *Evidence for Faith*

Historical Epoch, Time Period, Apologetical Issues	Apologists and Their Works
Postmodernity (continued)	J.P. Moreland, *Scaling the Secular City; Christianity and the Nature of Science; Does God Exist?: The Debate Between Theists & Atheists; Body & Soul: Human Nature & the Crisis in Ethics; Love Your God with All Your Mind: The Role of Reason in the Life of the Soul* Ronald Nash, *Faith and Reason; Worldviews in Conflict; Choosing Christianity in a World of Ideas* Clark Pinnock, *Set Forth Your Case; Reason Enough: A Case for the Christian Faith; A Defense of Biblical Infallibility* Alvin Plantinga, *God, Freedom, and Evil; The Nature of Necessity; Faith and Rationality; Warrant and Proper Function; Warranted Christian Belief; God and Other Minds: A Study of the Rational Justification of Belief in God* R.C. Sproul, *The Psychology of Atheism; Classical Apologetics; Faith Alone* Ravi Zacharias, *Can Man Live Without God? Jesus Among Other Gods; The Absolute Claims of the Christian Message; The Lotus and the Cross: Jesus Talks with Buddha; Deliver Us from Evil*

Appendix 2:
Was Irenaeus an Apologist
for Roman Primacy?

Given the profuse attention that has been given the Irenaean corpus in terms of the development of ecclesiology, an item concerning his apologetics is worthy of our consideration. This involves Roman Catholic apologists appropriating his writings, especially *Against Heresies*, in their attempt to establish the ecclesial primacy of Rome over all other churches. For example, the group Catholic Answers writes:

> In a wide variety of ways, the Fathers attest to the fact that the church of Rome was the central and most authoritative church. They attest to the Church's reliance on Rome for advice, for mediation of disputes, and for guidance on doctrinal issues . . . as Irenaeus explains, "because of its superior origin, all the churches must agree" with Rome. They are also clear on the fact that it is communion with Rome and the bishop of Rome that causes one to be in communion with the Catholic Church.[1]

While we may concede the possibility that Irenaeus subscribed to a kind of Roman priority, there is serious room for doubt—especially concerning the manner in which this priority is conceived by medieval and modern Roman Catholicism complete with magisterial and papal infallibility—for a number of reasons. I'll cover six.

First, to construe the Irenaean writings as an apology for the primacy of Mother Rome in contrast to the catholicity of the entire panoply of orthodox churches surrounding the Mediterranean seems at first to be a red herring. Irenaeus wrote *Against Heresies* to confute the errors of Gnosticism, not to argue for an ecclesiology proper. Indeed, though not unimportant, his mention of the Roman Church specifically was fleeting compared with the rest of his polemical corpus where his primary arguments were from the use and centrality of Scripture and sober reason. Thus, the contention of Roman primacy seems to distract from his true overall purpose.

Second, even in the most hotly debated Irenaean passage on this matter (3.3.2), where he recounted the episcopal lineage of the Roman see, he conceded beforehand that "it would be very tedious, in such a volume as this, to reckon up the successions of *all* the Churches." He focused, then, only on Rome. Another translator of *Against Heresies* puts it this way:

> So far from being "the mother and mistress" of even the West-
> ern Churches, Rome herself is a mission of the Greeks; South-
> ern Gaul is evangelized from Asia Minor, and Lyons checks the
> heretical tendencies of the Bishop at Rome. Ante-Nicene Chris-
> tianity, and indeed the Church herself, appears in Greek cos-
> tume which lasts through the synodical period; and Latin
> Christianity, when it begins to appear, is African, not Roman. It
> is strange, then, that those who have recorded this great histori-
> cal fact have so little perceived its bearings upon Roman preten-
> sions in the Middle Ages and modern times.[2]

This is no small matter. Even Roman Catholic scholars Berington and Kirk in their well-known work, *The Faith of Catholics*, concede that "to this Church, on account of more potent principality, it is necessary that every Church— that is, those who are on every side faithful—resort; in which Church ever, *by those who are on every side*, has been preserved that tradition which is from the apostles" (emphasis added).[3] Thus, when Irenaeus argued for a kind of Ro- man centrality, it was only to the extent that all true churches must be in agreement with one another. Irenaeus wanted those confused about the ram- pant doctrinal disputes to focus on the apostolic churches, those that keep- sake their teachings and remain in fidelity to Holy Writ.

Third, it appears that in his struggle against the Gnostics, Irenaeus found it expedient to marshal, in part, an appeal to apostolic lineage in which to ground the right teachings of the Church against the groundless teachings of Gnostic leaders. Thus, his aim was not to introduce global submission to Rome but rather her provincial representation of catholicity. In other words, the Gnostics *in Rome* should submit to Rome, become true Christians and place their stock in the authority of the Church *there*.

Fourth, Irenaeus did respect the authority of the Roman bishopric. As church historian Bruce Shelley points out, however, "This respect for Rome's traditions . . . did not prohibit able men like Irenaeus and Cyprian from dis- agreeing with Rome when they felt the church or bishop was in error."[4] In- deed, this was evidenced in Irenaeus' struggle against the Roman bishop Eleutherus, his flirtation with the errors of Montanism, his repudiation of his successor, Victor, and his stubbornness in the needless Easter controversy. Thus it seems that what Irenaeus really advocated was a respect for Rome as a member of all the apostolic churches and bishoprics. Moreover, from a strictly historical view, we have no conclusive evidence that Rome exercised authoritative jurisdiction outside her provincial territory.[5]

Fifth, Irenaeus' great respect for the Roman bishopric is a far cry from anything suggesting his support for what would become the late nineteenth century Vatican edict of papal infallibility. In my estimation, this doctrine would have seemed almost absurd to him considering the obvious errors that the "popes" of his day committed (as did other provincial bishops). No doubt, Irenaeus contended that all churches must submit to her (see 3.3.2). But given his mention of the multitudinous "successions" of the churches in all the Mediterranean basin, it seems more logical that he meant those churches in Roman jurisdiction. Irenaeus seemed to feel strongly that all the orthodox churches must act as "iron sharpening iron," providing checks and balances to one another and agreeing on serious matters jointly. This emphasis of his seems to militate, then, against the idea of a global Roman priority. Indeed, for one who stresses the catholicity of the church so strongly, "Roman Catholic" seems more akin to an oxymoron than a unifying and fostering dogma.

Our sixth and final—and perhaps most important consideration—is Irenaeus' unwavering commitment to the Holy Scriptures as the final court of appeal for all matters concerning faith and practice. If he disagreed and found error—even in the Roman bishop—he appealed to sacred Scripture. The binding authority of the Bible was a recurring theme, for example, in *Against Heresies*, where he wrote that "the Scriptures are indeed perfect, since they were spoken by the Word of God and His Spirit."[6] And, "We have learned from *none others* the plan of our salvation, than from those through whom the Gospel has come down to us, which they did at one time proclaim in public, and, at a later period, by the will of God, *handed down to us in the Scriptures, to be the ground and pillar of our faith*" (emphasis added).[7]

Finally, "the tradition from the apostles does thus exist in the Church, and is permanent among us, [therefore] let us revert to the *Scriptural proof* furnished by those apostles who did also write the Gospel, in which they recorded the doctrine regarding God, pointing out that our Lord Jesus Christ is the truth" (emphasis added).[8] This very same *modus operandi* was followed by the other great apologists both anterior and posterior to Irenaeus discussed in this book.

Notes

Introduction

1. John L. McKenzie, *The Two-Edged Sword* (Garden City, NY: Image Books, 1966), 7.

2. Letter from Cornelius Van Til to Francis Schaeffer, *Ordained Servant*, vol. 6, no. 4 (Sheldon, IA: Orthodox Presbyterian Church, October 1997), 79.

Chapter 1: Justin Martyr

1. Eusebius, *Ecclesiastical History*, 3.1.

2. Justo L. Gonzalez, *The Story of Christianity*, vol. 1 (San Francisco: Harper, 1984), 50.

3. Ibid.

4. Justin Martyr, *Second Apology*, chap. 12.

5. Eusebius, *Ecclesiastical History*, 6.19.

6. Justin Martyr, *Dialogue with Trypho*, chaps. 3-8.

7. Ibid.

8. Ibid.

9. Justin Martyr, *Second Apology*, chap. 12.

10. Gonzalez, *Story of Christianity*, 46.

11. Ibid., 46-7.

12. Justin, *Second Apology*, chap. 10.

13. James Kiefer, Christian Biographies. Available from: <http://elvis.rowan.edu/~kilroy/JEK/>.

14. Augustine, *Confessions*, 1.5.6.

15. Norman Geisler, "Justin Martyr," in *The Baker Encyclopedia of Christian Apologetics* (Grand Rapids, MI: Baker, 1999), 395. Used by permission of Baker Academic, a division of Baker Publishing Group.

16. Justin, *Second Apology*, chap. 13.

17. Justin, *Second Apology*, chap. 10.

18. Kenneth Boa and Robert Bowman, *Faith Has Its Reasons* (Colorado Springs: NavPress, 2001), 30.

19. Justin, *First Apology*, chap. 2.

20. Ibid., chaps. 5-6.

21. Ibid., chap. 32.

22. Ibid., chap. 53.

23. Justin, *Second Apology*, chap. 2.

24. Ibid.

25. Ibid.

26. Ibid.

27. Ibid., chap. 3.

28. Ibid., chap. 15.

29. Peter W. Stoner, *Science Speaks* (Chicago: Moody Press, 1958), 60.

30. Johannes Quasten, *Patrology*, vol. 1 (Allen, TX: Christian Classics, 1983), 202.

31. Ibid., 203.

32. Ibid.

33. Justin, *Dialogue with Tryphos*, chap. 99.

34. Ibid., chap. 136.

35. Ibid., chap. 142.

36. *The Martyrdom of the Holy Martyrs*, 1-2 in M. Dods, trans., Philip Schaff, *The Apostolic Fathers with Justin Martyr and Irenaeus* (Grand Rapids, MI: Christian Classics Ethereal Library, 2001), 439-40.

Chapter 2: Irenaeus

1. Matthew J. Slick, comp., *Interesting Quotes from New Age Sources* (Meridian, ID: Christian Apologetics & Research Ministry, 2003). Available from: <http://www.carm.org/nam/naquotes.htm>.

2. R.C. Sproul, *Renewing Your Mind* (radio broadcast), January 15, 2003.

3. Alexander Roberts and James Donaldson in "Introductory Note to Irenaeus," in Philip Schaff, trans., ed., *The Apostolic Fathers with Justin Martyr and Irenaeus* (Grand Rapids, MI: Christian Classics Ethereal Library, 2002), 443.

4. Ibid.

5. Irenaeus, *Letter to Florinus*, in Schaff, 825.

6. Eusebius, *Ecclesiastical History*, 5.1.

7. Patrick J. Healy, "Marcus Aurelius Antoninus," in *The Catholic Encyclopedia*, vol. 2 (online edition, Kevin Knight, 2002). Available from: <http://www.newadvent.org/cathen/02109a.htm>.

8. William Jurgens, *Faith of the Early Fathers*, vol. 1 (Collegeville, MN: Liturgical Press, 1998), 84.

9. Lumen Verum Apologetics, "St. Irenaeus," in *An Introduction to the Greatest Fathers of the Church*. Available from: <http://www.lumenverum.com/fathers/irenaeus.htm>.

10. Roberts and Donaldson, 444.

11. Johannes Quasten, *Patrology*, vol. 1 (Allen, TX: Christian Classics, 1983), 289.

12. Roberts and Donaldson, 442.

13. Irenaeus, *Against Heresies*, 1.25.3.

14. Ibid., 1.10.1.

15. Ibid., preface to book 3.

16. Ibid., 2.28.2.

17. Ibid., 3.1.1.

18. Ibid., 3.5.1.

19. Ibid., 5.20.2.

20. Ibid.

21. Ibid.,1.8.1.

22. Irenaeus, *Fragments from the Lost Writings of Irenaeus*, chap. 39.

23. Irenaeus, *Demonstration of Apostolic Preaching*, chap. 3.

24. Irenaeus, *Demonstration*, chap. 86, quoted in Quasten, *Patrology*, vol. 1, 292.

25. Quasten, *Patrology*, 292-3.

26. Eusebius, *Ecclesiastical History*, 5.23.

27. Irenaeus, *Epistle to Blastus*, in Schaff, 838.

28. Ward Gasque, *Handbook to the History of Christianity*, quoted in Bruce Shelley, *Church History in Plain Language*, 2nd ed. (Waco, TX: Word, 1996), 33.

Chapter 3: Origen

1. Celsus, *The True Discourse*, quoted in Origen, *Against Celsus*, 1.2.

2. Ibid.

3. See the Talmudic section, *Sanhedrin* 43a. Available from: <http://www.earlychristian writings.com/talmud.html>.

4. Steve Turner, *Creed*, cited in "A Puritan's Mind." Available from: <http://www.apuritans mind.com/Apologetics/SteveTurnerCreed.htm>.

5. Celsus, *The True Discourse*, quoted in Origen, *Against Celsus*, 6.34.

6. Ibid., 8.11.

7. Ibid., 8.75.

8. Eusebius, *Ecclesiastical History*, 6.3. Available from: <http://www.newadvent.org/fathers/250106.htm>.

9. F. Prat, "Origen and Origenism," in *The Catholic Encyclopedia*. Available from: <http://www.newadvent.org>.

10. Origen, *Against Celsus*, preface, 1.

11. Ibid., preface, 4.

12. Ibid., preface, 6.

13. Ibid., 1.2.

14. Ibid., 1.46.

15. Ibid., 6.2.

16. Ibid., 8.63.

17. Ibid., 8.64, 65.

18. Origen, *de Principiis*, 1.5.

19. Ibid., 2.2.2.

20. Origen, *Against Celsus*, 8.4.

21. Bruce Shelley, *Church History in Plain Language*, 2nd ed. (Waco, TX: Word, 1996), 86.

22. C.C. Kroeger, "Origen," in *The Evangelical Dictionary of Theology* (Grand Rapids, MI: Baker, 1984), 803.

23. Shelley, *Church History*, 86.

24. Eusebius, *Ecclesiastical History*, 6.39.

25. Origen, *Against Celsus*, 8.76.

Chapter 4: Athanasius

1. This quote is traditionally attributed to G.K. Chesterton.

2. Hank Hanegraaff, "Christmas Come, Celebrate Christ," in *The Plain Truth*. Available from: <http://www.ptm.org/98PT/NovDec/HHhankronyms.htm>.

3. "Diocletian," in *The Catholic Encyclopedia*. Available from: <http://www.newadvent.org/cathen/05007b.htm>.

4. Eusebius, *Ecclesiastical History*, 8.2, in "Diocletian," in *The Catholic Encyclopedia*, vol. 2 (online edition, Kevin Knight, 2002). Available from: <http://www.newadvent.org/cathen/02109a.htm>.

5. Eusebius, *Ecclesiastical History*, 8.11, in "Diocletian."

6. Athanasius, *Contra Gentes*, 1.1.

7. Athanasius, *On the Incarnation*, 10.4, 5.

8. Ibid., 53.1.

9. Loraine Boettner, "Arianism," in *The Wycliffe Dictionary of Theology* (Peabody, MA: Hendrickson, 1960), 63.

10. Ibid.

11. Athanasius, *Contra Gentes*, 1.1.

12. Athanasius, *Festal Letters*, 39.5-6.

13. The original *Nicene Creed*. Available from: <http://www.orthodox.co.uk/nicene.htm>.

14. Athanasius, *de Synodis*, 1.6.

15. Cornelius Clifford, "St. Athanasius," in *The Catholic Encyclopedia*. Available from: <http://www.newadvent.org/cathen/02035a.htm>.

16. Theodoret, *Ecclesiastical History of Theodoret*, 1.28.

17. Clifford, "St. Athanasius."

18. Athanasius, *Discourses Against the Arians*, 1.1.4.

19. Ibid., 2.14.1.

20. Ibid., 3.23.1.

21. Ibid., 4.30.1.

22. Ibid., 3.29.58.

23. Ibid., 4.30.36.

24. Athanasius, *On the Incarnation*, 10.5.

Chapter 5: Augustine

1. Eugène Portalié, *Life of St. Augustine of Hippo*. Available from: <http://www.newadvent. org/cathen/02084a.htm>.

2. B.B. Warfield, *Calvin and Augustine* (Philadelphia: Presbyterian & Reformed, 1956), 306. Cited in John Piper, *The Legacy of Sovereign Joy* (Wheaton, IL: Crossway, 2000), 43. Available from: <http://www.desiringgod.org/library/biographies/98augustine.html>.

3. R.C. Sproul, *The Consequences of Ideas* (Wheaton, IL: Crossway, 2000), 57.

4. Augustine, *Confessions*, 1.6.7.

5. Ibid., 3.1.1.

6. Ibid., 1.5.9.

7. Portalié, *Life of St. Augustine*.

8. Michael Mendelson, "Saint Augustine," *The Stanford Encyclopedia of Philosophy* (Winter 2000 ed.), Edward N. Zalta, ed. Available from: <http://plato.stanford.edu/archives/win2000/ entries/augustine/>.

9. Augustine, *Confessions*, 4.7.12, 13.

10. Ibid., 5.14.24.

11. Ibid., 8.12.28.

12. Ibid., 9.6.14.

13. Portalié, *Life of St. Augustine*.

14. Ibid.

15. Augustine, *Confessions*, 11.4.6.

16. Ibid., 11.9.11.

17. Ibid. 11.12.13.

18. Augustine, *On Faith and the Creed*, 1.1.

19. See, for example, Augustine, *Letters*, 120.1.

20. Kenneth Boa and Robert Bowman, *Faith Has Its Reasons* (Colorado Springs: NavPress, 2001), 32.

21. Augustine, *The City of God*, 1, preface.

22. Ibid.

23. Johannes Quasten, *Patrology*, vol. 4 (Allen, TX: Christian Classics), 363.

24. Augustine, *The City of God*, 1.35.

25. Norman Geisler, "Augustine," in *The Baker Encyclopedia of Christian Apologetics* (Grand Rapids, MI: Baker, 1999), 62.

26. Augustine, *The City of God*, 4.24.

27. Augustine, *Confessions*, 7.5.7.

28. Augustine, *The City of God*, 11.9.

29. Ibid., 12.6.

30. Ibid., 12.8.

31. Ibid., 22.1.

32. Ibid., 22.30.

33. Ibid., 19.18.

34. Augustine, *Confessions*, 13.15.16.

35. Augustine, *Letters*, 23.7.

36. Piper, *The Legacy of Sovereign Joy*, 9.

37. Augustine, *Confessions*, 6.5.7.

38. Ibid.

Chapter 6: Anselm

1. C.A. Beckwith, "Saint Anselm of Canterbury," in the *New Schaff-Herzog Encyclopedia of Religious Knowledge*, vol. 1. Available from <http://www.ccel.org/ccel/schaff/encyc/encyc01.htm>.

2. W.H. Kent, "St. Anselm," in *The Catholic Encyclopedia*, vol. 1 (online ed., Kevin Knight, 2002). Available from: <http://www.newadvent.org/cathen/01546a.htm>.

3. Eadmer, *Life of St. Anselm*, 1.1, in W.H. Kent, "St. Anselm," in *The Catholic Encyclopedia*.

4. Kent, "St. Anselm."

5. Ibid.

6. Ibid.

7. Ibid.

8. Ibid.

9. Anselm, *Monologium*, chap. 1.

10. Norman Geisler, *Baker Encyclopedia of Christian Apologetics* (Grand Rapids, MI: Baker, 1999), 25.

11. Anselm, *Monologium*, chap. 3.

12. Anselm, *Proslogium*, chap. 1.

13. Ibid., chap. 2.

14. Ibid., chap. 3.

15. James Fieser, ed., "Anselm of Canterbury," in *The Internet Encyclopedia of Philosophy*, 1996. Available from: <http://www.utm.edu/research/iep/a/anselm.htm>.

16. William Turner, *History of Philosophy*, chap. 30 (Athenaeum Press, 1903) (online ed., University of Notre Dame). Available from: <http://www.nd.edu/Departments/Maritain/etext/hop30.htm>.

17. Kent, "St. Anselm."

18. Ibid.

19. Beckwith, "Saint Anselm of Canterbury."

20. Kent, "St. Anselm."

21. Anselm, *Cur Deus Homo?* 1.3.

22. Ibid.

23. Ibid., 1.11.

24. Ibid., 1.19.

25. Ibid., 2.14.

26. Ibid., 2.20.

27. Kent, "St. Anselm."

28. Anselm, *Proslogium*, chap. 26.

29. Edward Augustus Freeman, *History of the Norman Conquest*, vol. 4, 444, in Kent, "St. Anselm."

30. Robert S. Hartman, "Prolegomena to a Meta-Anselmian Axiomatic," in *The Review of Metaphysics*, 14:4 (June 1961), 637.

31. Alvin Plantinga, *God and Other Minds* (Ithaca, NY: Cornell University Press, 1967), 26.

32. Hartman, "Prolegomena," 637.

33. Thomas Williams, "Saint Anselm," in *The Stanford Encyclopedia of Philosophy*. Available from: <http://setis.library.usyd.edu.au/stanford/archives/sum2000/entries/anselm/>.

Chapter 7: Thomas Aquinas

1. D.J. Kennedy, "St. Thomas Aquinas," in *The Catholic Encyclopedia*, vol. 14 (online ed., Kevin Knight, 2002). Available from: <http://www.newadvent.org/cathen/14663b.htm>.

2. Ibid.

3. G.K. Chesterton, *St. Thomas Aquinas: The Dumb Ox* (New York: Doubleday, 1956), 41.

4. Ibid., 43-4.

5. Kennedy, "St. Thomas Aquinas."

6. Ibid.

7. Chesterton, *St. Thomas Aquinas*, 49-50.

8. Kennedy, "St. Thomas Aquinas."

9. Ibid.

10. Thomas Aquinas, *De Veritate*, cited in Paul Horrigan, "Introduction to Philosophy." Available from: <http://www.paulhorrigan.0catch.com/>.

11. These points are adapted from Michael Sudduth's *The Thought of St. Thomas Aquinas: Intellectual Background, Faith and Reason, and God*. Available from: <http://www.homestead.com/philofreligion/files/Aquinashandout. html>.

12. Ibid.

13. Sudduth, *The Thought of St. Thomas Aquinas*.

14. Norman Geisler, *Baker Encyclopedia of Christian Apologetics* (Grand Rapids, MI: Baker, 1999), 725.

15. Thomas Aquinas, *Summa Contra Gentiles*, 1.4.

16. Thomas Aquinas, "On Truth," in *Providence and Predestination* (Chicago: Henery Regnery, 1953), 44.

17. Thomas Aquinas, *Summa Theologica*, 1.16.

18. Ellen Charry, ed., *Inquiring after God* (Malden, MA: Blackwell, 2000), 29.

19. Thomas Aquinas, *Summa Theologica*, 1.2.

20. Kennedy, "St. Thomas Aquinas."

21. Ibid.

22. The Center for Thomistic Studies (Houston: University of St. Thomas, 2004). Available from: <http://www.stthom.edu/cts/about.html>.

23. Kennedy, "St. Thomas Aquinas."

Chapter 8: Blaise Pascal

1. R.C. Sproul, *Renewing Your Mind*, radio broadcast, circa Fall 2003.

2. Rick Wade, *Blaise Pascal: An Apologist for Our Times*, Probe Ministries, 1994. <http://www.probe.org/docs/pascal.html>.

3. Some modern apologists are fond of referring to apologetics as "pre-evangelism." I present no real challenge to such a notion except to say that apologetics often extends its import beyond that of "pre-" status. For many, it satisfies a "present" and "post-" need as well.

4. Forrest Baird, "Blaise Pascal," in *Philosophic Classics*, vol. 3 (Upper Saddle River, NJ: Prentice Hall, 2000), 473.

5. Ibid.

6. Ibid.

7. Ibid.

8. Ibid.

9. J. Lataste, "Blaise Pascal," in *The Catholic Encyclopedia*, vol. 11 (online edition, Kevin Knight, 2003). Available from: <http://www.newadvent.org/cathen/11511a.htm>.

10. Ravi Zacharias, "Beyond Pleasure," in *A Slice of Infinity* (Norcross, GA: Ravi Zacharias International Ministries, 2003). Available from: <http://www.gospelcom.net/rzim/publications/slicetran.php?sliceid=60>.

11. Augustine, *Confessions*, 1.1.1.

12. Elizabeth J. Knuth, ed., "Pascal's Memorial." Available from: <http://www.users.csbsju.edu/~eknuth/pascal.html>.

13. Lataste, "Blaise Pascal."

14. Bill Tsamis, "Blaise Pascal." Available from: <http://www.apologetics.org/articles/pascal.html>.

15. Peter Kreeft, *Christianity for Modern Pagans: Pascal's Pensees Edited, Outlined and Explained* (San Francisco: Ignatius Press, 1993), 13, 189. Cited in Wade, *Blaise Pascal*.

16. Blaise Pascal, *Pensees*, 257.

17. Ibid., 194.

18. Ibid., 187.

19. Ibid., 434.

20. Ibid., 82.

21. Ibid., 187.

22. Les Walthers, "Reformed Sermons." Available from: <http://www.sermon.org/Articles/Philosophy/truth_denied.htm>.

23. Pascal, *Pensees*, 194, 195.

24. Wade, *Blaise Pascal*.

25. Pascal, *Pensees*, 233.

26. Lataste, "Blaise Pascal."

27. Pascal, *Pensees*, 194.

28. Wade, *Blaise Pascal*.

29. Pascal, *Pensees*, 347.

30. Ibid., 314.

31. Ibid., 227.

32. G.M. Savage, "Fideism," in *The Catholic Encyclopedia,* vol. 6 (online ed., Kevin Knight, 2003). Available from: <http://www.newadvent.org/cathen/06068b.htm>.

33. Wade, *Blaise Pascal*.

34. Ibid.

35. Alvin Plantinga, "Theism as a Properly Basic Belief" [online] (Addison, TX: Leadership University, 1995–2001). Available from: <http://www.leaderu.com/truth/3truth06.html>.

36. As recorded in Jimmy Williams, *Apologetics and Evangelism* (Probe Ministries, 1994). Available from: <http://www.probe.org/docs/apol-eva.html>.

37. Pascal, *Pensees*, 185.

38. Ibid., 430.

39. Ibid., 33.

40. Pascal, *Pensees*, 921, 922.

41. Lataste, "Blaise Pascal."

42. Edward T. Oakes, "Pascal: The First Modern Christian," in *First Things*, August/September 1999, 48.

43. T.S. Eliot as quoted in Oakes, 48.

44. Pascal, *Pensees*, 277.

45. Ibid., 185.

46. Hank Hanegraaff, "EQUIP: The Mission of the Christian Research Institute," *The Christian Research Institute*. Available from: <http://www.equip.org/inside/index.asp?view=goals>.

47. W. Robert Godfrey, R.C. Sproul, and Rod Rosenblatt, "Where Do We Start? A Conversation About Apologetics," *Modern Reformation*, March/April 1998. Available from <http://www.modernreformation.org/mr98/marapr/mr9802roundtable.html>.

Chapter 9: Joseph Butler and William Paley

1. Richard Hooker, *The European Enlightenment* (Pullman: Washington State University, 1996). Available from: <http://www.wsu.edu/~dee/ENLIGHT/>.

2. Francis Aveling, "Deism," in *The Catholic Encyclopedia*, vol. 4 (online edition, Kevin Knight, 2003). Available from: <http://newadvent.org/cathen/ 04679b.htm>.

3. Augustus H. Strong, *Systematic Theology* (Valley Forge, PA: Judson Press, 1985), 414.

4. David E. White, "Joseph Butler," in *The Internet Encyclopedia of Philosophy* (Martin, TN: University of Tennessee at Martin, 2001). Available from: <http://www.utm.edu/research/iep/b/butler.htm>.

5. L. Ross Buss, *Readings in Christian Apologetics* (Grand Rapids, MI: Zondervan, 1983), 327.

6. Joseph Butler, *Fifteen Sermons Preached at the Rolls Chapel*, Semon XV, Upon the Ignorance of Man. Available from: <http://www.vts.edu/BPL/Butlers%20Sermons/Fifteen_Sermons_ Preached_at_the_Rolls_Chapel.htm>.

7. Origen, *On First Principles*, quoted in Joseph Butler, *Analogy of Religion* (New York: M.H. Newman, 1851) [online] Making of America Digital Library. Available from: <http:// www.hti.umich.edu/m/moa.new/>.

8. Butler, *Fifteen Sermons*, Sermon XV.

9. Ibid.

10. Ibid.

11. James E. Kiefer, "Joseph Butler," in *Biographical Sketches of Memorable Christians* [online]. Provided by the Society of Archbishop Justus. Available from: <http://justus.anglican. org/resources/bio/187.html>.

12. Quoted in Norman Geisler, "Joseph Butler," in *Baker Encyclopedia of Christian Apologetics* (Grand Rapids, MI: Baker, 1999), 109.

13. Quoted in Butler, *Analogy of Religion*, 27.

14. Ibid., 32.

15. Geisler, "Joseph Butler,"109.

16. Butler, *Analogy of Religion*, 159.

17. B.F. Tefft, *The Analogy of Religion with an Analysis of the Work* (Cincinnati: Poe & Hitchcock, 1863), 25 [online] Making of America Digital Library. Available from: <http://www.hti. umich.edu /m/moa.new/>.

18. Ibid.

19. Ibid., 35-6.

20. Albert Barnes, "The Life of Dr. Butler," in *The Analogy of Religion*.

21. Tefft, *The Analogy of Religion with an Analysis of the Work*, 36.

22. Charles Darwin, "Autobiography," in *The Life and Letters of Charles Darwin*, F. Darwin, ed. (Singapore: National University of Singapore, 2003). Available from: <http://www.schol- ars.nus.edu.sg/landow/victorian/science/darwin/darwin_autobiography.html>.

23. William Paley, *Natural Theology*, chap. 1.

24. Norman Geisler, "William Paley," *Baker Encyclopedia of Christian Apologetics* (Grand Rapids, MI: Baker, 1999), 574.

25. Paley, *Natural Theology*, chap. 1.

26. William A. Dembski, "The Intelligent Design Movement" [online] (Addison, TX: Leadership University, 2002). Available from: <http://www.origins.org/articles/dembski_ide signmovement.html>.

27. Paley, *Natural Theology*, chap. 3.

28. Ibid., chap. 23.

29. Dembski, "The Intelligent Design Movement."

30. Geisler, "William Paley," 574-5.

31. Paley, *Natural Theology*, chap. 27.

32. Quoted in *Paley's Natural Theology with Selections from the Illustrative Notes, and the Supplementary Dissertations of Sir Charles Bell and Lord Brougham*, Elisha Bartlett, ed. (New York: Harper &, Brothers, 1847). Available from: <http://home.att.net/~p.caimi/Paley-preface.doc>.

33. Geisler, "William Paley," 574.

34. Quoted in *Paley's Natural Theology*.

35. "William Paley" entry in Wikipedia. Available from: <http://www.wikipedia.org/wiki/William_Paley>.

36. Michael Behe, *Darwin's Black Box: The Biochemical Challenge to Evolution* (New York: Free Press, 1996), 39.

37. See William Dembski, *No Free Lunch: Why Specified Complexity Cannot Be Purchased Without Intelligence* (Lanham, MD: Rowman & Littlefield, 2001).

38. Dembski, "The Intelligent Design Movement."

Chapter 10: C.S. Lewis

1. George Sayer, *Jack: A Life of C.S. Lewis* (Wheaton, IL: Crossway, 1994), as quoted in Ted Olsen, "C.S. Lewis," in *Christianity Today*, 19, no. 65 (2000). Available from: <http://www.christianitytoday.com/ch/2000/001/2.26.html>.

2. C.S. Lewis, *Surprised by Joy* (New York: Harcourt, Brace & World, Inc., 1956), 4. Copyright © 1956 by C.S. Lewis and renewed 1984 by Arthur Owen Barfield, reprinted by permission of Harcourt, Inc. World rights are C.S. Lewis Pte. Ltd., 1955. Extract reprinted by permission.

3. Scott R. Burson and Jerry L. Walls, *C.S. Lewis & Francis Schaeffer* (Downers Grove, IL: InterVarsity Press, 1998), 22.

4. Bruce L. Edwards, "C.S. Lewis: A Modest Literary Biography," in *Into the Wardrobe*. Available from: <http://cslewis.drzeus.net/bio/bio.html>.

5. Lewis, *Surprised by Joy*, 10.

6. Burson and Walls, *C.S. Lewis & Francis Schaeffer*, 25.

7. C.S. Lewis, *Introduction to Phantastes and Lilith* (Grand Rapids, MI: Eerdmans, 1964), 11.

8. Lewis, *Surprised by Joy*, 191.

9. Ted Olsen, "C.S. Lewis."

10. Lewis, *Surprised by Joy*, 228-9.

11. Edwards, "C.S. Lewis."

12. Ibid.

13. C.S. Lewis, *A Grief Observed* (London: Faber, 1966), 33.

14. Ryan Renn, "The Works of C.S. Lewis and the New Testament-Critical Context" (Ashland, OH: Purdue University Press, 2003). Available from: <http://web.ics.purdue.edu/~renn/musings-outlet/CSLrpFn.htm>.

15. C.S. Lewis, *Miracles: A Preliminary Study* (New York: Simon & Schuster, 1996), 215-6, quoted in Renn, "The Works of C.S. Lewis."

16. C.S. Lewis, *The Problem of Pain* (San Francisco: HarperSanFrancisco, 2001), 81.

17. C.S. Lewis, "Reflections on the Psalms," in *The Inspirational Writings of C.S. Lewis* (New York: Inspirational Press, 1994), 145.

18. Norman Geisler, "C.S. Lewis," in *Baker Encyclopedia of Christian Apologetics* (Grand Rapids, MI: Baker, 1999), 421.

19. Ibid.

20. C.S. Lewis, *Mere Christianity* (New York: Harper Collins, 2001), 38. Copyright C.S. Lewis Pte. Ldt. 1942, 1943, 1944, 1952. Extract reprinted by permission.

21. Geisler, "C.S. Lewis," 421.

22. Lewis, *Mere Christianity*, 25.

23. Ibid., 9-10.

24. Geisler, "C.S. Lewis," 422.

25. Lewis, *Mere Christianity*, 31.

26. C.S. Lewis, *The Weight of Glory* (New York: Harper Collins, 2001), 26.

27. Lewis, *Mere Christianity*, 135.

28. Ibid., 52.

29. C.S. Lewis, "What Are We to Make of Jesus Christ?" in *God in the Dock* (Grand Rapids, MI: Eerdmans, 1994), 157.

30. C.S. Lewis, *Miracles* (San Francisco: HarperCollins, 2001), 5.

31. Geisler, "C.S. Lewis," 423.

32. Ibid.

33. Olsen, "C.S. Lewis."

34. J.I. Packer, "Still Surprised by Lewis," in *Christianity Today* [online]. September 7, 1998. Available from: <http://www.christianitytoday.com/ct/8ta/8ta054.html>.

35. *Time*, April 7, 1980, 66, quoted in Kenneth Boa and Robert Bowman, *Faith Has Its Reasons* (Colorado Springs: NavPress, 2001), 75.

36. Packer, "Still Surprised by Lewis."

37. Ibid.

38. Boa and Bowman, *Faith Has Its Reasons* (Colorado Springs: NavPress, 2001), 75.

39. Bruce L. Edwards, "C.S. Lewis: Public Christian and Scholar," presented at the Frances White Colloquium on C.S. Lewis, Taylor University, November 12, 1998. Available from: <http://personal.bgsu.edu/~edwards/lewisdoc. html>.

40. Geisler, "C.S. Lewis," 420.

Appendix 2

1. Catholic Answers, "The Authority of the Pope: Part 1." Available from: <http://www. catholic.com/library/Authority_of_the_Pope_Part_1.asp>.

2. Alexander Roberts and James Donaldson in "Introductory Note to Irenaeus," in Philip Schaff, ed., *The Apostolic Fathers with Justin Martyr and Irenaeus* (Grand Rapids, MI: Christian Classics Ethereal Library, 2002), 442. Available from: <http://www.ccel.org/fathers2/ANF-01/anf01-56.htm#P6124_1360495>.

3. Joseph Berington and John Kirk, *The Faith of Catholics*, as quoted in Roberts and Donaldson, in "Introductory Note to Irenaeus," 596.

4. Bruce Shelley, *Church History in Plain Language*, 2nd ed. (Waco, TX: Word, 1996), 134.

5. Ibid.

6. Irenaeus, *Against Heresies*, 2.28.2.

7. Ibid., 3.1.1.

8. Ibid., 3.5.1.